EDUCATION AND THE POSTMODERN CONDITION

Critical Studies in Education and Culture Series

EDUCATION AND THE POSTMODERN CONDITION

Edited by Michael Peters

Foreword by Jean-François Lyotard

Critical Studies in Education and Culture Series
Edited by Henry A. Giroux and Paulo Freire

BERGIN & GARVEY
Westport, Connecticut • London

Library of Congress Cataloging-in-Publication Data

Education and the postmodern condition / edited by Michael Peters ;
    foreword by Jean-François Lyotard.
        p.   cm.—(Critical studies in education and culture series,
    ISSN 1064–8615)
        Includes bibliographical references and index.
        ISBN 0–89789–373–5 (alk. paper).—ISBN 0–89789–528–2 (pbk.)
        1. Education—Philosophy. 2. Education—Aims and objectives.
    I. Peters, Michael (Michael A.), 1948–   . II. Series.
    LB14.7.E38   1995

    370′.1—dc20   94–21996

British Library Cataloguing in Publication Data is available.

Library of Congress Catalog Card Number: 94–21996
ISBN: 0–89789–528–2 (pbk.)

First published in 1995

Bergin & Garvey, 88 Post Road West, Westport, CT 06881
An imprint of Greenwood Publishing Group, Inc.

Printed in the United States of America

The paper used in this book complies with the
Permanent Paper Standard issued by the National
Information Standards Organization (Z39.48–1984).

10 9 8 7 6 5 4 3 2 1

Dedicated to the memory of
Bill Readings

Contents

Series Foreword

For many theorists occupying various positions on the political spectrum, the current historical moment signals less a need to come to grips with the new forms of knowledge, experiences, and conditions that constitute postmodernism than the necessity to write its obituary. The signs of exhaustion are in part measured by the fact that postmodernism has gripped two generations of intellectuals who have pondered endlessly over its meaning and implications as a "social condition and cultural movement" (Jencks 1992, 10). The "postmodern debate" has spurned little consensus and a great deal of confusion and animosity. The themes are, by now, well known: master narratives and traditions of knowledge grounded in first principles are spurned; philosophical principles of canonicity and the notion of the sacred have become suspect; epistemic certainty and the fixed boundaries of academic knowledge have been challenged by a "war on totality" and a disavowal of all-encompassing, single world views; the rigid distinctions between high and low culture have been rejected by the insistence that the products of the so-called mass culture, popular, and folk art forms are proper objects of study; the Enlightenment correspondence between history and progress and the modernist faith in rationality, science, and freedom have incurred a deep-rooted skepticism; the fixed and unified identity of the humanist subject has been replaced by a call for narrative space that is pluralized and fluid; and, finally, though far from complete, history is spurned as a unilinear process that moves the West progressively toward a final realization of freedom.[1]

While these and other issues have become central to the postmodern debate, they are connected through the challenges and provocations they provide to modernity's conception of history, agency, representation, culture, and the responsibility of intellectuals. The postmodern challenge constitutes not only a diverse body of cultural criticism, it must also be seen as a contextual discourse that has challenged specific disciplinary boundaries in such fields as literary studies, geography, education, architecture, feminism, performance art, anthropology, and sociology.[2] Given its broad theoretical reach, its political anarchism, and its challenge to "legislating" intellectuals, it is not surprising that there has been a growing movement on the part of diverse critics to distance themselves from postmodernism.

Although postmodernism may have been elevated to the height of fashion hype in both academic journals and the popular press in North America during the last twenty years, it is clear that a more sinister and reactionary mood has emerged that constitutes something of a backlash. Of course, postmodernism did become something of a fashion trend, but such events are short lived and rarely take any subject seriously. But the power of fashion and commodification should not be underestimated in terms of how such practices bestow on an issue a cloudy residue of irrelevance and misunderstanding. There is more at stake in the recent debates on postmodernism than the effects of fashion and commodification; in fact, the often-essentialized terms in which critiques of postmodernism have been framed suggest something more onerous. In the excessive rhetorical flourishes that dismiss postmodernism as reactionary nihilism, fad, or simply a new form of consumerism there appears a deep-seated anti-intellectualism, one that lends credence to the notion that theory is an academic luxury and has little to do with concrete political practice. Anti-intellectualism aside, the postmodern backlash also points to a crisis in the way in which the project of modernity attempts to appropriate, prescribe, and accommodate issues of difference and indeterminacy.

Much of the criticism that now so blithely dismisses postmodernism appears trapped in what Zygmunt Bauman refers to as modernist "utopias that served as beacons for the long march to the rule of reason [which] visualized a world without margins, leftovers, the unaccounted for—without dissidents and rebels" (Bauman 1992, xi). Against the indeterminacy, fragmentation, and skepticism of the postmodern era, the master narratives of modernism, particularly Marxism and liberalism, have been undermined as oppositional discourses. One consequence is that "a whole generation of postwar intellectuals have experienced an identity crisis. . . . What results is a mood of mourning and melancholia" (Mercer 424).

The legacy of essentialism and orthodoxy seems to be reasserting itself on the part of left intellectuals who reject postmodernism as a style of cultural criticism and knowledge production. It can also be seen in the refusal on the part of intellectuals to acknowledge the wide-ranging processes of social and cultural transformation taken up in postmodern discourses that are appropriate to grasping the contemporary experiences of youth and the wide-ranging proliferation of forms of diversity within an age of declining authority, economic uncertainty, the proliferation of electronic-mediated technologies, and the extension of what I call consumer pedagogy into almost every aspect of youth culture.

Michael Peters's splendid book shifts the terms of the debate in which postmodernism is usually engaged, especially by its more recent critics. In doing so, various authors in the text argue that postmodernism as a site of conflicting ideas, practices, and tendencies becomes useful pedagogically when it provides elements of an oppositional discourse for understanding and responding to the changing cultural and educational shifts that are going on in the industrial world. *Education and the Postmodern Condition* will be invaluable in helping educators and others address the changing conditions of knowledge production in the context of emerging mass electronic media and the role these new technologies are playing as critical socializing agencies in redefining both the locations and the meaning of pedagogy.

My own concern with expanding the way in which educators and cultural workers understand the political reach and power of pedagogy as it positions youth within a postmodern culture suggests that postmodernism is to be neither romanticized nor casually dismissed. On the contrary, I believe that it is a fundamentally important discourse that needs to be mined critically in order to help educators to understand the modernist nature of public schooling in North America.[3] It is also useful for educators to comprehend the changing conditions of identity formation within electronically mediated cultures and how they are producing a new generation of youth who exists between the borders of a modernist world of certainty and order, informed by the culture of the West and its technology of print, and a postmodern world of hybridized identities, electronic technologies, local cultural practices, and pluralized public spaces.

But the debate about postmodernism has come into bad times. That is, there has emerged recently a backlash against postmodernism that reproduces rather than constructively addresses some of the pedagogical and political problems affecting contemporary education. It is against this backlash that *Education and the Postmodern Condition* appears as a welcome antidote.

WELCOME TO THE POSTMODERN BACKLASH

Whereas conservatives such as Daniel Bell (1976) and his cohorts may see in postmodernism the worst expression of the radical legacy of the 1960s, an increasing number of radical critics view postmodernism as the cause of a wide range of theoretical excesses and political injustices. For example, recent criticism from the British cultural critic John Clarke (1991) argues that the hyper-reality of postmodernism wrongly celebrates and depoliticizes the new informational technologies and encourages metropolitan intellectuals to proclaim the end of everything in order to commit themselves to nothing (especially the materialist problems of the masses).[4] Dean MacCannell (1992) goes further and argues that "postmodern writing [is] an expression of soft fascism" (p. 187). Feminist theorist Susan Bordo (1993) dismisses postmodernism as just another form of "stylish nihilism" and castigates its supporters for constructing a "world in which language swallows up everything" (p. 291). The nature of the backlash has become so prevalent in North America that the status of popular criticism and reporting seems to necessitate proclaiming that postmodernism is "dead." Hence, comments ranging from the editorial pages of the *New York Times* to popular texts such as *13thGen* to popular academic magazines such as the *Chronicle of Higher Education* alert the general public in no uncertain terms that it is no longer fashionable to utter the "p" word.

Of course, more serious critiques have appeared from the likes of Jürgen Habermas (1978), Perry Anderson (1984), David Harvey (1989), and Terry Eagleton (1985), but the current backlash has a different intellectual quality to it, a kind of reductionism that is both disturbing and irresponsible in its refusal to engage postmodernism in any kind of dialogical, theoretical debate.[5] Many of these left critics often assume the moral high ground and muster their theoretical machinery within binary divisions that create postmodern fictions, on the one side, and politically correct, materialist freedom fighters on the other. One consequence is that any attempt to engage the value and importance of postmodern discourses critically is sacrificed to the cold winter winds of orthodoxy and intellectual parochialism. I am not suggesting that all critics of postmodernism fall prey to such a position, nor am I suggesting that concerns about the relationship between modernity and postmodernity, the status of ethics, the crisis of representation and subjectivity, or the political relevance of postmodern discourses should not be problematized. But viewing postmodernism as a terrain to be contested suggests theoretical caution rather than reckless abandonment or casual dismissal.

What is often missing from these contentious critiques is the recognition that since postmodernism does not operate under any absolute sign, it might be more productive to reject any arguments that position post-modernism within an essentialized politics, an either-or set of strategies. A more productive encounter would attempt, instead, to understand how postmodernism's more central insights illuminate how power is produced and circulated through cultural practices that mobilize multiple relations of subordination. And it is precisely on this point that *Education and the Postmodern Condition* provides welcome theoretical relief.

Rather than proclaiming the end of reason, postmodernism can be critically analyzed for how successfully it interrogates the limits of the project of modernist rationality and its universal claims to progress, happiness, and freedom. Instead of assuming that postmodernism has vacated the terrain of values, it seems more useful to address how it accounts for how values are constructed historically and relationally, and how they might be addressed as the basis or "precondition of a politically engaged critique" (Butler 1991, 6–7). In a similar fashion, instead of claiming that postmodernism's critique of the essentialist subject denies a theory of subjectivity, it seems more productive to examine how its claims about the contingent character of identity, constructed in a mul-tiplicity of social relations and discourses, redefines the notion of agency. One example of this type of inquiry comes from Judith Butler, who argues that acknowledging that "the subject is constituted is not [the same as claiming] that it is determined; on the contrary, the constituted character of the subject is the very precondition of its agency (1991, 13). The now familiar argument that postmodernism substitutes represen-tations for reality indicates less an insight than a reductionism that refuses to engage critically how postmodern theories of representation work to give meaning to reality.

A postmodern politics of representation might be better served through an attempt to understand how power is mobilized in cultural terms, how images are used on a national and local scale to create a representational politics that is reorienting traditional notions of space and time. A postmodern discourse could also be evaluated through the pedagogical consequences of its call to expand the meaning of literacy by broadening "the range of texts we read, and . . . the ways in which we read them" (Berube 1992–93, 75). The fact of the matter is that mass media play a decisive role in the lives of young people, and the issue is not whether such media perpetuate dominant power relations but how youth and others experience the culture of the media differently, or the ways the media are "experienced differently by different individuals" (Tomlinson 1991, 40). Postmodernism pluralizes the meaning of culture, whereas modernism firmly situates it theoretically in apparatuses of power. It is precisely in this dialectical interplay between difference and power that postmodernism and modernism inform each other rather than cancel each other out. The dialectical nature of the relationship that postmodernism has to modernism warrants a theoretical moratorium on critiques that affirm or negate postmodernism on the basis of whether it represents a break from modernism. The value of postmodernism lies elsewhere. Homi Bhabha is very instructive on this issue and points to the importance of postmodernism as a way of translating the limits of modernism and Eurocentrism into a search for new analyses and translations. Postmodernism in this sense is useful less as a fixed tradition or discourse than a marker of transit, a boundary from which new investigations can begin. Bhabha writes:

If the jargon of our times—postmodernity, postcoloniality, postfeminism—has any meaning at all, it does not lie in the popular use of the "post" to indicate sequentiality after-feminism; or polarity-anti-modernism. These terms that insistently gesture to the beyond only embody its restless and revisionary energy if they transform the present into an expanded and excentric site of experience and empowerment. . . . The wider significance of the postmodern condition lies in the awareness that the epistemological "limits" of [modernism] are also the enunciative boundary of a range of other dissonant, even dissident histories and voices—women, the colonized, minority groups, the bearers of policed sexualities.[6]

Acknowledging both the reactionary and progressive moments in postmodernism, anti-essentialist cultural work might take up the challenge of "writing the political back into the postmodern" (Ebert 1991, 291), simultaneously radicalizing the political legacy of modernism in order to promote a new vision of radical democracy in a postmodern world. One challenge in the debate over postmodernism is whether its more progressive elements can further our understanding of how power works, how social identities are formed, and how the changing conditions of the global economy and the new informational technologies can be articulated to meet the challenges posed by progressive cultural workers and the new social movements.

More specifically, the issue for critical educators lies in appropriating postmodernism as part of a broader pedagogical project that reasserts the primacy of the political while simultaneously engaging the most progressive aspects of modernism. Postmodernism becomes relevant to the extent that it becomes part of a broader political project in which the relationship between modernism and postmodernism becomes dialectical, dialogic, and critical.

Although the authors in *Education and the Postmodern Condition* largely address the work of Jean-François Lyotard and postmodernism as a site of conflict and struggle, they do so from the perspective of a wide-ranging critical debate. In doing so, the authors display how differences provide the basis for new languages and make struggle imperative to any project that takes human agency seriously. Educators and students who want to understand how postmodern discourses have influenced educational theory through various theoretical discourses will find this book invaluable and very difficult to put down.

Henry A. Giroux

NOTES

1. For a particularly succinct examination of the postmodernist challenge to a modernist conception of history, see Vattimo 1992, especially Chapter 1.

2. A number of excellent books have appeared that provide readings in postmodernism that cut across a variety of fields. Some of the more recent examples include Jencks 1992, Natioli and Hutcheon 1993, and Docherty 1993.

3. I have taken this issue up in great detail in Giroux 1988 and Giroux 1992.

4. See Clarke 1991, especially Chapter 2. Clarke's analysis has little more to do with a complex reading of postmodernism than a defensive reaction of his own refusal to take seriously a postmodern critique of the modernist elements in Marxist theories.

5. Needless to say, one can find a great deal of theoretical material that refuses to dismiss postmodern discourses so easily and in doing so performs a theoretical service in unraveling its progressive tendencies from its reactionary ones. Early examples of this work can be found in Foster 1985, Hebdige 1988, Vattimo 1992, Ross 1988, Hutcheon 1988, Collins 1989, and Connor 1989; more recent examples include Nicholson 1990, Lasch 1990, Chambers 1990, Aronowitz and Giroux 1991, Best and Kellner 1991, Denzin 1991, and Owens 1992.

6. Homi Bhabha, "Beyond the Pale: Art in the Age of Multicultural Translation," *Kunst and Museumjournal* 5:4 (1994), p. 16.

WORKS CITED

Anderson, Perry. "Modernity and Revolution." *New Left Review*, No. 144 (1984): 96–113.

Anshaw, Carol. "Days of Whine and Poses." *Village Voice* 10 (November 1992): 25–27.

Aronowitz, Stanley, and Henry A. Giroux. *Postmodern Education*. Minneapolis: University of Minnesota Press, 1991.

Aronowitz, Stanley and Henry A. Giroux. *Education Still Under Siege*. 2nd ed. Westport, Conn.: Bergin and Garvey, 1993.

Bauman, Zygmunt. *Intimations of Postmodernity*. New York: Routledge, 1992.

Bell, Daniel. *The Cultural Contradictions of Capitalism*. New York: Basic Books, 1976.

Berube, Michael. "Exigencies of Value." *Minnesota Review*, No. 39 (1992–93): 63–87.

Best, Stephen, and Douglas Kellner. *Postmodern Theory*. New York: Guilford Press, 1990.

Bordo, Susan. *Unbearable Weight: Feminism, Western Culture, and the Body*. Berkeley: University of California Press, 1993.

Butler, Judith. "Contingent Foundations: Feminism and the Question of Postmodernism." In *Feminists Theorize the Political*, ed. Judith Butler and Joan Scott, 3–21. New York: Routledge, 1991.

Chambers, Iain. *Border Dialogues*. New York: Routledge, 1990.

Clarke, John. *New Times and Old Enemies: Essays on Cultural Studies and America*. New York: HarperCollins, 1991.

Clifford, John. "Museums in the Borderlands." In *Different Voices*, ed. Association of Art Museum Directors, 117–136. New York: Association of Art Museum Directors, 1992.

Collins, Jim. *Uncommon Cultures*. New York: Routledge, 1989.

Connor, Steven. *Postmodernist Culture*. Cambridge, Mass.: Blackwell, 1989.

Denzin, Norman. *Images of a Postmodern Society*. Newbury Park, Calif.: Sage, 1991.

Docherty, Thomas, ed. *Postmodernism: A Reader*. New York: Columbia University Press, 1993.

Eagleton, Terry. "Capitalism, Modernism, and Postmodernism" 185 (July 1985): 60–73.

Ebert, Teresa. "Writing in the Political: Resistance (Post)modernism." *Legal Studies Forum* 15, 4 (1991): 291–303.

Foster, Hal, ed. *Postmodern Culture*. London: Pluto Press, 1985.

Giroux, Henry. *Schooling and the Struggle for Public Life*. Minneapolis: University of Minnesota Press, 1988.

Giroux, Henry. *Border Crossings*. New York: Routledge, 1992.

Giroux, Henry. *Disturbing Pleasures: Learning Popular Culture*. New York: Routledge, 1994.

Habermas, Jürgen. *The Philosophical Discourse of Modernity*. Cambridge, Mass.: MIT Press, 1978.

Harvey, David. *The Conditions of Postmodernity*. Cambridge: Basil Blackwell, 1989.

Hebdige, Dick. *Hiding in the Light*. New York: Routledge, 1988.

Hunter, Ian. *Culture and Government: The Emergence of Literary Education*. London: Macmillan, 1988.

Hutcheon, Linda. *The Poetics of Postmodernism*. New York: Routledge, 1988.

Jencks, Charles. "The Postmodern Agenda." In *The Postmodern Reader*, ed. by Charles Jencks. New York: St. Martin's Press, 1992.

Lasch, Scott. *Sociology of Postmodernism*. New York: Routledge, 1990.

MacCannell, Dean. *Empty Meeting*. New York: Routledge, 1992.

Mercer, Kobena. " '1968': Periodizing Politics and Identity." In *Cultural Studies*, ed. Lawrence Grossberg, Cary Nelson, and Paula Treichler. New York: Routledge, 1992.

Natioli, Joseph, and Linda Hutcheon, eds. *A Postmodern Reader.* Albany, N.Y.: SUNY Press, 1993.

Nicholson, Linda, ed. *Feminism/Postmodernism.* New York: Routledge, 1990.

Owens, Craig. *Beyond Recognition: Representation, Power, and Culture,* ed. Scott Bryson et al. Berkeley: University of California Press, 1992.

Patton, Paul. "Giving up the Ghost: Postmodernism and Anti-Nihilism." In *It's a Sin,* ed. Lawrence Grossberg, 88–95. Sydney: Power Publications, 1988.

Ross, Andrew, ed. *Universal Abandon? The Politics of Postmodernism.* Minneapolis: University of Minnesota Press, 1988.

Smart, Barry. "Theory and Analysis after Foucault." *Culture and Society* 8 (1991): 144–45.

Smart, Barry. *Modern Conditions, Postmodern Controversies.* New York: Routledge, 1992.

Tomlinson, John. *Cultural Imperialism.* Baltimore: Johns Hopkins University Press, 1991.

Vattimo, Gianni. *The Transparent Society.* Baltimore: Johns Hopkins University Press, 1992.

Virilio, Paul. *Lost Dimension,* trans. Daniel Moshenberg. New York: Semiotext(e), 1991.

Worth, Fabienne. "Postmodern Pedagogy in the Multicultural Classroom: For Inappropriate Teachers and Imperfect Strangers." *Cultural Critique,* No. 25 (Fall 1993): 5–32.

Foreword: Spaceship

"Sometimes I dream that I am an astronaut. I land my spaceship on a distant planet. When I tell the children on that planet that on earth school is compulsory and that we have homework every evening, they split their sides laughing. And so I decide to stay with them for a long, long time. . . . Well anyway . . . until the summer holidays!"

On the first day back at school in September David, aged seven and a half, comes home with the following homework: He has to learn this little story by Erhardt Dietl. In the space of one hour he can recite it in the right tone of voice without any mistakes. He has drawn the distant planet in his exercise book and the spaceship approaching it. The first thing that school makes him learn is the happiness of a world without school, with no obligations and no homework. This world exists on another planet. It is reached in a spaceship. The story does not say whether the little dreamer had to study to learn how to pilot the spaceship. It seems just as natural as climbing onto a bicycle. Years ago my sister and I would go off with two or three little friends, on long bicycle rides into the blue Atlantic summer, with our parents' blessing and our day's supplies of food on our carriers.

Perhaps going to school has only ever been to fill in time between radiant holidays. Perhaps the freedom promised by the Enlightenment was really the grace of this summer light bestowed on all. And the process of learning had perhaps as its true goal to give to the child the beauty of the world, its colors, breaths, poems, theorems, and other people.

To educate is to lead out. The moderns have stressed the efforts necessary to lead and let oneself be led out of nature toward language. But "out" is possibly not "outside." It is no doubt within, far inside. One cannot reach it by uprooting oneself but by plunging deep within toward what is most intimate, where lies desire. The child knows a lot more than we do about this state of dependency not only in relation to adults, but to what he cherishes in itself, with or against "big people," well or badly.

When are we educated? When we know more or less which is the far-off planet that we desire, and when we do all that we can to set off for it. If adults are often tough and sad, it is because they are disappointed. They do not listen well enough to the invitation to grace which is in them. They let the spaceship rust.

They take their holidays on the Riviera or in Florida. They really need them for their work exhausts them. To carry out their work, they have to give up their desire. Yet giving it up is impossible. In each of us there is an unconquerable resistance to the serious "ends" that social life proposes, a profession, a career, success. These ends count for nothing against a bicycle ride to another planet. This does not mean that I am advocating spontaneity as a pedagogical method and I don't believe that children are angelic. We are in debt to them and there is only one way to clear this debt, by assisting them to take off in their spaceship to the planet of their dreams.

Jean-François Lyotard
(Translated by Rosemary Arnoux)

Preface to the Paperback Edition

In *The Postmodern Condition* Jean-François Lyotard was concerned with metanarratives which had grown out of the Enlightenment and had come to mark modernity. In *The Postmodern Explained to Children* Lyotard mentions "the progressive emancipation of reason and freedom, the progressive or catastrophic emancipation of labour . . . the enrichment of all through the progress of capitalist technoscience, and even . . . the salvation of creatures through the conversion of souls to the Christian narrative of martyred love."[1] These metanarratives which have the goal of legitimating our institutions and our practices all have centrally involved education. Indeed, education is not merely one of the institutions which have been shaped or legitimated by the dominant metanarratives: at the lower levels it has been instrumentally involved with their systematic reproduction, elucidation, and preservation and, at the higher levels, it has been concerned with their ideological production, dissemination, and refinement.

Certainly, the first mentioned of these metanarratives which we can also refer to as the complex skein of liberalism considered as both a political tradition and an economic doctrine, has been the dominant metanarrative in education in the West. Since the early 1980s a particularly narrow variant—neoliberalism—has become the dominant metanarrative. (The publication of Lyotard's *The Postmodern Condition* coincided with the election to power of Margaret Thatcher's Conservative Government in Britain.) This particular variant, which revitalizes the master discourse of neoclassical economic liberalism, has been remarkably successful in advancing a foundationalist and universalist reason as a basis for a radical global reconstruction of all aspects of society and economy. A form of economic reason encapsulated in the notion of *homo economicus*, with its abstract and universalist assumptions of individuality, rationality and self-interest, has captured the policy agendas of OECD countries. Part of its innovation has been the way in which the neoliberal master narrative has successfully extended the principle of self-interest into the status of a paradigm for understanding politics itself, and, in fact, not merely market but *all* behavior and human action. Consequently, in the realm of education policy, especially in OECD countries but also in developing countries, at every opportunity the market has been substituted for the state: students are now "customers" or "clients" and teachers are "providers." The notion of vouchers is suggested as a universal panacea to problems of funding and quality. The teaching/learning relation has been reduced to an implicit contract between buyer and seller. As Lyotard argued prophetically in *The Postmodern Condition*, not only have knowledge and research become commodified but so have the relations of the production of knowledge in a new logic of *performativity*.

Yet on any analysis of the commodification of education it is not clear what the student (or her family) is buying: Is it the skills of the teacher? Is it the program or course? Is it the certificate or qualification at the end of the course or program? In no other example can I think of a "product" (or service) where the "customer" actively participates and constructs the "product" she buys. Such active participation is an essential or inherent part of the "product" such that if the participation is missing, then there is no "product" (or service). What this suggests is that the teaching/learning relation is difficult (if not impossible) to adequately capture in market terms; that the relation can not logically be reduced to a mode of consumption, without distortion.

Lyotard has consistently pursued what he refers to as "the problem of capitalism" and its transformations after the Second World War since the publication of *The Postmodern Condition*. Indeed, his break with the radical Marxism of *Socialisme ou barbarie* after twelve years of commitment was due, in part, to what he considered was the inability of the master discourse of Marxism to explain why and how capitalism had succeeded in surviving the crisis of the thirties. The proletariat had not seized the opportunity to overturn the old order. On the contrary, modern capitalism, once its market and production capacities had been restored, had set up new relations of exploitation and taken on new forms. Lyotard lists the following new realities confronting Marxism: the reorganization of capitalism into bureaucratic or State monopolistic capitalism; the role of the modern State in the so-called mixed economy; the dynamics of the new ruling strata (bureaucratic or technocratic) within the bourgeoisie; the impact of the new techniques on work conditions and on the mentality of workers and employees; the effects of economic growth on daily life and culture; the appearance of new demands by workers and the possibility of conflicts between the base and apparatus in worker organizations.[2]

Lyotard breaks intellectually with radical Marxism because dialectical logic as "the machinery for overcoming alterity by negating and conserving it" had broken down. As he says:

Inasmuch as there was in Marxism a discourse which claimed to be able to express without residue all opposing positions, which forgot that differends are embodied in incommensurable figures between which there is no logical solution it became necessary to stop speaking this idiom at all. . . .[3]

And yet having given up on the discourse of Marxism as that which could explain the transformations of global capitalism after World War II, Lyotard never gives up on the "the problem of capitalism." He argues:

One hears talk everywhere that the great problem of society is that of the state. This is a mistake, and a serious one. The problem that overshadows all others, including that of the contemporary state, is that of capital.[4]

Lyotard argues, for instance, in "A Svelte Appendix to the Postmodern Question," that "capitalism is one of the names of modernity," and suggests that capitalism

has been able to subordinate to itself the infinite desire for knowledge that animates the sciences, and to submit its achievements to its own criterion of technicity: the rule of performance that requires the endless optimalization of the cost/benefit (input/output) ratio.[5]

In this context he speaks of the "penetration of capitalism into language" and "the transformation of language into a productive commodity" which reduces phrases to encoded messages with an exchange value—information which can be stored, retrieved, packaged, calculated, and transmitted. Lyotard therefore remains within the ambit of a commodification thesis (albeit as a *representational* system) as one of the main processes of rationalization which guides the development of the system as a whole and he recognizes the way in which the logic of performance, aimed at maximizing the overall efficiency of the system, generates socioeconomic contradictions. Yet he parts company with Marxists on the possibility of emancipation or of salvation expected to arise automatically from these contradictions. He jettisons what Readings calls the "politics of redemption" based upon "the Marxist desire to identify alienation as a reversible ideological distortion" in order to rethink politics and resistance in "minoritarian" terms, which forgoes an authoritative reading of events based on determinate judgements, to respect the differend and "to think justice in relation to conflict and difference" that admit of no resolution.[6]

Our role as thinkers in the situation of postmodernity, Lyotard suggests, "is to deepen what language there is, to critique the shallow notion of information, to reveal an irremediable opacity within language itself."[7] The issue for Lyotard is one of understanding and providing a critique of capitalist forms of the insinuation of will into reason and the way this is manifest primarily in language.

Lyotard holds that capitalist renewal and the upsurge of technology has led to a "crisis" of scientific knowledge and to an internal erosion of the very prospect of legitimation. He locates the seeds of such "delegitimation" in the decline of the legitimating power of the grand narratives of the nineteenth century. The speculative narrative of the unity of all knowledge held that knowledge is worthy of its name only if it can generate a second-order discourse that functions to legitimate it, otherwise such "knowledge" would amount to mere ideology. The process of "delegitimation" has revealed that not only does science play its own language game (and consequently is both on a par with and incapable of legitimating other language games) but also is incapable of legitimating itself as speculation assumed it could. Under these conditions and with the proliferation of new language games which no one person is able to master, philosophy is forced to relinquish its legitimation duties and is reduced to the study of logic or the history of ideas. European nihilism for Lyotard is represented in the process of cultural disintegration symbolized most clearly by the end of metaphysics or, more correctly, the end of philosophy as the universal metalanguage—as that master-discipline able to underwrite all claims to knowledge and, thereby, to unify the rest of culture.

Central to Lyotard's analysis is the revival or recovery of the notion of "narrative" which he develops at the *local* and *popular* level as a form of customary, cultural, or ethnic knowledge—a "knowing how," "knowing how to live," and "knowing how to listen"—against the *totalizing* and *globalizing* tendencies of older master-narratives of legitimation which operate, albeit in crisis mode, in the service of the great historical "actors" of the nation-state, the proletariat, the party, and increasingly (one might add), the world policy agencies (e.g., World Bank, OECD), the G-7, "the new world order." Lyotard develops what he calls a "pragmatics of narrative knowledge" in which narratives determine criteria of competence and performance, defining rights of what can be said and done in a particular culture. Local or little narratives (*petit récits*), in sharp contrast to the game of legitimacy played in the West, provide immediate legitimation: as he says, "they are legitimated by the simple fact that they do what they do."[8] In that statement there is a philosophy of education based on difference and an epistemology of performance not unlike Wittgenstein's account of the relation of knowing to the mastery of a technique, waiting to be elaborated.

Lyotard's work and specifically the analysis he offers in *The Postmodern Condition*, even at a time when neoliberalism is on the wane, will remain relevant and politically significant for the new "flexible cultures of per-formance" which are in the process of being established in universities and other tertiary institutions, to the detriment of knowledge and diversity. This constitutes, in large measure, why I am pleased that Bergin and Garvey has decided to publish a paperback edition of this collection of essays. I would like to thank Maureen Melino and Lisa Reichbach at Bergin and Garvey for their editorial help and support.

NOTES

1. Jean-François Lyotard, *The Postmodern Explained to Children, Correspondence 1982–1985*. Ed. and trans. J. Pefanis and M. Thomas (Sydney: Power Publications, 1992), p. 29.

2. Jean-François Lyotard, "A Memorial for Marxism," in *Peregrinations: Law, Form, Event* (New York: Columbia University Press, 1988), p. 66.

3. Lyotard, "A Memorial for Marxism," in *Peregrinations: Law, Form, Event*, p. 61.

4. Jean-François Lyotard, "A Svelte Appendix to the Postmodern Question," in *Political Writings*. Trans. Bill Readings and Kevin Paul (Minneapolis: University of Minnesota Press, 1993), p. 25.

5. Lyotard, "A Svelte Appendix to the Postmodern Question," in *Political Writings*, p. 27.

6. Lyotard, "A Svelte Appendix to the Postmodern Question," in *Political Writings*, p. xxiv.

7. Lyotard, "A Svelte Appendix to the Postmodern Question," in *Political Writings*, p. 27.

8. Jean-François Lyotard, *The Postmodern Condition: A Report on Knowledge*. Trans. G. Bennington and B. Massumi (Minneapolis: University of Minnesota Press, 1984), p. 23.

Acknowledgments

I would like to thank Jean-François Lyotard for his support for this project. I first approached him with the idea of such a collection in 1990. He not only supported the general idea but also agreed to write a foreword for the book. My acknowledgment goes also to Rosemary Arnoux of the Romance Languages Department at the University of Auckland for translating Lyotard's foreword.

I am especially grateful to Peter McLaren for support for this project and to Lynn Flint at Bergin and Garvey for her enthusiasm, support, and guidance. Last but not least my thanks go to Tina Besley, who lived with me through the period of the book's gestation.

Introduction: Lyotard, Education, and the Postmodern Condition

Michael Peters

When Jean-François Lyotard's *La Condition Postmoderne: Rapport sur le Savoir* was first published in Paris in 1979, it became an instant *cause célèbre.*[1] It was written as an occasional text and presented to the Conseil des Universitiés of the government of Quebec at the request of its president. It is, as Lyotard himself makes clear in his own introduction, "a report on knowledge in the most highly developed societies" written by "a philosopher, not an expert."[2] An expert, Lyotard tells us, "knows what he knows and what he does not know"; the philosopher does not. The former concludes, whereas the latter questions. As Lyotard remarks, in terms entirely consistent with his approach to the pragmatic analysis of narratives, of ethicopolitical discourses of legitimation that underlie the report, these are two quite different language games with different rules and expectations. Lyotard thus expresses his own disquiet at the uneasy combination of the two.

The book was important for a number of reasons. It developed an original philosophical interpretation of the changing state of knowledge and education in the most highly developed societies, reviewing, synthesizing, and presenting information on contemporary science within the broader context of the sociology of postindustrial society and studies of postmodern culture. Lyotard brought together for the first time diverse threads and previously separate literatures in a prophetic analysis that many commentators and critics believed to signal an epochal break not only with the so-called modern era but also with various traditionally "modern" ways of viewing the world.

Education has been addressed by philosophers and experts. Most, if not all, of these contributions have viewed education in modernist terms. Historically, for instance, liberal institutions (prisons, courts, psychiatric institutions), including the school and the modern university, have legitimated themselves and their practices by reference to discourse of subject-centered reason. The project of liberal mass schooling and higher education in the late twentieth century is built around the intellectual authority inherited from the Enlightenment. It is grounded in a European universalism and rationalism heavily buttressed by highly individualistic assumptions. It is these assumptions and the authority that rests upon them that is now being called into question and with it both neoconservative and left radical attempts to reform education. "Postmodernism" is the broad cultural phenomenon of Western societies that best typifies this questioning and the attempt to find new cultural and political orientations. Such a questioning is fundamental to Lyotard's work, and the essays that comprise this volume stand in the same line of radical questioning that provides critique and reinterpretation of the significance and role of education in the postmodern condition.

The publication of Lyotard's work and its translation into English in 1984 marked important stages in the globalization of what came to be known as the "modernity/postmodernity debate"—phrased, misleadingly, in the singular—a philosophical debate given a distinct form and interpretation by Lyotard, and one that contemporaneously involved, in one way or another, most of the central thinkers of the late twentieth century. It is a debate now officially some fifteen years old and one that despite the occasional obituary still dominates the intellectual landscape. The tremendous outpouring of publications in the English language alone, in architecture, the arts and humanities, in fields of literary and art theory, in the traditional disciplines of history, sociology, education, psychology, economics, political economy, geography, and in fields of feminist theory, cultural studies, communications theory, and so on, is so staggeringly diverse that few academics can master the different genres of discourse or absorb the circulation and recirculation of ideas, theory, and information.

Lyotard's *The Postmodern Condition* is important, in retrospect, not least for sparking and reformulating a debate that has proved to be a most durable and persistent set of themes, both accessible and open to wide participation and conversation. In a strong sense one could argue that the reason why Lyotard's work has given rise to such controversy is that it epitomizes, self-referentially, the very conditions for discourse in the "postmodern condition" elaborated in *The Differend*: "that a universal rule of judgement between heterogeneous genres is lacking in general,"[3] or that "there is no genre whose hegemony over others would be just."[4] A *differend*, as Lyotard defines it, is "a case of conflict, between (at least) two parties, that cannot be equitably resolved for lack of a rule of judgement applicable to both arguments."[5] Where multiple parties are involved from a variety of genres of discourse, each with a different perspective or argument, as is the case in the modernity-postmodernity debate, it is, perhaps, no wonder that there is no one ruling or hegemonic genre, no overarching metadiscourse, language game or metanarrative, and no rule of judgment applicable to all arguments (in spite of claims and counterarguments to the contrary). The explosion of the modernity-postmodernity debate is itself a differend, and the essays in this volume are no exception. The aim of philosophy in this situation, Lyotard argues, is to detect differends (a cognitive task) and to bear witness to them (an ethical obligation).

It is the aim also guiding this collection of essays, which brings together for the first time a number of contributions on Lyotard's work made by educationalists, philosophers, and sociologists in the English-speaking world around the special focus of education. The initial collective intent behind these essays was to examine Lyotard's notion of the postmodern condition—its relevance and special significance for education. Although these essays are advertised in terms of the title as *Education and the Postmodern Condition*, a clear reference to Lyotard's major work incorporating the now-famous phrase, they are not restricted to a consideration of *The Postmodern Condition*, which since its publication has tended to overshadow both Lyotard's earlier and later work. These essays themselves do not constitute anything like a unity or standard interpretation of Lyotard, except in the material sense of comprising a single volume. They are also too diverse in their interpretations to constitute a single orthodoxy. Written by a range of academics from a variety of disciplines, the essays approach Lyotard's work from a variety of perspectives and genres; some more sympathetically than others; some concentrating on Lyotard's early rather than his later work or vice versa; some contesting Lyotard's most basic notions; others significantly developing or building upon an aspect of his thinking. The reader is left the philosophical task of detecting and bearing witness to the differends.

DISCOURSE, PHILOSOPHY, AND THE POSTMODERN CONDITION

Lyotard originally adopted the most highly charged word postmodern from its then-current use among American sociologists and critics. In the first footnote to *The Postmodern Condition*, Lyotard acknowledges the contemporary sources of the usage of this term, which has since become embedded in so many different phrase regimes: the sociology of postindustrialism, mentioning the work of Alain Touraine,[6] as well as Daniel Bell,[7] and, loosely speaking, the literary theory of Ihab Hassan,[8] together with the emphasis on "performance" in postmodern culture by Michel Benamou and Charles Caramello.[9] He mentions, in addition, the now classic essay by M. Köhler.[10] These sources date from the late 1960s and themselves suggest an intellectual genealogy of the term that dates back much further.

Lyotard uses the term to describe "the condition of knowledge in the most highly developed societies" and asserts that "it designates the state of our culture following the transformations which, since the end of the nineteenth century, have altered the game rules for science, literature, and the arts."[11] These transformations have altered the game rules not only for science, literature, and the arts but also for the field, practices, and institutions of education that are responsible for their transmission and production. Most fundamentally, they have altered the game rules for the discourse of legitimation, which returns us to one of the main themes of *The Postmodern Condition* that bears centrally on education.

The discourse of legitimation is cast within the general context of the crisis of narratives that, in turn, becomes the fulcrum for distinguishing the "modern" from the "postmodern." As Lyotard writes in a passage that is often quoted: "I will use the term *modern* to designate any science that legitimates itself with reference to a metadiscourse . . . making explicit appeal to some grand narrative, such as the dialectics of Spirit, the hermeneutics of meaning, the emancipation of the rational or working subject, or the creation of wealth."[12] By contrast, he defines *postmodern* simply as "incredulity toward metanarratives."[13] The rule of consensus that governed the Enlightenment narratives and cast truth as a product of agreement between rational minds has finally been rent asunder. The narrative function has been dispersed into many language elements, each with its own pragmatic valencies. We are left only with "language particles," a heterogeneity of language games (a "particle" theory of language?). There is no neutral ground upon which to adjudicate between competing claims, no synthesizing master discourse that can reproduce the speculative unity of knowledge. Simply put, the linguistic turn of twentieth-century philosophy and the social sciences does not warrant the assumption of a metalinguistic neutrality or foundational epistemological privilege.

The logico-linguistic turn taken by twentieth-century philosophy was motivated by the concern to find a permanent and neutral framework for inquiry, one that would enable rational agreement amongst philosophers and sanction the authority of their inquiries. In this sense, modern analytic philosophy can be viewed as a linguistic variant of the epistemological enterprises of John Locke and Immanuel Kant, at least to the extent that it has inherited a doctrine of philosophical autonomy based on a similar critical or reflexive turn. On this basis metaphysical claims, it was argued, could be evaluated solely in terms of their formal or logical features and such "second-order" thinking aimed at the analysis of the languages used in the sciences, literature, and the arts would occasion agreement or, at least, eliminate disagreement. In Lyotard's terms, the "semantic assent"[14]—the strategy of a metalanguage—has failed to provide the necessary foundations for epistemological certainty or privilege. Lyotard would undoubtedly agree with Ludwig Wittgenstein, who in the *Philosophical Investigations* forcefully attacks the cartesian, or modern, view that philosophy is a foundational discipline[15]—a metadiscourse or metadiscipline that provides foundations for first-order disciplines. For both Lyotard and Wittgenstein philosophy is not something that one needs to do before doing anything else. Above all philosophy is not a metaactivity. At one point in the *Investigations*, for instance, Wittgenstein writes: "One might think: if philosophy speaks of the use of the word 'philosophy' there must be a second-order philosophy. But this is not so: it is, rather, like the case of orthography which deals with the word 'orthography' among others without then being second-order."[16] At another, he plainly asserts, "The philosophy of logic speaks of sentences and words in exactly the same sense in which we speak of them in ordinary life."[17] The impossibility of a metalanguage, of philosophy's metalinguistic strategy, was already forecast in the *Tractatus* in the doctrine of showing.[18] Wittgenstein asserts that the sense of a proposition can only be shown,[19] and the propositions of the *Tractatus* itself are themselves to be viewed as nonsensical, as a ladder to be thrown away once we have ascended.[20]

It is, of course, no accident that I speak of Lyotard and Wittgenstein in the same breath, for Lyotard champions Wittgenstein's language games as the basis of his analysis of the crisis of narratives in *The Postmodern Condition* and acknowledges the strong sense in which his own work takes place "after" Wittgenstein.[21] In "Wittgenstein 'After,'" Lyotard likens Wittgenstein to Kant and writes in terms that foreshadow the account he presents in *The Differend*:

The examination of language games, just like the critique of the faculties, identifies and reinforces the separation of language from itself. There is no unity to language; there are islands of language, each of them ruled by a different regime, untranslatable into others. This dispersion is good in itself, and ought to be respected.[22]

Further on, he adds:

In ordinary language, a multiplicity of phrases obeys different regimes. Giving someone an order does not have the same stakes or the same rules for success as describing a landscape to him or her, telling him or her a story, providing the blueprint of a piece of machinery, or promising him or her something. Each set (or family) of phrases brings specific pressures to bear on the interlocutors, which push them to make phrase linkages in one way rather than another. In principle, after any given phrase, any phrase whatsoever may occur. If this is not generally the case, if some linkages are more expected than others, it is because rules for making linkages have been fixed and learned under the aegis of tradition.[23]

It is clear that Lyotard in *The Postmodern Condition* has taken on board the Wittgensteinian understanding of language games, yet his reading is both playful and innovative rather than simply exegetical. He emphasizes the pluralistic nature of language games to advance an attack on the conception of universal reason, of the unity of language and of the subject. There is no one reason, only reasons, in the plural, where no one form of reason takes precedence over others. The traumatic aspect of *The Postmodern Condition* here points to the tearing apart of old organic bodies that regulate thinking. Where Jürgen Habermas and critical theory emphasizes the bifurcation of reason into its instrumental (positivistic) and moral-practical forms, Lyotard (following Wittgenstein) and Michel Foucault emphasize the (postmodern) multiplicity and proliferation of forms of reason, defined by the rules of particular discourses or language games. Each of the various types of utterance—denotative, prescriptive, performative, and so on—comprises a language game with its own body of rules. The rules are irreducible, and there exists an incommensurability among different games. Further, Lyotard argues in true Wittgensteinian fashion that the rules do not have a bedrock justification, nor do they carry with them their own legitimation. Where Wittgenstein might say they are constituted in practice, Lyotard claims they are the object of a contract, explicit or not, between players that gives rise to an "agonistics" of language. As Lyotard suggests:

After Wittgenstein, the first task is that of overcoming this humanist obstacle to the analysis of phrases regimes, to make philosophy inhuman. Humanity is not the user of language, nor even its guardian; there is no more one subject than there is one language. Phrases situate names and pronouns (or their equivalent) in the universes they present. Philosophy is the discourse that has as its rule the search for its rule (and that of other discourses), a discourse in which phrases thus try themselves out without rules and link themselves guided only by amazement at the fact that everything has not been said, that a new phrase occurs, that it is not the case that nothing happens.[24]

Lyotard argues that this "inhumanity," its implications for the "social bond," yet remains to be analyzed and that the principal difficulty is not that of the State but the "functioning of capital, which is a regime of linking phrases far more supple and far more 'inhuman' (oppressive, if you will) than any political or social regime."[25]

CAPITALISM AND THE PROBLEM OF LEGITIMATION

The problem of capitalism is one that has occupied Lyotard since his early political involvement with *Socialisme ou Barbarie*, later in *Libidinal Economy*,[26] and consistently thereafter in his "post-Marxist" writings. He argues, for instance, in "A Svelte Appendix to the Postmodern Question," "Capitalism is one of the names of modernity," and continues in a vein highly reminiscent of *The Postmodern Condition*: "Capitalism has been able to subordinate to itself the infinite desire for knowledge that animates the sciences, and to submit its achievements to its own criterion of technicity: the rule of performance that requires the endless optimalization of the cost/benefit (input/output) ratio."[27]

Lyotard thus speaks of the "penetration of capitalism into language," "the transformation of language into a productive commodity" that reduces phrases to encoded messages with an exchange value—information that can be stored, retrieved, packaged, calculated, and transmitted. Lyotard acknowledges his debt to Karl Marx and remains within the ambit of commodification (albeit as a *representational* system) as one of the main processes of rationalization that guides the development of the system as a whole: the Marxian analysis of commodity fetish as it applies to knowledge and education. And he recognizes the way in which the logic of performance, aimed at maximizing the overall efficiency of the system, generates socioeconomic contradictions, but he parts company with Marxists on the possibility of emancipation or of salvation expected to arise automatically from these contradictions.[28] He jettisons what Bill Readings[29] calls the "politics of redemption" based upon "the Marxist desire to identify alienation as a reversible ideological distortion" in order to rethink politics and resistance in "minoritarian" terms, which forgoes an authoritative reading of events based on determinate judgments, to respect the differend and "to think justice in relation to conflict and difference" that admit of no resolution.[30] "Our role as thinkers" in the situation of postmodernity, Lyotard suggests, "is to deepen what language there is, to critique the shallow notion of information, to reveal an irremediable opacity within language itself."[31] The issue for Lyotard is one of understanding and providing a critique of capitalist forms of the insinuation of will into reason and the way this is manifest in language.

This is a question he addresses clearly in *The Postmodern Condition* in terms of the performativity principle, which, he suggests, reduces difference, ignores the differend, and treats all language games as commensurable, and the whole as determinable. The logic of performance, of optimizing the system's overall performance based on the criterion of efficiency, does violence to the heterogeneity of language games and "necessarily involves a certain level of terror: be operational (that is, commensurable) or disappear."[32] The notion of performance and its criterion of efficiency is technological; it cannot provide us with a rule for judging what is true or just or beautiful. Here, then, is a trenchant critique of capitalism, of capitalism's penetration of language, and of the way thought is managed, packaged, and commodified in "the new postmodern technologies insofar as they express the most recent application of capitalist rules to language."[33]

It is a critique that leads us back to the central question of legitimation of knowledge and education. If the Enlightenment idealist and humanist metanarratives have become bankrupt and the State and Corporation must abandon or renounce them, wherein can legitimacy reside? Lyotard, in his critique of capitalism, suggests that the State has found its only credible goal in power. Science and education are to be legitimated, in de facto terms, through the principle of performativity, that is, through the logic of maximization of the system's performance, which becomes self-legitimating in Niklas Luhmann's sense.

It is this account that has proved so potent in prophesizing and analyzing the changes to economic and social policy that have taken place in the Western world with the ascendancy of the so-called new right, beginning, perhaps, with Margaret Thatcher's rise to power in 1979 and her ability to wield an alliance between neoliberal and neoconservative factions. The commitment by the Thatcher and Reagan administrations during the 1980s and by world agencies such as the Organization for Economic Cooperation and Development (OECD), World Bank, and International Monetary Fund, to monetarism and supplyside economics, precipitated a general move by Western governments toward economic rationalism and provided a general context for structural reform based upon the idea of self-limiting government and new strategies for capital accumulation. Neoliberalism as an international development during the 1980s and early 1990s represents a renewal of the main article of faith underlying classical economic liberalism based on the assumption of *homo economicus*. Its major innovation is to apply this assumption of self-interest to all behavior: economic, social, and political. Thus, for example, public choice theory, originating at Virginia State University, extends the principle of self-interest to the status of a paradigm for understanding politics (politics as exchange); and a rejuvenated human capital theory with an emphasis on private and individual investment, rather than public investment, commodifies education, viewing it as a major strategy for enhancing labor flexibility and, therefore, for improving the overall competitiveness of the economy. On this view individuals are rational utility maximizers and it is accepted that the pursuit of self-interest in the marketplace will yield socially and economically desirable outcomes.

Neoliberals and advocates of new right policies have increasingly focused their attention on the rising and apparently irreversible tide of welfare expectations, arguing that the welfare state has evaded both investment and work incentives and has directly contributed to economic recession. The combined effects of social policies—including guaranteed minimum wages, superannuation, and the exponential growth of health and education sectors—has allegedly strengthened organized labor vis-à-vis capital, augmented wages as against capital goods, and increased state borrowings from itself, leading to a decline of profitability. Neoliberals argue that the so-called perverse effects lead to greater State interventionism in both social and economic terms; but the more the State helps, they argue, the more it will have to help and at diminishing levels of effectiveness. It is alleged that increasing levels of intervention, while leading to the current crisis of an imbalance between State receipts and expenditure, tend in the long term to rob economic liberalism of its vitality. The bottom line is that the perverse effects of economic and social intervention represent to these critics a fundamental threat to individual political and economic freedom.

Education, not so long ago regarded as a universal welfare right under a social democratic model, has been recast as a leading subsector of the economy and one of the main enterprises of the future "postindustrial" economy. Lyotard's *The Postmodern Condition* provides an understanding and critique of the neo-liberal marketization of education in terms of the systemic, self-regulatory nature of global capitalism.[34] His concern is that critical theory, based upon the traditional critique of political economy, has been used as a way of reprogramming the system and that it has lost its theoretical standing and been reduced to a utopia.

His response to this state of affairs is to emphasize legitimation by paralogy. He argues: "Postmodern knowledge is not simply a tool of the authorities; it refines our sensitivity to differences and reinforces our ability to tolerate the incommensurable. Its principle is not the expert's homology, but the inventor's paralogy."[35] In contrast to the models of legitimation based on the principle of consensus, Lyotard suggests a kind of legitimation based on difference understood as paralogy. Against the possibility of consensus either defined as dialogical agreement between rational minds (based on the narrative of emancipation) or as the logic of maximum performance, Lyotard theorizes the legitimation of postmodern science in terms of paralogy, where "the little narrative remains the quintessential form of imaginative invention."[36] Paralogy includes the study of open systems, local determinism, and antimethod.[37] It is what Readings[38] calls "the pragmatics of discursive legitimation" and what Lyotard explains in the following terms: "Postmodern science—by concerning itself with such things as undecidables, the limits of precise control, conflicts characterized by incomplete information, '*fracta*,' catastrophes, and pragmatic paradoxes—is theorizing its own evolution as discontinuous, catastrophic, nonrectifiable, and paradoxical."[39]

Lyotard stands against the legitimation of education in terms of consensus or performance, forms of legitimation linked, on the one hand, to a reductive homogenization of interests that produces in a single overriding, transparent, and dialectical conclusion an inversion of the capitalist hierarchy of values and class positions and, on the other, to its opposite—an equally "monological" version based upon the performance of a system as a whole. Both forms of legitimation offer the promise of utopia (literally "no place"), in terms of a metanarrative—a single master language and reason according to which the community must be shaped. By contrast, if we view the question of paralogy as being linked to a version of education, in accordance with Lyotard, we might begin to bear witness to the differend, to a form of education based on difference, where the little narratives, still largely unwritten, are not forced to resolve themselves into a monologue.

LYOTARD ON LYOTARD

What, then, is the postmodern? . . . It is undoubtedly a part of the modern. . . . postmodernism thus understood is not modernism at its end but in the nascent state, and this state is constant.[40] I have said and will say again that "postmodern" signifies not the end of modernism, but another relation to modernism.[41]

The reception and appraisal of Lyotard's *The Postmodern Condition* in the English-speaking world has occasioned a great deal of criticism, some sympathetic and constructive, some vitriolic and accusatory. Rather than engage this literature here (a function performed by a number of essays in this collection), the strategy followed has been to allow Lyotard himself to reappraise his own work, which he has undertaken in published correspondence and interviews. Even in *The Postmodern Condition* itself, Lyotard enters a number of caveats: He makes it quite clear, for instance, that the scenario he presents is not as simple as he has made it appear; he also makes no claims to his account's being original, predictive, or even true; rather, the hypothesis of the changing status of knowledge is presented as having "strategic value" in relation to the problem of legitimation.[42]

In an interview with Willem van Reijen and Dick Veerman in 1987, Lyotard strongly indicates that many of his critics received *The Postmodern Condition* as a book of philosophy that sought to put an end to reflection as it had been established by Enlightenment rationalism. His response to this kind of reception took a number of forms: first, he emphatically denied that *The Postmodern Condition* was indeed a book of philosophy; it was rather, he suggests, a book "marked by sociology, by a certain historicism, and by epistemology"—subjects that were imposed by the nature of "a report on the actual state of the sciences in the advanced countries."[43] He further suggests that the philosophical basis of the report could be found in *Le Differend*, which provides readings of the great tradition. Second, he remarks that the "postmodern" as he theorized the notion did not signify the end of modernism, nor the end of philosophical reflection, a remark amply justified by the guiding quotations referred to at the beginning of this section. It is therefore clear that although Lyotard bases his use of the notion in part on its past sociological uses, he explicitly denies that he is using the term as a periodizing concept. Postmodernity is not simply that which comes after modernity; postmodernism is not simply that which comes after modernism, in a continuous, unbroken chronology marking a specific historical configuration. He detemporalizes both the modern and the postmodern by rehabilitating the term *postmodern* as a philosophical category.[44] For Lyotard, the postmodern is not a different historical epoch but, rather, a critical attitude or mode of thought about time and history. Lyotard defines modernism also as a mode of thought about time (rather than a period) that rests on two features: time as succession and time as an atemporal subject. As Readings explains: "The discourse of history is thus structured as a narrative sequence around an 'I' dedicated to the possession and control of both nature and itself through the organization of time as a sequential series of phrases."[45] The point that Lyotard is making is that the postmodern is a critical way of thinking about a conception of time, history, and, indeed, the very urge to periodize, which is characteristic of modernity. This critical approach should be construed as a reevaluation and problematization of the modernist notion of time and history as an ordered, stable, sequential, temporal succession of events synthesized in an atemporal subject and, therefore, also a rethinking of the modernist notion of history as the continuous chronology of reason.

Third, Lyotard suggests that the attack of his critics, who focused upon *The Postmodern Condition* at the expense of his other works, "bears the marks of a summary and totalizing idea of reason."[46] And he responds, following a Kantian (and Wittgensteinian) line of argument: "I would oppose them simply with the following principle (which seems to me much more rationalist than they think): there is no reason, only reasons."[47] Lyotard opposes Kant to G. W. Hegel, the Kantian sublime to the Hegelian dialectic, the principle of difference against the power of totalizing reason: "It is never a question of *one* massive and unique reason—that is nothing but an ideology. On the contrary, it is a question of plural rationalities, which are, at the least, respectively, theoretical, practical, aesthetic."[48] Referring to the "crisis of reason" in the sciences, brought to our attention by epistemologists such as Thomas Kuhn and Paul Feyerabend, Lyotard suggests that this crisis, which constitutes "a continual interrogation of reason," is, in fact, "certainly the most rational thing around."[49]

Fourth, in "Apostil on Narratives" Lyotard acknowledges that in *The Postmodern Condition* he exaggerated the importance of the narrative genre and, he says, "specifically, . . . went too far in identifying knowledge with narrative."[50] He argues that on the whole, scientific theory does not take the form of narrative and that within general narratology there remains an ineliminable metaphysics that accords hegemony to the genre of narrative over all others. In accordance with the passage to *Le Différend*, Lyotard now wishes to forgo this metaphysical element by emphasizing the different regimes of phrases and different genres of discourse without attributing any one regime or genre privilege or precedence. In "Missive on Universal History" Lyotard writes:

It is inadvisable to grant the narrative genre an absolute privilege over other genres of discourse in the analysis of human, and specifically linguistic (ideological), phenomena, particularly when the approach is philosophical. Some of my earlier reflections may have succumbed to this "transcendental appearance," "Presentations," *Instructions Païennes*, even *The Postmodern Condition*.[51]

This revision is treated as an occasion to explore the question of the Idea of a universal history of humanity, and he claims that if we treat the world in historical terms we cannot help but organize events in narrative terms. Modernity considered as a mode within thinking and speech is governed by the Idea of emancipation expressed variously in narrative form: the Christian narrative of redemption; the *Aufklärer* narrative of emancipation through knowledge; the speculative narrative of the realization of the universal Idea; the Marxist narrative of emancipation from exploitation through the socialization of work; the capitalist narrative of emancipation from poverty through development. Yet "between these narratives there are grounds for litigation and even for differends,"[52] even if they all participate in the call for universal freedom.

The differends within the narrative of universal emancipation promised by modernity are to be found in a questioning and abandonment of the "linguistic structure of communication (I/you/he)," which serves as the ontological and political model of the moderns. Lyotard elaborates:

A different way of dealing with the universal emancipation promised by modernity would be to "work over" (in the Freudian sense) not just the loss of this object but the loss of the subject to whom this goal was promised. It would not only be a matter of recognizing our finitude but of elaborating the status of *we*, the question of the subject. That is, of escaping both an unrevised renewal of the modern subject and its parodical or cynical repetition (tyranny).[53]

EDUCATION AND THE POSTMODERN CONDITION

Lyotard's foreword to this volume, entitled "Spaceship" ("Fusée"), is a brief, elegantly written, even poetic piece that questions and reverts the metaphor of childhood as one of dependency and unreason. In deceptively simple terms, Lyotard turns upside down the Kantian definition of Enlightenment as the escape from immaturity through reason. This is a theme he has developed before in "The Grip" (*Mainmise*): "We are held by the grasp of others since childhood, yet our childhood does not cease to exercise its *mancipium* [the gesture of taking hold] even when we imagine ourselves to be emancipated."[54] By the term childhood Lyotard does not mean a stage characterized by the lack of reason. He means a condition of being *affected* "at a time when we do not have the means—linguistic and representational—to name, identify, reproduce, and recognize what it is that is affecting us. By childhood, I mean the fact that we are born before we are born to ourselves."[55] We are, to paraphrase Lyotard, born in the grip of others: fathers, mothers, siblings, ministers, teachers, philosophers, themselves always in the grip of their own childhood, from which they can never attain emancipation.[56]

It is this sense of childhood that motivates Lyotard to dismiss the parallel between minds and computers and to remark that the questions of children are not unlike those of the philosopher.[57] One might say also that *The Postmodern Explained to Children* is given that title precisely in the same spirit, as the translators explain in their foreword to the English edition:

So the promise of the title to "explain to children" what adults find obscure is surely ironic and not to be taken literally. It will not have explained the postmodern. Rather, it will have shown why it is necessary to approach the philosophical questions raised by postmodernity both with patience and with the mind of the child. For childhood is the season of the mind's possibilities and of the possibility of philosophy.[58]

William Bain in the opening chapter examines the "loss of innocence" by reference to Lyotard's definition of the postmodern as "incredulity toward narratives" and Foucault's notion of the "limit-attitude" in order to focus on the changed relationship between education and enlightenment, which, he argues following Foucault, assumes the unique form of a "critical ontology of ourselves." In these terms Bain establishes that the postmodern condition represents not the end of the enlightenment, nor the end of the symbiotic relationship between education and enlightenment, but its continuance by other means. The second enlightenment tradition, understood as a "critical ontology of ourselves," is not a depth hermeneutic preoccupied with the cartesian question "Who am I?" a question that sets out to reveal foundations of the self. It is, as Bain makes abundantly clear, guided by the Kantian question "Who are we?" and directed at investigating in a critical manner the contingent ways we are constituted in and through discourse. This reading of Lyotard and postmodernism, therefore, is one that is both critical and still within the enlightenment tradition. Foucault, I am reminded, commented that the thread connecting us to the Enlightenment is not one primarily of doctrine but of attitude, as he says, "of a philosophical ethos that could be described as a permanent critique of our historical era."[59]

In providing some background to the modernism-postmodernism debate in Chapter 2, I make reference to Foucault in a similar way to Bain, with the general purpose of fleshing out some of the general issues that impinge upon Lyotard's discussion of the problem of the legitimation of knowledge, and, therefore, also of education. I attempt to provide the appropriate context within the English-speaking philosophical world for viewing Lyotard's epistemological claims. It is a context that, I think, is dominated by the figure of the later Wittgenstein and, thereafter, linked to Wittgensteinian-inspired epistemologists: Thomas Kuhn, Stephen Toulmin, and Paul Feyerabend. The thought of the later Wittgenstein is also championed by Peter Winch and Richard Rorty who, although in different ways, make similar claims to Lyotard concerning the radical contingency of our culture and warn us against the philosophical urge to eternalize a particular language game or practice.

In the following two companion chapters A. T. Nuyen and J. M. Fritzman explicitly compare the positions of Lyotard and Rorty. Nuyen examines Lyotard's claim that the postmodern condition means the death of the Professor, and he argues that in so far as epistemology determines pedagogy, Lyotard's model of education is not entailed by the epistemology Lyotard diagnoses as part of the postmodern condition. If this is the case, Nuyen argues, then we are obliged to listen more closely to Rorty, who assigns the Professor the crucial role of edification based on imagination, a sense of poetic wonder, and conversational engagement—a kind of socialization.

J. M. Fritzman, by contrast, sides with Lyotard against Rorty, arguing that "the differend overcomes the deficiencies of pragmatism." Rorty, it appears, is committed to a notion of consensus at the level of procedural rationality: He believes that consensus can be obtained in a rational fashion over the criteria that will regulate conflicts and differences. Whereas Lyotard agrees that such consensus is possible, it does not exist in all cases: Specifically, the differend constitutes the very type of dispute or conflict where procedural rationality, in the sense of agreement on the rules or criteria governing discourse, breaks down. In such cases of dispute where there are no agreed-upon rules of procedure, there can be no fair adjudication of differences. Fritzman provides an account of the differend between Rorty and Lyotard—an instantiation of the very argument at stake—and he investigates the implications of the differend for pedagogy. In so doing he raises the central question for education in the postmodern condition: Can all differences be legislated for, regulated, or resolved through litigation? The question is central because it bears directly on the issue of oppression of cultural minorities and, indeed, all

Others, whose identities, traditions, literatures, histories—in general, forms of life—have been systematically occluded or suppressed. As Fritzman makes clear, Rorty has come to accept the possibility that not all disputes can be resolved through shared criteria, and thus "he implicitly recognizes the ineliminatable presence of differends."

Women in general, and groups of women marked by differences of color, nationality, and sexual orientation, have suffered from exactly this problem, essentially one of inequality expressed in the refusal to recognize their "voices" and political concerns as distinct and different, both within the intellectual tradition of the Enlightenment and within feminism itself. Postmodernism has been viewed by feminists in ambivalent terms: at one and the same time providing the theoretical apparatus to understand gender differences—and differences within gender—while seemingly eroding the traditional metanarrative of emancipation as a universal basis for political action. Carol Nicholson locates her theoretical concerns squarely within this tangled problematic. She provides historical background on the modernism-postmodernism debate, tracing the arguments that separate Lyotard from Rorty and Habermas before detailing feminist responses to postmodernism and focusing on the challenge represented by the work of Camille Paglia to both feminist theory and postmodernism. On the basis of Paglia's work Nicholson argues for an interdisciplinary and multicultural approach to education that avoids "the pitfalls of 'political correctness' on the one hand and cynical nihilism on the other."

In the next three chapters, which are grouped together because of their Marxist or neo-Marxist orientations, Peter McLaren, John Hinkson, and Barry Kanpol take issue with Lyotard over the political ramifications involved in relinquishing the grand narrative of emancipation. In a wide-ranging essay that surveys much of the relevant literature, Peter McLaren defends the claim of a nascent critical pedagogy based loosely on Marxist categories against Lyotard's dissolution of universal political agency and the possibility of a general theory of politics. McLaren summarizes the claims of critical pedagogy that "has its roots in Marxian analyses of class" while at the same time "appropriating deconstructive readings of discursive formations and certain strands of poststructuralist thinking." He focuses on the fundamental question of agency, working through the critique of the subject and Lyotard's notion of the "subaltern" in order to highlight the concerns of multiculturalists. His argument is that "Lyotard's celebration of multiplicity and plurality . . . can fall prey to the very liberal pluralist stance he is criticizing," and he attempts to rescue a sense of universal justice grounded in the notion of "specific" agency mediated by history and the politics of social relations.

John Hinkson also is concerned with the question of agency. He approaches the question by drawing a distinction between postmodernity as idea and postmodernity as social reality and using it as the means for rethinking theories of postmodernity and Lyotard's contribution in particular, especially in so far as they bear on the practice of education. He argues that it is possible to separate the fact of the "communications revolution"—the technologization of the image and information, and the emergence of its observable institutional practices—from the meanings or interpretations that we trace upon them. His point, following from this, is that Jean-François Lyotard in *The Postmodern Condition* did not "attempt to differentiate the observable structural transformations associated with the information revolution from arguments about what they meant." Hinkson maintains that by accepting the reality of the information revolution as *the* reality, Lyotard tacitly and unquestioningly accepts the resulting model of social relations in education as never being other than what it is. Hinkson traces the implications of this analysis for educational research and the curriculum, stressing the limits of a purely "linguistic" analysis of social relations.

In the final essay of this "Marxist" trilogy, Chapter 8, Barry Kanpol takes up themes similar to those of McLaren and Hinkson. He perhaps more baldly points to the necessity for critical pedagogy to base itself upon a new "sovereign" story—a moral and spiritual narrative—that can ground new democratic possibilities. What is distinctive of Kanpol's essay is the way he attempts to reintroduce spiritual themes by reference to liberation theology as a means of anchoring normative criteria for the exercise and practice of democracy within schools.

James Marshall and Bill Readings complement each other as the final two chapters of this collection. Marshall returns to the events of May–June 1968 to examine Lyotard's involvement at Nanterre and his notion of "apedagogy," formulated in response to these events, against the local background of French educational reforms of the 1960s. In an essay that is both strongly historical and biographical, he examines Foucault's and Lyotard's responses to Fouchet's university reforms, and he concludes that Lyotard proposed "a more appropriate pedagogy to attain educational aims" consistence with a position on the left that was better able to resist the oppressive modernizing tendencies of the reforms. Marshall's essay thus speaks to the personal history of Lyotard's political engagement with educational issues and the way in which Lyotard understood that the role of the teacher and pedagogy required rethinking.

Bill Readings's contribution is oriented to the future, rather than to the past, and he, by contrast, is concerned to provide a "sketch for a heteronomous politics of education" informed by Lyotard's *Political Writings*, which he translated (with Kevin Geiman) and for which he provides a foreword. He concentrates on Lyotard's attention to the "pragmatic scene of pedagogy," its structure of an asymmetrical relation, and the idea that this relation must be addressed in *ethical* terms as belonging to "the sphere of justice rather than of truth." Readings argues that Lyotard's decentering of the pedagogical situation leads to a reappraisal of dialogue as a form that is not designed dialectically to arrive at a single conclusion or a synthesis. It is "to listen, to do justice to the pole of the addressee," which is to avoid both turning "the students into the locus of a simple reproduction" and "subjugating education to a Marxist grand narrative" (students as proletariat). Such a conception of dialogue, which is as Readings remarks akin to M. M. Bakhtin's notion,[60] sets up a network of ethical obligations that avoids a simple replication of the *magister's* authority or autonomy. It is a network, which as Readings explains, "extends to all four poles of the pragmatic linguistic situation: the sender, the addressee, the referent, and the signification."

What is addressed in the essays that comprise this collection is the nature of the differend, not only of Lyotard's original concept but of the arguments that are presented here. It is with some hope that readers can listen to and respect the differends at work, for the lack of consensus, as Ronald Bogue remarks in respect of both Gilles Deleuze's work and the instability of the concept of postmodernism itself, is a sign of intellectual health:

For Deleuze, genuine thought only begins with a disturbance that impinges on thought, with a perplexing and paradoxical question that forces thought into motion. Such a paradoxical question is not amorphous, nor is the field of problems it delineates vague and without contours. But that disturbance is a difference rather than an identity, and the field it reveals is likewise a field of unfolding differences rather than fixed entities. When such a paradoxical question is finally settled, when all the problems of a domain are solved, then thought is dead and difference has played itself out. At present, postmodernism is a generative difference that is disclosing a specific field of problems; once its multiple and contradictory senses are resolved, its use will be over. Then it will be merely another reductive period concept that helps us master history by emptying it of its contradictions.[61]

NOTES

I would like to thank Bill Readings and James Marshall for helpful comments on an earlier version of this introduction.

1. Originally published in France as *La Condition Postmoderne: Rapport sur le Savoir* (Paris: Les Editions de Minuit, 1979); published in English as *The Postmodern Condition: A Report on Knowledge*, trans. Geoff Bennington and Brian Massumi, Foreword by Fredric Jameson (Minneapolis: University of Minnesota Press, 1984). Henceforth referred to as *PMC*.

2. Ibid., p. xxv.

3. Jean-François Lyotard, *The Differend: Phrases in Dispute*, trans. Georges Van Den Abbeele (Minneapolis: University of Minnesota Press, 1988), p. xi.

4. Ibid., p. 158.

5. Ibid., p. xi.

6. Alain Touraine, *La Société Postindustrielle* (Paris: Denoël, 1969).

7. Daniel Bell, *The Coming of Post-Industrial Society* (London: Wildwood House, 1974).

8. Ihab Hassan, *The Dismemberment of Orpheus: Towards a Post Modern Literature* (New York: Oxford University Press, 1971).

9. Michel Benamou and Charles Caramello, eds., *Performance in Postmodern Culture* (Wisconsin: Center for Twentieth Century Studies and Coda Press, 1977).

10. M. Köhler, "Postmodernismus: ein Begriffgeschichtlicher Überblick," *Amerikastudien* 22, 1 (1977).

11. *PMC*, p. xxiii.

12. Ibid., p. xxii.

13. Ibid., p. xxiv.

14. The term is Willard Quine's, *Word and Object* (Cambridge, Mass.: MIT Press, 1960). In the 1981 edition, he writes, "The strategy of semantic assent is that it carries the discussion into the domain where both parties are better agreed on the objects (viz., words) and on the main terms concerning them" (pp. 271–72).

15. Ludwig Wittgenstein, *Philosophical Investigations*, trans. G.E.M. Anscombe (Oxford: Basil Blackwell, 1953; repr. of English text, 1972). Henceforth referred to as *PI*.

16. Ibid., #121.

17. Ibid., p. 108.

18. Ludwig Wittgenstein, *Tractatus Logico-Philosophicus*, trans. D. F. Pears and B. F. McGuiness, with Introduction by Bertrand Russell (London: Routledge & Kegan Paul, 1961; first German edition, 1921).

19. Ibid., #4.022.

20. Ibid., #6.54, which reads: "My propositions serve as elucidations in the following way: anyone who understands me eventually recognizes them as nonsensical, when he has used them—as steps—to climb up beyond them. (He must, must so to speak, throw the ladder after he has climbed up it)."

21. See my essay "Philosophy and Education: 'After' Wittgenstein," in *Philosophy and Education: Accepting Wittgenstein's Challenge*, ed. Paul Smeyers and James Marshall (Dordrecht: Kluwer, in press). The "'After' Wittgenstein" is taken from J.-F. Lyotard, "Wittgenstein 'After,'" in *Political Writings*, trans. Bill Readings and Kevin Paul Geiman, Foreword by Bill Readings (Minneapolis: University of Minnesota Press, 1993), pp. 19–22. (*Political Writings* henceforth referred to as *PW*.) In that essay I propose a Lyotardian reading of Wittgenstein as a basis for a poststructuralist philosophy of education.

22. J.-F. Lyotard, "Wittgenstein 'After,' " *PW*, p. 20.

23. Ibid., p. 21.

24. Ibid.

25. Ibid., p. 22.

26. J.-F. Lyotard, *Libidinal Economy* (Bloomington: Indiana University Press, 1993).

27. *PW*, p. 25.

28. "The logic of maximum performance is no doubt inconsistent in many ways, particularly with respect to contradiction in the socioeconomic field: It demands both less work (to lower production cost) and more (to lesson the social burden of the idle population). But our incredulity is now such that we no longer expect salvation to rise from these inconsistencies, as did Marx," *PMC*, p. xxiv.

29. Bill Readings, "Foreword: The End of the Political," *PW*, pp. xiii–xxvi.

30. Ibid., p. xxiv.

31. J.-F. Lyotard, *PW*, p. 27. In "An Interview with Jean-François Lyotard" (with Willem van Reijen and Dick Veerman), *Theory, Culture and Society* 5, (1988), p. 302, Lyotard argues: "The real political task today, at least in so far as it is also concerned with the cultural . . . is to carry forward the resistance that writing offers to established thought, to what has already been done, to what everyone thinks, to what is well-known, to what is widely recognized, to what is 'readable,' to everything which can change its form and make itself acceptable to opinion in general."

32. *PMC*, p. xxiv.

33. J.-F. Lyotard, "Interview" (with Georges Van Den Abbeele), *Diacritics* 14, 3 (Fall 1984), p. 18.

34. See my "Performance and Accountability in 'Post-Industrial Society': The Crisis of British Universities," *Studies in Higher Education* 17, 2 (1992): 123–39; "Re-reading Touraine: Postindustrialism and the Future of the University" *Sites* 23 (Spring 1991): 63–83; Michael Peters, James Marshall, and Bruce Parr, "The Marketization of Tertiary Education in New Zealand," *Australian Universities' Review* 36 (1993): 34–39.

35. *PMC*, p. xxv.

36. Ibid., p. 60.

37. Ibid., see footnote 211, p. 100.

38. Bill Readings, "Foreword," *PW*, p. xxi.

39. *PMC*, p. 60.

40. Ibid., p. 79.

41. "An Interview with Lyotard," p. 277.

42. *PMC*, p. 5, 7.

43. "Interview with Lyotard," p. 277.

44. See Clayton Koelb, "Introduction: So What's the Story?" in *Nietzsche as Postmodernist: Essays Pro and Contra*, ed. Clayton Koelb, pp. 2–3 (New York: SUNY Press, 1990).

45. Bill Readings, *Introducing Lyotard: Art and Politics* (London: Routledge, 1991), p. 161.

46. "Interview with Lyotard," p. 278.

47. Ibid.

48. Ibid., p. 279.

49. Ibid., p. 280.

50. J.-F. Lyotard, *The Postmodern Explained to Children: Correspondence 1982–1985* (Sydney: Power Publications, 1992), p. 31.

51. Ibid., p. 35.

52. J.-F. Lyotard, "The Missive on Universal History," in *The Postmodern Explained to Children*, p. 36.

53. Ibid., p. 39.

54. J.-F. Lyotard, "The Grip" ("Mainmise"), in *PW*, p. 148.

55. Ibid., p. 149.

56. Lyotard, drawing on Freud, distinguishes two meanings of infancy: "the infancy that is not bound in time and that is the heavenly model of those who do not need to be emancipated, having never been subjected to a grip other than that of the father; and an infancy inevitably subjected to scandal or offense [in Freud's term, 'seduction'], and thus subject to the abjection of not belonging to the truth of this call," *ibid.*, p. 154.

57. See J.-F. Lyotard, "Oikos," *PW*, p. 3.

58. Julian Pefanis and Morgan Thomas, "Foreword to the English Edition," *The Postmodern Explained to Children*, p. 7.

59. Michel Foucault, "What Is Enlightenment?" in *Foucault Reader*, ed. Paul Rabinow (New York: Pantheon Books, 1984), p. 42.

60. Michael Holquist in his introduction to M. M. Bakhtin's *Speech Genres and Other Late Essays* (trans. Vern W. McGee, ed. Caryl Emerson and Michael Holquist, Austin, University of Texas Press, p. xviii) comments upon how Bakhtin's later concept of dialogue disperses "the cloud of binaries" characterizing his early statement. He writes:

> Working as always with a specular subject (a self derived from the other), he makes it clear that speakers always shape an utterance not only according to the object of discourse (*what* they are talking *about*) and their immediate addressee (whom they are talking *to*), but also according to the particular image in which they model the belief they will be understood, a belief that is the *a priori* of all speech. Thus, each speaker authors an utterance not only with an audience-addressee, but a *superaddressee* in mind: " . . . in addition to [the immediate addressee] the author of the utterance, with a greater or lesser awareness, presupposes a higher *superaddressee* (third), whose *absolutely just and responsive understanding* [my emphasis] is presumed, either in some metaphysical distance or in distant historical time . . . In various ages and with various understandings of the world, this superaddressee and his ideally true responsive understanding assumes various ideological expressions (God, absolute truth, the court of dispassionate human conscience, the people, the court of history, science, and so forth)." "The Problem of the Text"

See also David Carroll, "Narrative, Heterogeneity, and the Question of the Political: Bakhtin and Lyotard," in *The Aims of Representation: Subject/Text/History*, ed. Murray Krieger (New York: Columbia University Press, 1987), pp. 69–106.

61. Ronald Bogue, "Gilles Deleuze: Postmodern Philosopher?" *Criticism* 32, 4 (Fall 1990): 402.

EDUCATION AND THE POSTMODERN CONDITION

1 The Loss of Innocence: Lyotard, Foucault, and the Challenge of Postmodern Education

William Bain

> A will to the thinkability of all beings: this *I* call your will. You want to *make* all beings thinkable, for you doubt with well-founded suspicion that it is already thinkable. But it shall yield and bend for you. Thus your will wants it. It shall become smooth and serve the spirit as its mirror and reflection. That is your whole will, you who are wisest: a will to power—when you speak of good and evil too, and of valuations. You still want to create the world before which you can kneel: that is your ultimate hope and intoxication.[1]

> What is familiar is what we are used to; and what we are used to is most difficult to "know"—that is, to see as a problem; that is, to see as strange, as distant, as "outside us."[2]

> Thinking only takes place by listening in [sic] attentively to the question: "Is it happening that . . . ?"[3]

A LITTLE BACKGROUND

Rather than begin immediately with the question of postmodernism, I thought it might be helpful to provide some perspective on the issue by briefly comparing and contrasting it with Matthew Arnold's perspective in the latter third of the nineteenth century.

England in the mid-1860s seemed headed for trouble. Religious divisiveness had long ago undermined the role of religion in providing an anchor for social relations and national community. Industrialization was wreaking havoc on nature and promoting a bureaucratization and mechanization of society. The working classes were demanding greater control over their own lives, governmental reform, and voting rights, flexing their political muscle with numerous outdoor rallies and protests. Colonial crises, particularly the "Irish question," the Jamaica rebellion in 1865, agricultural disasters, and financial instabilities all precipitated a pervasive sense of crisis.

In 1869 Matthew Arnold, educator, school inspector, and social critic, zeroed in on the source of this turmoil. He realized that the old medieval system of hierarchy, authority, and legitimation—based on "the strong feudal habits of subordination and deference"[4]—and firmly grounded in the authority of religion had finally dissolved as a force of social cohesion. For Arnold, the smoking gun that clearly indicated the final dissolution of the medieval system was the noisy irruption "of the working class which, raw and half-developed, has long lain half-hidden amidst its poverty and squalor,"[5] and now dared speak out in public on issues of social, economic, and political fairness and justice. Within the old political cosmology, "the strong feudal habits of subordination and deference continued to tell upon the working class." However, by Arnold's time, "the modern spirit has now almost entirely dissolved those habits."[6] The irruption and public displays of the working class evidenced an anarchic threat to "that profound sense of settled order and security, without which a society like ours cannot live and grow at all."[7] As William Spanos remarks, Arnold confronted this dangerous, "modern" condition by "substituting a 'new' . . . center for the divine *Logos* which the intellectual and political history of his century had de-centered and rendered untenable."[8] In effect, for the metanarrative of religion, Arnold appropriated the Kantian idea of reason and installed it in a new form—the metanarrative of Culture. If God had made "man" in his image and bound him to a system of faith and obedience, culture was to remake "man" in Man's image and bind him in a system of knowledge and self-knowledge, grounded in what David Lloyd labels a new "idea of the universal formal identity of the human,"[9] effectively aligned with and enforced through State/Norm/Law. In effect, culture, as the nineteenth century manifestation of Reason, is conceived (and made to prevail) as the secular manifestation of "the will of God."[10]

In arguing for his alliance of culture and "right reason," Arnold claimed that the English had become all too comfortable with the status quo, with what appeared to them as self-evident truths. He wrote:

And to any of these impulses we soon come to give that same character of a mechanical, absolute law, which we give to our religion; we regard it, as we do our religion, as an object for strictness of conscience, not for spontaneity of consciousness; for unremitting adherence on its own account, not for going back upon, viewing in its connexion with other things, and adjusting to a number of changing circumstances.[11]

Jean-François Lyotard has termed our contemporary tendency for "going back upon" our mechanical, absolute laws, viewing them in connection with other things, and adjusting to a number of changing circumstances, the "postmodern condition."

THE POSTMODERN CONDITION

A highly volatile debate has been provoked by Lyotard's designation of "the state of our culture following the transformations which, since the end of the nineteenth century, have altered the game rules for science, literature, and the arts" as the "postmodern condition."[12] What does this so-called end of modernity mean for the project of the Enlightenment? What is the relation between the modern and the postmodern? What is the relation between postmodernism and poststructuralism? What is the significance of the postmodern for feminist theory and politics, for theory and politics of peoples of color? Is postmodernism implicated in postcolonialism? In other words, what exactly is the meaning of "post"? It is well beyond the scope of this chapter to survey these debates. These issues have been well documented elsewhere.[13] Rather, I wish here to focus on how the postmodern condition transforms both enlightenment and the relationship between education and enlightenment and what this means in terms of our relationship to knowledge. I will do this by examining the constellation of ideas surrounding Lyotard's general pronouncement of the postmodern as an "incredulity toward metanarratives" and Michel Foucault's ethos of the "limit-attitude." In doing so, I will suggest that the traditional understanding of the symbiotic relationship between enlightenment and education is not severed, does not undergo an untenable rupture, but rather assumes a unique form, one that Foucault characterizes as a "critical ontology of ourselves."

Postmodernism and the Loss of Innocence

On one level, Lyotard locates the postmodern condition through a Kantian reading of the "signs of history." Immanuel Kant formulated his idea of general human progress toward universal emancipation by reading the enthusiasm with which spectators viewed the French Revolution as a sign that indicated (but did not prove) the continuous progression of a common humanity. That is, Kant postulated that the universal history of humanity was a history of general progress guided by the natural laws of Reason. Under the banners of reason and progress, all humanity would be able to overcome the particularities of cultural identities "in favor of a universal civic identity."[14] For Lyotard, the apodictic certainty of this "cosmopolitical" vision has been severely eroded. "Auschwitz" is the key sign in Lyotard's reading of contemporary history. Lyotard notes that for each metanarrative—speculative doctrine, Marxist, liberal-political, capitalist economic—one could also point to countersigns that refute the prognostication of the end of history as the general emancipation of something called a universal humanity.[15] However, a sign of history need not be a spectacular event. We have all seen how the "progress" of the West, what Lyotard calls development because its consequences cannot by any stretch of the imagination be called progress, has been predicated throughout history upon the subjugation, domination, exploitation, enslavement, and near-genocide of all those who are not the West. We recognize now that we have "progressed" so far, at least in the United States, that we imprison a greater percentage of our population than any other "developed" country and specialize in imprisoning poor people and people of color; that the disparity between rich and poor is growing; that xenophobia is on the rise in a nation of immigrants; that we have "progressed" so far that our primary visions of the "end of history" are nuclear or ecological annihilation. As Lyotard understands it, the development of knowledge, particularly technoscientific knowledge has not brought us closer to emancipation. Rather, for some in the West, at least, it has led to a complexification of life. As Lyotard remarks, "Humanity is divided into two parts. One faces the challenge of complexity, the other that ancient and terrible challenge of its own survival. This is perhaps the most important aspect of the failure of the modern project—a project that, need I remind you, once applied in principle to the whole of humanity.[16]

From this perspective, Lyotard announces that the metanarratives of emancipation have liquidated themselves. It is not a question of abandoning the project of modernity. The internal dynamics of the metanarratives themselves have produced their own liquidation.[17]

However, Lyotard also notes that the metanarratives of modernity are not simply collapsing from exhaustion. The smooth, homogeneous lines of universal history have always been subject to deformation and transformation by those who did not see themselves reflected in the mirror of humanity. Lyotard writes that "the canonic story has suffered the effects of erosion, if only to a minor extent as yet, and has been eaten away by . . . thousands of little stories."[18] These thousands of little stories are emerging from "the diverse and disorderly Others beginning to speak and beginning to chip away at the social and political power of the Theorizer."[19] These are the disorderly voices that the homogenizing discourses of modernity thought to either domesticate, eliminate, or ignore. The postcolonial voices of non-Western peoples, women, African-Americans, gays, lesbians, the physically challenged, all those who somehow did not meet the criteria for being the universal subject of history, these have, in effect, blown open the continuum of History.[20] They have unrepentently revealed its ragged edges, its scars, its fundamental fears and suspicions, its initial forgettings. In so doing, such voices have reopened what Gilles Deleuze has called "the problem of existence."[21] Paradoxically, the fundamental task of metanarratives had been to foreclose that question.

For Lyotard, whatever seeks to set itself up as a metanarrative "will inevitably inspire us to lift up our souls to some major absence, and will therefore lead to the degradation of reality."[22] This is a precise allusion to what Friedrich Nietzsche recognized as the ascetic ideal. For Nietzsche, the ascetic ideal posits an "afterworld" in which repose Truth and Reality. It is a "sacred, timeless, cosmic reality" that hovers around human reality but is not of human reality.[23] This sacred realm may exist in some originary past or some redemptive future. Most generally it assumes the names Ideal Forms, Being, God, Tradition, Enlightenment, or Culture. In positing the domain of Truth and Reality as beyond the flesh-and-blood existence of a human world, the ascetic ideal necessarily degrades this world, subordinating the materiality, sensuousness, contradiction, and struggle of this world to an ethereal and sacred domain of disembodied Truth. In so doing, the ascetic ideal provokes "the delusory and dangerous recurrent hope of redemption [in] a world not of our own making."[24] The ascetic ideal thus posits a truth or reality uncontaminated by mere human reality/error. Truth is beyond all contingency, all "interests." Situated beyond the fractious world of human affairs, this Truth, by definition, cannot be implicated with power. As Jane Flax remarks, such truth is presented as innocent, and those who invoke its name, who speak under its authorization, are innocent. In other words, in speaking in the name of an antiseptic truth, one is safely innoculated against having to assume any responsibility in relation to this truth other than making sure that its benevolence is made to prevail over all humankind.[25]

Further, the ascetic ideal operates with such potency "because truth was posited as being, as God, as the highest court of appeal—because truth was not *permitted* to be a problem at all."[26] However, the untamed discourses of "diverse and disorderly others" no longer abide by that prohibition. In effect, postmodernism dislodges a self-confident and self-referential truth from its spectral throne and confronts it with the claim that "truth is a thing of this world."[27] In so doing, postmodernism absolves us of the blinding task of looking toward the heavens for some blazing sun of Truth and opens our senses and recalls our responsibilities to the "colours and beauties and enigmas and riches of significance" in this life.[28]

Thus, metanarratives also serve as the god-point from which to understand history. They provide the framework within which to decipher the multitudinous events of human reality. All metanarratives claim a privileged insight into the nature of History and portray it as ultimately homogeneous and universal; announce a single subject whose words, actions, struggles, and concerns represent a universal subject; posit an end-point from which to recognize and judge what they deem as the significant aspects of human history; and put forth a telos of "authentic" human being toward which all possibilities of human becoming should aspire or be directed (i.e., the truth of human nature). In other words, metanarratives offer a promised land of unity and harmony—a place of final repose at the end of history.[29]

In many respects, metanarratives function as discourses (in a Foucauldian sense). They stipulate a reality to be looked for and the means whereby it can be judged, measured, and controlled. Discourse is not the unmediated representation of a preexistent reality. Discourses operate via restrictive systems of exclusion and inclusion that establish the parameters of the discourse. As Michel Foucault states, "We must conceive discourse as a violence that we do to things, or, at all events, as a practice we impose on them; it is in this practice that the events of discourse find the principle of their regularity."[30] That is, discourse functions to stabilize and fix an otherwise incessant flood of phenomena, perceptions, and sensations into selectively recognizable forms. Discourse does not re-present the world. It orders it.

Discourse is a socially constructed "systematic set of relations" within which statements, practices, and corresponding institutions are given meaning and their self-evident reality.[31] That is, a discourse establishes the norms for determining which statements, objects, and practices will be admitted for discussion; the elaboration of forms, languages, and procedures for discussion; the criteria by which to judge the truth or falsity of admissible statements; the regulations on who can be admitted to the discourse; the role of speakers and addressees in the discourse; who is able to speak the truth of the discourse; and the rules for its distribution. Further, "discursive practices are not purely and simply ways of producing discourse. They are embodied in technical processes, in institutions, in patterns of general behavior, in forms of transmission and diffusion, and in pedagogical forms, which, at once, impose and maintain them."[32]

Foucault further maintains that in examining the meanings, valuations, and practices supported by discourse "we are not to burrow to the hidden core of discourse, to the heart of the thought or meaning manifested in it." Rather, "we should look for its external conditions of existence."[33] That is, meaning (truth) "is produced only by virtue of multiple forms of constraint."[34] These constraints are internal to the discourse itself and external in their imbrication with power relations in society. Discourse is not the sacred vessel of meaning.[35] On the contrary, discourse polices meaning and disciplines it.

Consequently, the metanarratives of modernity seek to curb the potential proliferation of meanings, especially those created by unauthorized others. For Lyotard, one of the most noxious effects of metanarratives is the increasing homogenization of language, thought, and sensibility. He gives the examples of Orwellian bureaucratic newspeak, capitalist technoscience, and claims to a metalanguage, all as forces intent on reducing language to conformity with some variable of performativity. Newspeak fixes meaning in doctrine. It claims to have surveyed the whole field of the human and to have accounted for all possible events. Thus, Lyotard writes that "nothing must happen but what is announced, and everything that is announced must happen."[36] Elsewhere, Lyotard notes the tendency of new postmodern technologies to apply "capitalist rules to language."[37] The intention is to shrink language (and meaning) to the "binary logic of Boolean algebra" in order to reduce it to a "commercial unit of information" that can be rendered sensible in account books.[38] In the case of universal language, Lyotard sees the project of modernity as the imposition of a "metalanguage capable of collecting together every shred of meaning established in specific languages." He argues that "the doubt cast on 'reason' springs not from the sciences but from the critique of metalanguage, that is, from the decline of metaphysics (and therefore of metapolitics as well)."[39]

Newspeak cannot tolerate idiomatic expressions. Universal language claims to digest all idioms. Capitalism wants to reduce language to an input-output function. What all want to preempt and defuse is the question of the event, the question that something may be happening that is not accounted for.[40] All want to create and enforce a "basic" language that neatly squares off and smooths over existence; and as Lyotard rightly observes, " 'Basic language' is the language of surrender and forgetting."[41]

The reduction of possible interpretations to the demands of "basic language" or the increased surveillance of unauthorized interpretations through the imposition of a metalanguage create definitively favorable conditions for "consensus." In other words, once we learn the right use of language (as put forth through the performativity principle of capitalist technoscience or a universal normativity), the "true" meaning behind the proliferation of second-order meanings will shine forth. With only "correct" meanings in circulation, consensus would be "natural." As Lyotard understands it, to postulate "consensus" as the telos of language, one must collapse the heterogeneity of "regimes of phrases" into conformity with a metalanguage capable of universal mediation between all phrase universes.[42] Lyotard sees two problems with this. First is the supposed possibility of all situated speakers "to come to agreement on which rules or metaprescriptions are universally valid for language games."[43] Second, Lyotard recognizes consensus as "only a particular state of discussion."[44] In order for the discussion to go further, to take different directions, to open it up to "the event," dissensus or paralogy must be introduced. However, within the domain of performativity (which both "basic language" and metaprescriptive norms enforce), paralogy would be reduced to mere innovation of contents within the ordained form. If paralogy is understood as the invention of new, imaginative moves not prescripted by the norms, then paralogy is directed at the forms themselves.[45] The intent of paralogy is the creation of new idioms (forms and expressions) for thought. Paralogical moves ensure that any metanarratives do not terminally congeal into totalitarian imperatives whereby

you are officially assigned to three positions in the master narrative, and in every aspect of your own life. Your imagination is fettered, as a narrator, as a listener and as an actor. . . . There is no avoiding it, as it is not within your power to control the meaning of the narrative or that of what you have to listen to or do. Its meaning is beyond the limits of your understanding.[46]

Thus, for Lyotard, the heterogeneity of phrases and the idea of dissensus/paralogy calls into question the hypothesis that "humanity as a collective (universal) subject seeks its common emancipation through the regularization of the 'moves' permitted in all language games and that the legitimacy of any statement resides in its contributing to that emancipation."[47]

Hubert L. Dreyfuss and Paul Rabinow see this metanarrative of consensus as another (Kantian) search "for the structure of human finitude which would provide universal norms for human activity."[48] Lyotard also sees it as another way to provide "the solace of good forms," that is, the "formal identity of the human." Lyotard notes that one form of modern aesthetics "allows the unpresentable to be put forward only as the missing contents; but the form, because of its recognizable consistency, continues to offer to the reader or viewer matter for solace and pleasure."[49] We recognize here another variant of metanarrative in terms of the ideality of the form. Dreyfuss and Rabinow locate this problematic "in the radical Kantian distinction between the empirical and the transcendental. Kant attempts to rescue the pure *form* of knowing from history and factuality by relegating all contingency and obscurity to the side of the *content* of knowledge."[50] However, this ideality of the form does much more than provide solace. It in effect determines what qualifies for presentability and under what conditions. Consequently, it also determines what and how something is to be made unpresentable and provides the grounds for the justification of these exclusionary moves. It effectively silences the voices of those made unpresentable by authorizing the specific idioms within which claims for presentation must be made and by validating only specific contents that may be considered as claims. That is, ideal forms set the rules of the game wherein differends (difference) cannot possibly be heard.[51] Thus, the ideality of the form prevents any critical interrogation of the meaning or the status of the *we*.

However, the postmodern threatens both the meaning and the status of this universal and self-evident *we*. Within the horizon of modernity, the identity and status of the *we* was ensured, since the *we* was marked by "the control of speech and meaning."[52] The *we* maintained the sovereign right to parcel out meanings and identities and the institutional and imperial means to enforce them. However, with the dissolution of the meta-narratives' power to organize the meanings and practices of human life, not only is the great object (universal humanity) of the metanarratives lost, so too is the very subject to whom this object had been promised. This postmodern condition prompts three responses: either mourning (the absence of meaning in history); secondary narcissism (whereas Western culture was made to prevail under the innocence of universal truth, it now is made to prevail as raw conquest and Terror); or a "working over" the loss of the modern *we*.

This process of "working over" the loss of the modern *we* suggests that postmodernism is not a rupture with modernity. It is not a wholesale rejection or a totalizing critique.[53] It is not a radical overcoming (*Uber-windung*) but rather a transformation, a working through (*Verwindung*) the conceptual and institutional apparatuses of modernity. It is also a remembering, a recollection (*An-denken*) of the presuppositions and forgettings that modernity cannot or will not face. As Lyotard remarks, to classify the postmodern as a rupture "is in fact a way of forgetting or repressing the past, that is, repeating it and not surpassing it."[54] In fact, postmodernism suggests a responsibility to elaborate modernity's " 'initial forgetting,' "[55] working through the very identities, knowledges, and practices distributed under the auspices of modernity's privileged claim to universal meaning.

Thus, the decline of the metanarratives and the dissolution of their power to legislate, legitimate, and universalize modern forms of Western thought, rationality, sensibility, institutions, practices, and morality leads Lyotard to define postmodernism as "a change in people's relation to the problem of meaning."[56] On one level, this entails the question, "Is it happening that . . . ?" "Is it happening that . . . ?" refers precisely to the problematic of "the event," of a meaning no longer constrained to that which had already been announced in advance. Lyotard remarks that this denotes a particular condition of postmodern thought and action, one that can no longer "be inflected by a purposiveness (anthropological, cosmological, or ontological) which would legitimate it."[57] With meaning no longer ultimately legitimated in a guaranteed future, one modality of postmodern thought is a "thinking of the proximity." As Gianni Vattimo interprets it, such a process "no longer deals with the ultimate foundations and principles (*archai*) but with the 'errors,' interpretations and cultural constructions inherited from humankind's past."[58]

This direction of a postmodern form of thought highlights the fact that postmodernism signifies a change in people's relation not just to meaning but to the *problem* of meaning. That is, given the demise of transcendental, foundational discourses, meaning itself—its appearance, its effects, its legitimation—becomes a problem. It is not that meaning suddenly disappears in a dense fog of nihilism, but that the "conditions of existence" of meaning(s) can no longer be taken for granted or blithely assumed. Meaning must be understood as implicated in power relations.[59] In other words, meaning/knowledge/truth has lost its innocence, and so have we. Perhaps accepting our responsibility to confront this "loss" is a "sign" of some degree of maturity?

WORKING THROUGH ENLIGHTENMENT

In 1784 in his brief essay "What Is Enlightenment?" Kant described enlightenment as "man's release from his self-incurred tutelage. Tutelage is man's inability to make use of his understanding without direction from another."[60] Enlightenment is a process whereby we move from a state of immaturity characterized by our subservient obedience to "Statutes and formulas, those mechanical tools" to a state of "maturity."[61] This process itself is marked by the free use of public reason. However, in Kant's critical philosophy, the relationship between enlightenment, freedom, and reason could be secured only if critical thought could establish the formal limits of reason. As Foucault understands it, Kant provided an analytic of finitude in which "the limits of knowledge provide the positive foundation for the possibility of knowing."[62] Thus, Kant proceeded to reinscribe statutes and dogma by establishing the canonical boundaries beyond which reason ought not venture. Consequently, the universal enlightenment and emancipation of a general humanity is ultimately grounded in the postulation of a natural reason, which, given the opportune conditions, will be able to fulfill its inner telos of self-realization. Thus, paradoxically, the escape from our self-incurred tutelage involves bonding ourselves to a natural, yet quasi-divine Reason. In 1980 Foucault observed that "two centuries later, the Enlightenment returns: but now not at all as a way for the West to take cognizance of its present possibilities and of the liberties to which it can accede, but as a way of interrogating it on its limits."[63]

The Limit-Attitude

In his own writings on Kant, Foucault brings a novel interpretation to the question (and possibility or direction) of enlightenment. Foucault notes that Kant's critical philosophy is the basis for "the two great critical traditions between which modern philosophy is divided." One tradition follows an "analytics of truth," whose role is to establish "the conditions in which true knowledge is possible."[64] Its project is "that of defining the conditions under which the use of reason is legitimate in order to determine what can be known, what must be done, and what may be hoped."[65] The second enlightenment tradition can be understood as "an ontology of the present, an ontology of ourselves."[66] This particular direction of enlightenment Foucault terms "limit-attitude."

Foucault describes the limit-attitude as an *ethos*, that is, as "a mode of relating to contemporary reality,"[67] which is "oriented toward the 'contemporary limits of the necessary,' that is, toward what is not or is no longer indispensable for the constitution of ourselves as autonomous beings" (43). For Foucault such an ethos amounts to a "critical ontology of ourselves" (47). A critical ontology of ourselves entails examining "in what is given to us as universal, necessary, obligatory, what place is occupied by whatever is singular, contingent, and the product of arbitrary constraints" (45). As such, it is a corollary to Lyotard's question, "Is it happening that . . . ?"

The limit-attitude, as a critical ontology of ourselves, is opposed to any depth hermeneutic of the self. For Foucault the Cartesian question, "Who am I?" is transformed into the critical Kantian question, "What are we?"[68] This latter question does not set out to discover "the positive foundation of the self."[69] It is not meant to ferret out our hidden truths or confirm us in our mode of being. On the contrary, the limit-attitude points out "what kinds of assumptions, what kinds of familiar, unchallenged, unconsidered modes of thought" our understandings of ourselves and others rest upon.[70] The limit-attitude does not seek to "deduce from the form of what we are what it is impossible for us to do and to know." Rather, "it will separate out from the contingency that has made us what we are, the possibility of no longer being, doing, or thinking what we are, do, or think."[71] The limit-attitude thus announces a "politics of ourselves."[72] On one level, this involves "the questioning of 'what we are' in the name of a principle of permanent contingency."[73] On another level, it entails resisting any form of power that "applies itself to immediate everyday life which categorizes the individual, marks him by his own individuality, attaches him to his own identity, imposes a law of truth on him which he must recognize and which others have to recognize in him."[74] Finally, on a third level, the idea of a "politics of ourselves" solicits "new forms of subjectivity,"[75] the opening up of possibilities to "set about creating something else to be."[76] In this sense, the "politics of ourselves" emerges as "a practical critique that takes the form of a possible transgression"[77] of limits that would disclose new alternatives for "recontextualizing ourselves" and consequently new options "for a 'common cultural territory,' and within it put into practice new models of communication and association."[78]

For Foucault, this direction of critique is not concerned with regrounding reason or returning reason to its true form. He does not believe "in a kind of founding act whereby reason, in its essence, was discovered or established and from which it was subsequently diverted by such and such an event."[79] Rather, within the horizon of the limit-attitude, critical thought is directed toward the historical limits imposed on us through the deployment of given forms of rationality that "reside on a base of human practice and human history."[80] Thus, "since these things have been made, they can be unmade, as long as we know how it was that they were made."[81] The goal of such knowledge is to "open up the space of freedom understood as a space of concrete freedom, i.e., of possible transformation."[82] Such historicopractical interrogations are "genealogical in [their] design and archaeological in [their] method."[83]

Both archaeology and genealogy are differential, paralogical "antisciences." The quest is not to establish the solace of good forms but, rather, to investigate all that goes under the names of continuity, identity, unity, and being. Foucault explains that archaeology "does not establish the fact of our identity by the play of distinctions. It establishes that we are difference, our history the difference of times, our selves the difference of masks. That difference, far from being the forgotten and recovered origin, is this dispersion that we are and make."[84] Thus, rather than once again trying to delineate universal forms and possibilities of human becoming, archaeology "will seek to treat the instances of discourse that articulate what we think, say, and do as so many historical events."[85]

Then, genealogy tries to recover the emergence of those events. It works as a countermemory, brushing history against the grain, so to speak. This countermemory is also a "dangerous memory,"[86] in that "it is a painstaking rediscovery of struggles together with the rude memory of their conflicts."[87] Thus, while archaeology establishes the "difference" of discourses in their singularity as events, genealogy links this difference of discourses to "various systems of subjection . . . the hazardous play of dominations."[88] Genealogy does not seek to establish "indefinite teleologies" that would unite all events under the authority of "ideal significations."[89] Further, genealogy rejects the search for origins that would comfortably verify authenticity. In displacing the practice of total history to pursue "that which was already there," genealogy finds "something altogether different" behind things: not a timeless and essential secret, but the secret that they have no essence or that their essence was fabricated piecemeal fashion from alien forms."[90]

Foucault calls genealogy "effective history." One way to grasp this term is to view the events of history—our discourses, practices, bodies, identities, differences—as the "effects" of what Foucault calls (rather cavalierly, I think) "haphazard conflicts."[91] Conflicts are haphazard in that they are not organized within a suprahistorical perspective. What appears to us in its solidity as a self-evident reality is shown to be the effects of numerous struggles, conflicts, accidents, reversals, and appropriations. These apply to all aspects of human life and history. For genealogy, nothing is more suspect than the taken-for-granted, and the taken-for-granted is nothing more than the sanctification of a particular interpretation. And for Foucault, the installation of such canonical interpretations involves "the violent or surreptitious appropriation of a system of rules, which in itself has no essential meaning, in order to impose a direction,"[92] in other words, to give human life and history an "essential" form. It is the purpose of genealogy to dismantle this "consoling play of recognitions."[93]

Thus, archaeology and genealogy create a new relationship between ourselves, knowledge, and "reality." In exposing the history of events as one of struggles, conflicts, contingencies, and reversals, the limit-attitude reconceives reality as "a difficult interplay between the truth of what is real and the exercise of freedom." Given the paralogical character of the limit-attitude, this interplay is coupled with the responsibility of imagining reality "otherwise than it is."[94] This is definitely not to suggest a passive withdrawal into the "artificial paradise" of an aesthetic subjectivism. Foucault stresses that to imagine reality otherwise requires not the annulment of reality but precisely "grasping it in what it is."[95] Genealogically, this means grasping the reality of "events" by analyzing the conditions of their emergence, their propagation within "regimes of truth," the circuits of power/knowledge that give them force, their forms of institutionalization, and their axes of circulation in discourses and practices, and the different positions we occupy in regards to such. Colin Gordon suggests that what emerges from such analyses is an ethic of "refusing what we are." However, he finds it "advisable to emphasis" that this "does not mean a mere leap into the void, an immoralism of the gratuitous act." He argues, "The form of freedom which Foucault envisages requires a form of knowledge obtainable only by means of exacting historical and political investigation."[96]

In other words, the postmodern condition signaled by the demise of metanarratives, the loss of innocence suffered by truth/knowledge/meaning and consequently by our own selves, the contingencies that invade our representations of ourselves, others, and the world, and the "certain fragility" the limit-attitude discovers in "the very bedrock of [our] existence,"[97] does not mean the triumph of nihilism, irrationalism, or the loss of hope. It does not mean that nothing is true or false. What it does mean is that "everything is dangerous."[98] To which Friedrich Nietzsche would reply, well, then, "live dangerously."[99]

The postmodern requires that we shed our priestly robes of innocence and confront the world as ultimately one that we made and that we can remake; to confront ourselves not as isolated, self-contained vessels of a unique essence but as always already implicated with each other. It requires that we affirm the fact that "the world in which we were at home up till now with our reverences" is being transformed into "another world *that consists of us.*"[100] It thus requires of us a new relationship between ourselves, others, and the world that we must develop along coordinates that as yet have not been set in place. As such, it demands of us not an allegiance to truth but a responsibility to interrogate the conditions and effects of truth. It demands of us an attention to, and responsibility for, those "colours and beauties and enigmas and riches of significance" that it was previously our job to outlook.

Foucault captures the essence of these new, dangerous responsibilities and relationships in his unique understanding of "curiousity." He writes:

It evokes "care"; it evokes the care one takes of what exists and what might exist; a sharpened sense of reality, but one that is never immobilized before it; a readiness to find what surrounds us strange and odd; a certain determination to throw off familiar ways of thought and to look at the same things in a different way; a passion for seizing what is happening now and what is disappearing; a lack of respect for the traditional hierarchies of what is important and fundamental.[101]

It is with this combination of dangerousness, curiosity, and care that the limit-attitude seeks "to give new impetus, as far and wide as possible, to the *undefined* work of freedom."[102]

NOTES

1. Friedrich Nietzsche, "Thus Spoke Zarathustra," in *The Portable Nietzsche*, trans. Walter Kaufmann (New York: Penguin Books, 1976), p. 225.

2. Friedrich Nietzsche, *The Gay Science*, trans. Walter Kaufmann (New York: Vintage Books, 1974), p. 301.

3. Jean-François Lyotard, "Interview" (with Georges Van Den Abbeele), *Diacritics* 14, 3 (Fall 1984): 16.

4. Matthew Arnold, *Culture and Anarchy*, ed. Ian Gregor (Indianapolis: Bobbs-Merrill, 1971), p. 61.

5. Ibid., p. 87.

6. Ibid., pp. 61–62.

7. Ibid., p. 66.

8. William V. Spanos, "The Apollonian Investment of Modern Humanist Education: The Examples of Matthew Arnold, Irving Babbitt, and I. A. Richards," *Cultural Critique* 1 (Fall 1985): 19.

9. David Lloyd, "Arnold, Ferguson, Schiller: Aesthetic Culture and the Politics of Aesthetics," *Cultural Critique* 2 (Winter 1985–86): 139.

10. Arnold, *Culture and Anarchy*, p. 36.

11. Ibid., p. 131.

12. Lyotard, *The Postmodern Condition: A Report on Knowledge*, trans. Geoff Bennington and Brian Massumi (Minneapolis: University of Minnesota Press, 1984), p. xxiii.

13. Jochen Schulte-Sasse, "Modernity and Modernism, Postmodernity and Post-modernism: Framing the Issue," *Cultural Critique* 5 (Winter 1986–87): 5–22; Scott Lash and Jonathan Friedman, eds., *Modernity and Identity* (Cambridge: Basil Blackwell, 1992); Linda J. Nicholson, ed. *Feminism/Postmodernism* (New York: Routledge, 1990); E. Ann Kaplan, ed., *Postmodernism and Its Discontents* (New York: Verso, 1988); Deborah Cook, "Remapping Modernity," *British Journal of Aesthetics* 30, 1 (January 1990): 35–45; Stanley Aronowitz and Henry A. Giroux, *Postmodern Education: Politics, Culture, and Social Criticism* (Minneapolis: University of Minnesota Press, 1991); Mustafa U. Kiziltan, William J. Bain, and Anita Canizares M., "Postmodern Conditions: Rethinking Public Education," *Educational Theory* 40, 3 (Summer 1990): 351–69; Patti Lather, "Postmodernism and the Politics of Enlightenment," *Educational Foundations* 3, 3 (Fall 1989): 7–28; *Education and Society* 9, 1 & 2 (special issues on postmodernism);

and Peter McLaren, "Multiculturalism and the Postmodern Critique: Towards a Pedagogy of Resistance and Transformation," *Cultural Studies* 7, 1 (January 1993): 118–46.

14. Lyotard, "Missive on Universal History," in J.-F. Lyotard, *The Postmodern Explained*, ed. Julian Pefanis and Morgan Thomas (Minneapolis: University of Minnesota Press, 1993), p. 34.

15. Ibid., p. 29.

16. Lyotard, "Note on the Meaning of 'Post,'" in *The Postmodern Explained*, p. 79.

17. Lyotard, "Apostil on Metanarratives," in *The Postmodern Explained*, p. 18; and "Memorandum on Legitimation," ibid., p. 51.

18. Lyotard, "Lessons in Pragmatism," in Lyotard, *The Lyotard Reader*, ed. Andrew Benjamin (Cambridge: Basil Blackwell, 1989), p. 128.

19. Nancy Hartsock, "Rethinking Modernism: Minority and Majority Theories," *Cultural Critique* 7 (Fall 1987): 195; see also Cornel West, "The New Politics of Difference," in *Out There: Marginalization and Contemporary Cultures*, ed. Russell Ferguson, Martha Gever, Trinh T. Minh-ha, and Cornel West (Cambridge, Mass.: MIT Press, 1990), pp. 19–36; and Cornel West, "Decentering Europe: A Memorial Lecture for James Snead," *Critical Quarterly* 33, 1 (Spring 1991): 1–19.

20. Lyotard writes that the failure of modernity to homogenize history in its image "could be connected to a resistance on the part of what I shall call the multiplicity of worlds of names, the insurmountable diversity of cultures." See "Missive on Universal History," in *The Postmodern Explained*, pp. 30–31.

21. Gilles Deleuze, *Nietzsche and Philosophy*, trans. Hugh Tomlinson (New York: Columbia University Press, 1983).

22. Lyotard, "Lessons in Paganism," in *The Lyotard Reader*, p. 134. See also Lyotard's brief discussion of Socrates and Protagoras in "On the Strength of the Weak," in Lyotard, *Toward the Postmodern*, ed. Robert Harvey and Mark S. Roberts (New Jersey: Humanities Press, 1993), pp. 71–72.

23. Francis Ballinger, "*Ambigere*: The Euro-American Picaro and the Native American Trickster," *MELUS* 17, 1 (Spring 1991–92): 31.

24. Jane Flax, "The End of Innocence," in *Feminists Theorize the Political*, ed. Judith Butler and Joan W. Scott (New York: Routledge, 1992), p. 460.

25. Flax, ibid.: "Speaking in knowledge's voice or on its behalf, we can avoid taking responsibility for locating our contingent selves as the producers of knowledge and truth claims," p. 458; see also pp. 447–48.

26. Friedrich Nietzsche, *On the Genealogy of Morals*, ed. Walter Kaufmann (New York: Vintage Books, 1969), p. 153.

27. Michel Foucault, "Truth and Power," in Foucault, *Power/Knowledge*, ed. Colin Gordon (New York: Pantheon Books, 1980), p. 131.

28. Friedrich Nietzsche, *Daybreak*, trans. R. J. Hollingdale (Cambridge: Cambridge University Press, 1982), p. 46.

29. Lyotard writes, "But in all of them, the givens arising from events are situated in the course of a history whose end, even if it remains beyond reach, is called universal freedom, the fulfillment of all humanity." See "Missive on Universal History," in *The Postmodern Explained*, p. 25. In Foucault's words, metanarratives posit "the form of history that reintroduces (and always assumes) a suprahistorical perspective: a history whose function is to compose the finally reduced diversity of time into a totality fully closed upon itself; a history that always encourages subjective recognitions and at-

tributes a form of reconciliation to all the displacements of the past; a history whose perspective on all that precedes it implies the end of time, a completed development." Michel Foucault, "Nietzsche, Genealogy, History," in Foucault, *Language, Counter-Memory, Practice*, ed. Donald F. Bouchard (Ithaca, N.Y.: Cornell University Press, 1977), p. 152.

30. Michel Foucault, *The Archaeology of Knowledge and the Discourse on Language*, trans. A. M. Sheridan Smith (New York: Pantheon Books, 1972), p. 229.

31. Ernesto Laclau and Chantal Mouffe, "Post-Marxism without Apologies," *New Left Review* 166 (1987): 79–136.

32. Michel Foucault, "History of Systems of Thought," in *Language, Counter-Memory, Practice*, p. 200.

33. Foucault, *The Archaeology of Knowledge*, p. 229.

34. Foucault, "Truth and Power," in *Power/Knowledge*, p. 131.

35. As James W. Bernauer remarks, it is not the case that "the world speaks meanings that our language merely reflects." James W. Bernauer, *Michel Foucault's Force of Flight: Toward an Ethics for Thought* (New Jersey: Humanities Press International, 1990), p. 93.

36. Lyotard, "Gloss on Resistance," in *The Postmodern Explained*, p. 90.

37. Lyotard, "Interview," p. 18.

38. Lyotard, "Rules and Paradoxes and Svelte Appendix," *Cultural Critique* 5 (Winter 1986–87): 210, 213; see also Lyotard, "The Sign of History," in *The Lyotard Reader*, p. 410.

39. Lyotard, "The Confusion of Reasons," in *The Postmodern Explained*, p. 65. Compare this with Judith Butler's statement that:

given the contested character of the term, to assume from the start a procedural or substantive notion of the universal is of necessity to impose a culturally hegemonic notion on the social field. To herald that notion then as the philosophical instrument that will negotiate between conflicts of power is precisely to safeguard and reproduce a position of hegemonic power by installing it in the metapolitical site of ultimate normativity. Butler, "Contingent Foundations: Feminism and the Question of 'Postmodernism,' " in *Feminists Theorize the Political*, pp. 7–8

40. Gianni Vattimo, "Verwindung: Nihilism and the Postmodern in Philosophy," *SubStance* 16, 2 (1987): 13, explains that "in thinking which is no longer metaphysical, Being no longer appears as presence but as an event (*Ereignis*), the disclosure of an epochal horizon which is historical and cultural (as in Foucault's *epistemai*)." Compare this with Foucault's description of the event and history:

As for the philosophy of history, it encloses the event in a cyclical pattern of time . . . it treats the present as framed by the past and the future: the present is a former future where its form was prepared and the past, which will occur in the future, preserves the identity of its content. First, this sense of the present requires a logic of essences (which establishes the present in memory) and of concepts (where the present is establishes as a knowledge of the future, and then a metaphysics of a crowned and coherent cosmos, of a hierarchical world. Michel Foucault, "Theatrum Philosophicum," in *Language, Counter-Memory, Practice*, pp. 175–76

41. Lyotard, "Gloss on Resistance," in *The Postmodern Explained*, p. 94.

42. Lyotard, "The Confusion of Reasons," in *The Postmodern Explained*, p. 65.

43. Lyotard, *The Postmodern Condition*, p. 65.

44. Ibid.

45. On the question of imagination in relation to modernity and postmodernity, see Jochen Schulte-Sasse, "Imagination and Modernity: The Taming of the Human Mind," *Cultural Critique* 5 (Winter 1986–87): 23–48; and Richard Kearney, *The Wake of Imagination* (Minneapolis: University of Minnesota Press, 1988).

46. Lyotard, "Lessons in Paganism," in *The Lyotard Reader*, p. 131. It is interesting to note in this light that Andreas Huyssen states that "Habermas' notion of modernity— the modernity he wishes to see continued and completed—is purged of modernism's nihilistic and anarchic strain." Andreas Huyssen, "Mapping the Postmodern," in *Feminism/Postmodernism*, ed. Nicholson, p. 252. Deborah Cook concludes that "Habermas expunges from the history of modernity those features which do not conform to his view of it." Deborah Cook, "Remapping Modernity," p. 37. Hubert L. Dreyfuss and Paul Rabinow also criticize the reductionist moves that Habermas makes in "privileging the communicative use of language" and his theoretical attempt "to exclude the perlocutionary effect of what is said and assert that ideally only the illocutionary content should play a role in reaching agreement." Hubert L. Dreyfuss and Paul Rabinow, "What Is Maturity? Habermas and Foucault on 'What Is Enlightenment?' " in *Foucault: A Critical Reader* ed. David Couzens Hoy (New York: Basil Blackwell, 1986), p. 119.

47. Lyotard, *The Postmodern Condition*, p. 66. For an excellent discussion and review of the "politics of consensus," see Peter McLaren, "Postmodernism, Post-Colonialism and Pedagogy," *Education and Society* 9, 1 (1991): 3–22.

48. Dreyfuss and Rabinow, "What Is Maturity?" p. 118.

49. Lyotard, "Answering the Question: What Is Postmodernism?" in *The Postmodern Condition*, p. 81.

50. Hubert L. Dreyfuss and Paul Rabinow, *Michel Foucault: Beyond Structuralism and Hermeneutics* (Chicago: University of Chicago Press, 1983), p. 32.

51. See Hartsock, "Rethinking Modernism: Minority and Majority Theories."

52. Lyotard, "Missive on Universal History," in *The Postmodern Explained*, p. 26.

53. Jürgen Habermas, "The Entwinement of Myth and Enlightenment: Rereading *Dialectic of Enlightenment*," *New German Critique* 26 (Spring–Summer 1982): 13–31.

54. Lyotard, "Note on the Meaning of 'Post,' " in *The Postmodern Explained*, p. 76.

55. Ibid., p. 80.

56. Lyotard, "Rules and Paradoxes and Svelte Appendix," p. 209. See also Lyotard, "Note on the Meaning of 'Post,' " in *The Postmodern Explained*, p. 79: "The question of postmodernity is also, or *first of all* a question of expressions of thought: in art, literature, philosophy, politics" (emphasis added).

57. Lyotard, "Interview," p. 18. Compare this with Colin Gordon's assessment of Foucault's use of genealogy as "focussing powerful analytical resources on the detailed, localised problems [which] demands an ability to interrogate the present without recourse to apocalyptic meta-narratives." Colin Gordon, "Question, Ethos, Event: Foucault on Kant and Enlightenment," *Economy and Society* 15, 1 (February 1986): 79.

58. Vattimo, "Verwindung: Nihilism and the Postmodern in Philosophy," p. 10.

59. This reflects Foucault's classic statement that "there is no power relation without the correlative constitution of a field of knowledge, nor any knowledge that does not

presuppose and constitute at the same time power relations." Foucault, *Discipline and Punish: The Birth of the Prison*, trans. Alan Sheridan (New York: Vintage Books, 1979), p. 27.

60. Immanuel Kant, "What Is Enlightenment? in *Foundations of the Metaphysics of Morals and What Is Enlightenment?* trans. Lewis White Beck (New York: Macmillan, 1990), p. 83.

61. Ibid., p. 84.

62. Michel Foucault, *The Order of Things: An Archaeology of the Human Sciences* (New York: Vintage Books, 1973), p. 317.

63. Foucault, "Georges Canguilhem: Philosopher of Error," quoted in Gordon, "Question, Ethos, Event," p. 72.

64. Michel Foucault, "The Art of Telling the Truth," in Foucault, *Politics, Philosophy, Culture*, ed. Lawrence D. Kritzman (New York: Routledge, 1988), p. 95.

65. Michel Foucault, "What Is Enlightenment?" in Foucault, *The Foucault Reader*, ed. Paul Rabinow (New York: Pantheon Books, 1984), p. 38.

66. Foucault, "The Art of Telling the Truth," in *Politics, Philosophy, Culture*, p. 95.

67. Foucault, "What Is Enlightenment?" in *The Foucault Reader*, p. 39. (Further references in text.)

68. Foucault, "The Subject and Power," in *Beyond Structuralism and Hermeneutics*, p. 216.

69. Michel Foucault, "About the Beginning of the Hermeneutics of the Self," *Political Theory* 21, 2 (May 1993): 222.

70. Foucault, "Practicing Criticism," in *Politics, Philosophy, Culture*, p. 154.

71. Foucault, "What Is Enlightenment?" in *The Foucault Reader*, p. 46.

72. Foucault, "About the Beginning of the Hermeneutics of the Self," p. 223.

73. Gordon, "Question, Ethos, Event," p. 76.

74. Foucault, "The Subject and Power," in *Beyond Structuralism and Hermeneutics*, p. 212. See also, Minh-ha, "Cotton and Iron," in *Out There*, pp. 327–36.

75. Foucault, "The Subject and Power," in *Beyond Structuralism and Hermeneutics*, p. 216.

76. Toni Morrison, quoted in Teresa de Laurentis, "Issues, Terms, and Context," in *Feminist Studies/Critical Studies*, ed. Teresa de Laurentis (Bloomington: Indiana University Press, 1986), p. 10.

77. Foucault, "What Is Enlightenment?" in *The Foucault Reader*, p. 45.

78. Guillermo Gomez-Pena, "Documented/Undocumented," in *Multi-Cultural Literacy: Opening the American Mind*, ed. Rick Simonson and Scott Walker (Saint Paul: Greywolf Press, 1988), p. 134.

79. Foucault, "Critical Theory/Intellectual History," in *Politics, Philosophy, Culture*, p. 28; also p. 29.

80. Ibid., p. 37. Deborah Cook observes that "if reason is not its own ground, then the possibility of a new form of reason lies in the critique of the grounds of reason." Deborah Cook, "Remapping Modernity," p. 45.

81. Foucault, *Politics, Philosophy, Culture*, p. 37.

82. Ibid., p. 36.

83. Foucault, "What Is Enlightenment?" in *The Foucault Reader*, p. 46.

84. Foucault, *The Archaeology of Knowledge*, p. 131.

85. Foucault, "What Is Enlightenment?" in *The Foucault Reader*, p. 46.

86. Sharon Welch, *Communities of Resistance and Solidarity: A Feminist Theology of Liberation* (Maryknoll, New York: Orbis Books, 1985), pp. 32–54.

87. Foucault, "Two Lectures," in *Power/Knowledge*, p. 83.

88. Foucault, "Nietzsche, Genealogy, History," in *Language, Counter-Memory, Practice*, p. 148.

89. Ibid., p. 140.

90. Ibid., p. 142; see also Foucault, *The Archaeology of Knowledge*, pp. 3–15.

91. Foucault, "Nietzsche, Genealogy, History," in *Language, Counter-Memory, Practice*, p. 154.

92. Ibid., pp. 151–52.

93. Ibid., p. 153.

94. Foucault, "What Is Enlightenment?" in *The Foucault Reader*, p. 41.

95. Ibid., p. 41.

96. Gordon, "Question, Ethos, Event," p. 76.

97. Foucault, "Two Lectures," in *Power/Knowledge*, p. 80.

98. Foucault, "On the Genealogy of Ethics: An Overview of Work in Progress," in *The Foucault Reader*, p. 343.

99. Nietzsche, *Gay Science*, p. 228.

100. Ibid., p. 287.

101. Foucault, "The Masked Philosopher," in *Politics, Philosophy, Culture*, p. 328.

102. Foucault, "What Is Enlightenment?" in *The Foucault Reader*, p. 46.

2 Legitimation Problems: Knowledge and Education in the Postmodern Condition

Michael Peters

The field of study is knowledge and the status of knowledge in the computerized societies of the postindustrial West. The problem is the legitimation of science in the postmodern age where the traditional legitimating "myths" or "metanarratives" of the speculative unity of all knowledge and its humanist emancipatory potential have allegedly fallen away. Knowledge and power have been revealed as two sides of the same question. The method is the analysis of language games signaling both a return to pragmatics and an elevation of narrative as a mode of thinking in its own right. The subtext is a polemic against Jürgen Habermas and his attempts to complete the "project of modernity"—to preserve the Enlightenment's emancipatory impulse in a fully transparent communicational society where validity claims implicit in ordinary talk can be discursively redeemed at the level of discourse.[1]

In this series of criss-crossing themes, at the intersection between issues concerning the status of scientific research and the existence of a postmodern culture, arise a welter of pragmatic questions concerning higher education and the future role of the university: Who transmits learning? What is transmitted? To whom? Through what medium? In what form? With what effect? Jean-François Lyotard maintains that a university policy is formed by a coherent set of answers to these questions.[2]

It is the purpose of this chapter to isolate Lyotard's contribution to the modernism-postmodernism debate, singling out the educational implications of his major working hypothesis: "that the status of knowledge is altered as societies enter what is known as the postindustrial age and cultures enter what is known as the postmodern age."[3]

In the course of exploring this hypothesis Lyotard—one of a number of French postmodernist thinkers along with Jacques Derrida, Gilles Deleuze, and Michel Foucault—makes a series of epigrammatic and provocative claims concerning the future of the university. For instance, at the end of the introduction Lyotard dedicates his report to the Institut Polytechnique de Philosophie at the Universite de Paries VIII (Vincennes), adding, "At this very postmodern moment that finds the University learning what may be its end, . . . the Institute may just be beginning."[4] It is the intent of this chapter to outline the conceptual basis that has led Lyotard to make conclusions of this sort.

The first section provides some background to the modernism-postmodernism debate in philosophical terms. It sketches some of the issues as they have surfaced between the antagonists, Habermas and Foucault, and provides a brief description of the position adopted by the American pragmatist Richard Rorty in this ongoing conversation.

The second section raises the problem of the legitimation of science in the postmodern age explicitly in Lyotard's terms. It also points to an interpretation of Ludwig Wittgenstein that Lyotard makes in order to assert his position.

In the final section, the notion of the performative as it figures in Lyotard's pragmatics is examined, and the questions of the legitimation of research and higher education are broached in terms of what Lyotard calls "the performativity criterion."

THE MODERNISM-POSTMODERNISM DEBATE

The terms *postmodernism* and *postmodernity* are catch-all concepts, allegedly signaling an epochal break not only with the so-called modern era but also with various traditionally "modern" ways of viewing the world. The epithet *postmodern* and its cognates have been used by a number of scholars in the English-speaking world since the historian Arnold Toynbee first coined the term in the early 1950s, although the notion of the modern era coming to an end is, of course, given thematic treatment by Friedrich Nietzsche, the spiritual grandfather of postmodernism, and by Oswald Spengler and Karl Marx among others. In Toynbee's thought the term *postmodern* suggests "irrationality, anarchy, and threatening indeterminacy."[5] Since that time in art and literary theory the term has been used with increasing frequency to indicate a completely distinctive aesthetic, philosophical, and political program.[6] Both Irving Howe[7] and

Harry Levin[8] use the concept *postmodern* in a derogatory sense to indicate the shift to "mass society" and to detect the "anti-intellectual undercurrent" threatening the humanism and Enlightenment characteristics of the culture of modernism. The term has also been used extensively in the sociological theories of both left- and right-wing persuasions. Boris Frankel[9] quotes Krishan Kumar's summary:[10]

Amitai Etzioni speaks of "the post-modern era," George Lichthelm of "the post-bourgeois society," Herman Kahn of "post-economic society," Murray Bookchin of "the post-scarity society." Daniel Bell simply of "the post-industrial society." Others, putting the point more positively have spoken of "the knowledge society" (Peter Drucker), "the personal service society" (Paul Halmos), "the service class society" (Ralf Dahrendorf), and "the technetronic era" (Zbigniew Brzezinski). Taken as a whole, these labels tell us what is in the past that has now been or is being suspended—e.g. scarcity, the bourgeois order, the predominance of the economic motive; and also what can be expected to be the main principle of the future society—e.g. knowledge, personal services, the electronic technology of computers and telecommunications.

It is surprising that Alan Touraine, who also talks of "the post-industrial society," should be omitted from this list along with Rudolf Bahro, Alvin Toffler, Barry Jones, and André Gorz, who form the basis of Frankel's study.[11]

Peter Bürger criticizes the sociological concept of the postmodern as historically premature:

Deep economic, technical and social changes can be observed when compared with the second half of the nineteenth century, but the dominant mode of production has remained the same: private appropriation of collectively produced surplus value. Social democratic governments in Western Europe have learned only too clearly that, despite the increasing significance of government intervention in economic matters, the maximisation of profit remains the driving force of social reproduction. We should therefore be cautious about interpreting the current changes and not evaluate them prematurely as signs of an epoch-making transformation.[12]

More recently, the term *postmodern* has figured as a key term in a more specifically philosophical debate. On one side, preeminently, is Jürgen Habermas, defender of what he calls "the project of modernity," which he traces back to Immanuel Kant and Max Weber, against the "antimodern sentiments" of a variety of self-styled postmodernist thinkers. Habermas attributes the term *postmodernity* to the French current of thought, the tradition, as he says "running from [Georges] Bataille to Derrida by way of Foucault" (it is to this line that Lyotard also belongs), and he compares the critique of reason of these French philosophers to the *Young Conservatives* of the Weimar Republic:

The *Young Conservatives* recapitulate the basic experience of aesthetic modernity. They claim as their own the revelations of a decentered subjectivity, emancipated from the imperatives of work and usefulness, and with this experience they step outside the modern world. . . . To instrumental reason, they juxtapose in manichean fashion a principle only accessible through evocation, be it the will to power or sovereignty, Being or the dionysiac force of the poetical.[13]

Habermas may be astray in christening Foucault "a postmodernist." Foucault, in an interview with Gerard Raulet, professes he does not understand what either the term *modernity* (at least, after Baudelaire) or *postmodernity* means or what kind of problem is common to postmodern or poststructural thinkers. His interviewer, Raulet, however, has no such problem. In putting the question to Foucault of whether he belongs to such a current, Raulet sketches *his* own understanding of postmodernity:

It is the idea of modernity, of reason, we find in Lyotard: a "grand narrative" from which we have finally been freed by a kind of salutory awakening. Postmodernity is a breaking apart of reason; Deleuzian schizophrenia. Postmodernity reveals, at last, that reason has only been one narrative among others in history; a grand narrative, certainly, but one of many, which can now be followed by other narratives.[14]

While Foucault professes not to understand the problem behind postmodernism, his sympathetic critics certainly take him to be a poststructuralist/postmodernist thinker who, along with Derrida and Lyotard, teaches that the values of the modern era were essentially logo- and homocentric illusions. Certainly both Mark Poster[15] and Nancy Fraser[16] understand Foucault's examination of "the philosophy of the subject"—by which he means a *problematique* dominating the modern *episteme* that privileges the subject as the foundation of all knowledge and signification—as bearing centrally on discussions of modernity. Both argue that Foucault's geneological analysis of modern power operates on the basis of a radical decentering that denies an epistemic or historical privilege to either the traditional Cartesian notion of a "centered" subjectivity or the humanist ideal of a rational, autonomous, and responsible self. Poster, for instance, writes, "In place of the continuous chronology of reason . . .

there have appeared scales that are sometimes very brief, distinct from one another, irreducible to a single law, scales that bear a type of history peculiar to each one, and which cannot be reduced to the general model of consciousness that acquires, progresses and remembers."[17]

They understand that Foucault's method allows us to see power very broadly in the development of a plurality of incommensurable discursive regimes, each with its multiplicity of "micropractices," which ultimately directs us to study the "politics of everyday life" and suspends the problematic of legitimacy understood in terms of the standard modern liberal normative framework with its talk of rights grounded as it is in the "nature of persons."

The issue between Habermas and Foucault, as Habermas sees it at least, concerns their respective evaluation of modernity. Locating himself in the tradition of Marxist social criticism reflected in the work of the Frankfurt School, Habermas argues that we should attempt to preserve the "emancipatory impulse" behind the Enlightenment:

The project aims at a differentiated relinking of modern culture with an everyday praxis that still depends on vital heritages. . . . This new connection, however, can only be established under the conditions, that societal modernization will also be steered in a different direction. The life-world has to become able to develop institutions out of itself which sets limits to the internal dynamics and to the imperatives of an almost autonomous economic system and its administrative complements.[18]

In contrast, he sites Foucault in a tradition of a line of thinkers, including Nietzsche, Martin Heidegger, and the French poststructuralists, who wish for a total break with the Enlightenment and "criticise the constitutive norms of modernity, rejecting the very commitments to truth, rationality, and freedom that alone make critique possible."[19]

This evaluation and siting of Foucault by Habermas is, perhaps, too simplistic an account of Foucault's position, for on the basis of his own assessment Foucault aligns himself with an attitude that clearly links his historical thinking with Kant.

To seek to define the internal teleology of time and the direction in which the history of humanity is moving, Foucault argues, is essentially a *modern* preoccupation—"modern" in the Kantian sense.[20] The Kantian sense of "modern," Foucault tells us, is derived from the question, *Was ist Aufklärung?* which is posed in terms of the difference "today" introduces with respect to yesterday." This is not, however, to make any glib statements about the historical relation between the Enlightenment and the modern era conceived of as a separate and distinct epoch of Western culture. Still less is it an opportunity to pronounce on high modernism as the liberal humanist legacy of the Enlightenment.

We are given a clue to Foucault's position in a reading he proposes of a crucial but minor text of Kant's. Foucault asks: "What, then, is the event that is called the Aufklärung and that has determined, at least in part, what we are, what we think, and what we do today?"

In an ironic inversion, posing the question, "What is modern philosophy?" Foucault answers: "Perhaps we could respond with an echo: modern philosophy is the philosophy that is attempting to answer the question raised so imprudently two centuries ago: *Was ist Aufklärung?*"[21] We are informed that Kant defines enlightenment in a negative way as the process that releases us from the status of immaturity. Enlightenment, then, is the moment when we come of age in the use of reason, when there is no longer the need to subject ourselves to forms of traditional authority. The notion of critique is also required at exactly this moment, for its role is that of defining the conditions under which the use of reason is legitimate "in order to determine what can be known, what must be done, and what may be hoped."[22]

The reading of Kant's text allows Foucault to characterize modernity as an *attitude* rather than an epoch (or a style) and to assert that the (unbroken?) thread connecting us to the Enlightenment if *not* "faithfulness to doctrinal elements, but rather the permanent reactivation of an attitude— that is, of a philosophical ethos that could be described as a permanent critique of our historical era."[23]

By defining the Enlightenment in such terms Foucault precludes much of the oppositional thinking that has typified philosophical discussions of modernity-postmodernity. In an instructive way Foucault draws our attention to the idea that defining the Enlightenment thus "means precisely that one has to refuse everything that might present itself in the form of a simple and authoritarian alternative: you either accept the Enlightenment and remain within the tradition of rationalism . . . ; or else you criticise the Enlightenment and then try to escape from its principles of rationality."[24]

Foucault's remarks here are salutory. They represent to a significant degree a different assessment of the differences separating Habermas and Foucault than the account offered by Habermas himself. They also serve to remind us of how easily a debate may become artificially polarized. Certainly, the oppositional thinking that Foucault described has become an entrenched feature of the debate, not only in terms of explicitly drawn "sides"—modernists versus postmodernists—but also of much of the discussion over rationality in the English-speaking world.

The oppositional thinking of which Foucault speaks is, to a large degree, characteristic of one line of the debate carried on between Jürgen Habermas, perhaps the leading voice of Critical Theory, and Jean-François Lyotard, a leading representative of a French postmodernism. As Rorty explains:

From Lyotard's point of view, Habermas is offering one more metanarrative, a more general and abstract "narrative of emancipation" than the Freudian and Marxian metanarratives. For Habermas, the problem posed by "incredulity towards metanarratives" is that unmasking only makes sense if we "preserve at least one standard for (the) explanation of the corruption of all reasonable standards." If we have no such standard, one which escapes a "totalising self-referential critique," then distinctions between the naked and the masked, or between theory and ideology, lose their force.[25]

Rorty himself is not merely an observer of the French-German debate on the status of modernity and its aftermath; he is embroiled in it, arguing for the destruction of the Cartesian-Kantian tradition with the aim of showing the pointlessness of talk of foundations of knowledge. He wants to remind us of the common message of Wittgenstein, Dewey, and Heidegger "that investigations of the foundations of knowledge or morality or language or society may be simply apologetics, attempts to eternalise a certain contemporary language-game, social practice or image."[26]

In one very real sense, Rorty sides with Lyotard against Habermas. He is suspicious of Habermas's transcendentalism, of Habermas's project of saving the emancipatory impulse of the Enlightenment by offering principles to ground and provide foundations for his reconstructive theory of communicative action. Habermas's appeal to rational consensus and discursively redeemable validity claims is just one more attempt to "eternalise the discourse of the day," one more self-deceptive effort to ground the European form of life and its institutions by glorifying social practices.

Rorty clearly aligns himself with Lyotard when he christens his own position as that of the postmodernist bourgeois liberal. "I use 'postmodernist' in a sense given to this term by Jean-François Lyotard, who says that the postmodern attitude is that of 'distrust of metanarratives,' narratives which describe or predict the activities of such entities as the noumenal self of the Absolute Spirit or the Proletariat."[27]

For the postmodernist bourgeois liberal the notion of moral self is regarded, not as a Rawisian rational chooser, but simply as "a network of beliefs, desires, and emotions with nothing behind it—no substrate behind the attributes."[28] This is not to say that Rorty, however, accepts Lyotard's interpretation of the character of modern science or his arguments based on it against Habermas.

THE FIELD OF KNOWLEDGE AND THE PROBLEM OF LEGITIMATION OF SCIENCE

Lyotard's single point of departure in attempting to describe and chart the transition in Western societies to the postindustrial age is scientific knowledge. He argues that the "leading" sciences and technologies—cybernetics, telematics, informatics, and the growth of computer languages—are all *significantly language based* and have transformed the two principal functions of knowledge: research and the transmission of acquired learning.

Knowledge is changed or redefined within this context of general transformation. Anything in the constituted body of knowledge that is not translatable into *quantities* of information, that is, into a computer language, will be abandoned. Knowledge, in other words, loses its "use-value," and the old principle that the acquisition of knowledge is dissociable from the training of minds becomes obsolete.

The technical transformations wrought by a continued miniaturization and commercialization of knowledge machines will further change the way in which "learning is acquired, classified, made available, and exploited." Knowledge is exteriorized with respect to the "knower," and the status of the learner and the teacher is transformed into a commodity relationship of "supplier" and "user": "Knowledge is and will be produced in order to be sold, it is and will be consumed in order to be valorised in a new production: in both cases, the goal is exchange."[29]

Already knowledge has become the principal force of production, severely altering the composition of the workforce in developed countries. The mercantilization of knowledge will further widen the gap between developed and developing countries. It will disrupt the traditional view that learning falls within the purview of the state and raise new legal and ethical questions for the relationship between the state and "information-rich" multinational corporations. This scenario, Lyotard admits, is not original or even necessarily true, but it does have *strategic value* in allowing us to see the effects of the transformation of knowledge on public power and civil institutions, and it raises afresh the central problem of legitimation. Who decides what is "true" or what is to be regarded as "scientific," as belonging to the discourse of a scientific community? Who has the right to decide what is just? In the postindustrial society, where knowledge and power are simply two sides of the same question, the question of double legitimation necessarily comes to the fore: "In the computer age, the question of knowledge is now more than ever a question of government."[30]

In the immediate past, in the *modern* as opposed to the postmodern era, science had been legitimated by the master discourse of philosophy. Lyotard writes, "I will use the term *modern* to designate any science that legitimates itself with reference to a metadiscourse of this kind making an explicit appeal to some grand narrative, such as the dialectics of the Spirit, the hermeneutics of meaning, the emancipation of the rational or working subject, or the creation of wealth."[31]

Lyotard then defines *postmodern* as "incredulity toward metanarratives," a distrust of "stories" that purport to justify certain practices or institutions by grounding them upon a set of transcendental, ahistorical, or universal principles. This incredulity is a product, Lyotard maintains, of progress in the sciences, specifically, a change in the way we practice science. Here Lyotard is linking up and referring in an anecdotal way to the crisis in metaphysical philosophy, pointed to in the English-speaking world by the historical theories of Thomas Kuhn and Paul Feyerabend. It seems, however, that Lyotard takes such theories as indicating that we actually conduct scientific research in a way different from the one used by those who practiced science in the Newtonian period, rather than thinking of the recent debunking of the empiricist model of science as simply repudiating a bad account.[32]

The metanarrative provided by the "crowning" science of speculative philosophy legitimated the university institution that was modeled along principles of emancipationist humanism. Youth from the liberal élite—"the heroes of knowledge"—were trained in the great task of pursuing good ethico-political ends and leading their countries toward social progress. This is part of the legacy of the Enlightenment narrative now under scrutiny: "To the obsolescence of the metanarrative apparatus of legitimation corresponds, most notably, the crisis of metaphysical philosophy and of the university institution which in the past relied on it."[33]

The crisis of metaphysical philosophy and the bankruptcy of ahistorical theories of justification are linked up, by way of an aesthetic thematic in Lyotard's work, with the so-called crisis of representation, in which an essentially realist epistemology based on a mirror theory of knowledge and art conceives of representation as the reproduction of an external reality. English-speaking readers will recognize the theme as it has been recently explored by the American "pragmatist" Richard Rorty in his reworking of the history of modern analytic philosophy.[34] Beginning his interpretation with a quotation from Wittgenstein's *Vermischte Bemerkungen*, which likens progress in philosophy to the finding of a remedy for itching, a physicianlike Rorty diagnoses modern analytic philosophy as simply one more variant of Kantian philosophy that is distinguished from its parent predecessor by its thinking of representation in linguistic terms and of philosophy of language as exhibiting the "foundations of knowledge."

Significantly, Rorty argues for a position termed "epistemological behaviorism," which explains rationality and epistemic authority by reference to what society lets us say rather than vice versa. Divested of the captivating mirror imagery, philosophy can then be seen simply as part of the social practice of conversation.

The reference to Rorty is not merely accidental. It is central to an emphasis on pragmatics in language shared by Lyotard and also motivated by a reading of the later Wittgenstein. Lyotard's assertion that the great legitimating myths are being dispersed in "clouds of . . . language elements," each with "pragmatic valencies specific to its kind," is squarely based on the "method of language games" he clearly attributes to Wittgenstein.[35] The relation of the later Wittgenstein to French theory, more generally, has been noted by a number of scholars. Gregory Ulmer in an article entitled "The Object of Post-Criticism," which discusses the import of Derrida's grammatology, writes, "Post-criticism, then, functions with an 'epistemology' of performance—knowing as making, producing, doing, acting, as in Wittgenstein's account of the relation of knowing to the 'mastery of a technique.' Thus post-criticism writes 'on' its object in the way that Wittgenstein's knower exclaims, 'Now I know how to go on!' "[36]

In a rather different vein, Peter Munz, reviewing Bloor's social theory of knowledge, also acknowledges the strong parallels between Wittgenstein's "epistemology" and French postmodernist theories of literature.[37] Having described Wittgenstein's social naturalism, he lists the works of members of "the Wittgenstein-inspired movement in Germany, England and America": Thomas Kuhn, Karl-Otto Apel, Richard Rorty, Saul Kripke, Peter Winch;[38] and then he draws our attention to the emergence of a similar philosophical movement in France.

Derrida argues that we can understand a text only by deconstructing it into the metaphor and idioms of which it is composed. It cannot be understood by comparing it to anything outside itself, i.e., by looking at the world it purports to describe. With this doctrine that 'Il n'y a pas hors texte,' Derrida echoes Wittgenstein's insistence that there are no pre-linguistic meanings and that anything we say constitutes its meaning but does not reflect or describe a pre-linguistically intuited or pictured state of affairs.[39]

Munz also sees Foucault's work as "something very similar to Kuhn's elaboration of Wittgenstein." His purpose is, however, not to elaborate French theory but, rather, to argue the poverty of Wittgenstein's "philosophy of closed circles" versus the intellectual superiority of Karl Popper's evolutionary epistemology.[40]

It is clear that at the heart of Lyotard's position is a playful reading of the later Wittgenstein, which emphasizes the pluralistic nature of language games. Each of the various types of utterance—denotative, prescriptive, performative, and so on—comprises a language game with its own body of rules defining its properties and uses. The rules are irreducible, and there exists an incommensurability among different games. Lyotard adds three further observations about language games. First, the rules do not have a bedrock justification, nor do they carry with themselves their own legitimation. Where Wittgenstein might say that they are constituted by agreement in practice, Lyotard says they are the object of a contract, explicit or not, between players. Second, "if there are no rules there is no game"; and third, "every utterance should be thought of as a 'move' in a game."[41] Two principles underlie the method as a whole: "To speak is to fight, in the sense of playing, and speech acts fall within the domain of a general agonistics."[42] As Fredric Jameson explains, utterances are not conceived of either as a process of the transmission of information or messages, or a network of signs, or signifying systems (structuralism, semiotics); rather, they are seen as an *agonistics of language*, as an unstable exchange between communicational adversaries.[43] The example Lyotard uses is that of playing cards: a "move" in the game is like the taking (or trumping) of a trick. The second principle elevates this conflictual view of language as a model for understanding the nature of the social bond (and science itself).

While there are many different language games, Lyotard asserts, and each of us lives at the intersection of many of these, the decision makers proceed on the assumption that there is commensurability and common ground among them and that the whole is determinable.

They allocate our lives for the growth of power. In matters of social justice and scientific truth alike, the legitimation of that power is based on its optimising the system's performance—efficiency. The application of this criterion to all of our games necessarily entails a certain level of terror, whether soft or hard: be operational (that is, commensurable) or disappear.[44]

In a later work, Lyotard more openly acknowledges his intellectual debt to the later Wittgenstein. Taking his cue from Theodor Adorno, he champions the "micrologic" in opposition to the speculative—the grand narrative of Hegelian philosophy—and asserts that "another perspective has been opened up through which it may be possible to measure up to the crisis [of metaphysics] and the reflective response it demands. This perspective is pointed to notably in the *Philosophische Untersuchungen* and *Zettel*, under the programmatical name of *Sprachsielen*."[45]

Lyotard proceeds to argue for his interpretation and to enumerate characteristics of the language game: The concept has its home in the language game; the language game is to be taken in the plural (they are "numerous, even unnumerable"); the rules of various language games are irreducible to one another; a sentence is a move in the game and can establish a new rule (and so a new game). He claims, "We are worlds away from necessary linkages, but are at the heart of equivocity," an equivocity "such that the task of expressing it . . . runs into an indefinite number of series of other moves belonging to an irreducibly heteronomous multiplicity of games."[46]

Lyotard's interpretation of the language games as heteronomous ("the untranslatability of one game into another") and paralogous ("the search for the limit between the tolerable and the intolerable by way of moves lacking any given model") shatters the grand legitimating metanarrative of science as the supreme voice of reason. Lyotard writes: "Science plays its own game; it is incapable of legitimating the other language games. The game of prescription, for example, escapes it. But above all it is incapable of legitimating itself, as speculation assumed it could."[47]

For Lyotard there is no principle of unitotality; there is no universal metalanguage. The reality is that there are many languages and, as Wittgenstein argued (Lyotard notes), new languages are added to the old ones, like suburbs of an old town. Lyotard acknowledges Wittgenstein's examples of the symbolism of chemistry and the notation of infinitesimal calculus. Less than fifty years on, he argues, we can substantially add to the list: Lyotard mentions the growth of machine languages, the matrices of game theory, new systems of musical notation, systems of notation for nondenotative forms of logic, the language of the genetic code, graphs of phonological structures, and so on.[48]

The proliferation and splintering of language games, which prevents an overall mastery, allows him to claim that "speculative or humanistic philosophy is forced to relinquish its legitimation duties, which explains why philosophy is facing a crisis wherever it persists in arrogating such functions and is reduced to the study of systems of logic or the history of ideas where it has been realistic enough to surrender them."[49]

PERFORMATIVITY

In terms of a theory of the performative (J. L. Austin) Lyotard elaborates a "pragmatics" of science and research. The end of science is not "consensus," as Habermas would have us believe, but *paralogy*. The practice of paralogism is a search for "instabilities" the point of which is not to reach agreement but, rather, to seek to undermine internally the very framework in which the previous "normal science" had been undertaken. The justification of science does not rest on a representational view of language, where knowledge expressed in a set of denotative statements mirrors states of affairs in the world (either truthfully or falsely). Rather, it is, as Jameson explains, "simply to produce *more* work, to generate new or fresh scientific *enoncés* or statements, to make you have new ideas (P. D. Medawar) or best of all (and returning to the more familiar aesthetics of high modernism), again and again to 'make it new.' "[50]

Jameson claims that by recasting postreferential epistemology in terms of a theory of the performative, Lyotard has "ingeniously saved," the coherence of the scientific enterprise. Rorty, however, as previously noted, takes issue with Lyotard's account, suggesting that we should view the recent debunking of the empiricist model of science as repudiating an inadequate account rather than indicating that we practice science differently from our Newtonian ancestors.[51] Jameson is correct, however, to note the close parallel between Lyotard's and Rorty's positions. Witness Rorty's claim, for instance, that "from an educational point of view, as opposed to the epistemological or technical, point of view, the way things are said is more important than the possession of truths."[52] In the project of "subordinating truth to edification," of giving up the traditional picture of knowing as having an essence, we will more readily come to regard knowing simply as a set of contingent social practices, as a right, by current standards, to believe. Once we have reached this point, "then we are well on the way to seeing *conversation* as the ultimate context within which knowledge is to be understood."[53]

Where Lyotard and Rorty differ is in describing the nature of the conversation as the ultimate context within which we can legitimate our European form of life. For Rorty there is always the hope of agreement so long as the conversation lasts. For Lyotard, "agreement," "consensus," and "undistorted communication" disguise the basic conflictual nature of the language game.

Let us return to science and begin by examining Lyotard's notion of the pragmatics of research. Lyotard argues that the essential mechanisms of research are undergoing two important changes, "a multiplication in methods of argumentation and a rising complexity in the process of establishing proof."[54] The first development is tantamount to a challenge to classical reason through an examination of the status of rules governing the class of denotative utterances. By reference to modern developments in logic and arithmetic, Lyotard attempts to show that the principle of a universal metalanguage required for demonstrating the truth of denotative statements has given way to the principle of a plurality of formal and axiomatic systems. In terms of the properties required of the syntax of any formal system (consistency, completeness, decidability, and independence of axioms), it is possible to generalize from Kurt Gödel's incompleteness theorem that all formal systems have internal limitation.[55] The shift from the principle of a universal metalanguage to one of plurality is at the heart of the break from a universal rationality (with its classical metanarrative of legitimation given in the course of philosophy) to a "breaking apart" of reason and the development of microrationalities confined in terms of the multiplicity of language games, defined by their irreducible rules. Scientific research does use, and already has used, methods (languages) outside the concept of classical reason. These languages, however, are subject to the pragmatic condition; that is, "each must formulate its own rules and petition the addressee to accept them."[56]

The pragmatic condition, therefore, means that the acceptability of moves in a language game depends upon a contract drawn between the players. It follows that "progress" in knowledge is of two different kinds: the first (normal science?) is construed as a *new* move within the established rules; the second is construed as the invention of *new* rules, that is, the change to a new game.

The second development—the production of proof—which is in Lyotard's pragmatic terms "only part of an argumentation process designed to win agreement from the addressees of scientific messages"—has increasingly fallen under the sway and control of another game, that of technology. The game of technology, as opposed to science, whose goal is truth, follows the principle of optimal performance (maximizing output, minimizing input). Its goal or criterion is efficiency rather than truth (the denotative game) or justice (the prescriptive game).

Technology (e.g., computers) requires research funding but it "optimises the efficiency of the task to which it is applied . . . and the surplus-value derived from this improved performance."[57] Progress in knowledge is thus subordinated to investment in technology, and "since performativity increases the ability to produce proof, it also increases the ability to be right: the technical criterion, introduced on a massive scale into scientific knowledge, cannot fail to influence the truth criterion."[58]

"Being right" is seen to be a product of research expenditure, especially in the new information science areas of the technology of data storage and accessibility. The self-reinforcement of science and technology, where funds from sales of technological improvements are recycled into a further improved performance, sets up "an equation between wealth, efficiency and truth."[59] Science thus becomes a force of production—"a movement in the circulation of capital"—and the old humanist (emancipatory) narratives of legitimation are replaced by the new ideological legitimation of science promulgated by the state and corporations in terms of the value of efficiency, which has as its goal power rather than truth.

A similar scenario can be plotted for education—the transmission of knowledge—which is also to be legitimated in terms of the performative (i.e., efficiency) criterion. It is at this point that Lyotard answers the questions that pertain to a university policy (mentioned in the introduction of this article). The goal for the university becomes its optimal contribution to the best performance of the social system. This goal demands the creation of two kinds of skills indispensable to the maintenance of the social system: Those necessary to enhance competitiveness in the world market and those necessary for fulfilling the need for its internal cohesion. The first, Lyotard predicts, will lead to the growth of demand for middle-management executives in leading sectors and priority in education being given to any discipline that can demonstrate an applicability to training in "telematics" (computer science, sybernetics, mathematics, and so on). The second, within the context of delegitimation, will no longer regard the transmission of knowledge as the training of an elite capable of guiding society toward its emancipation but will simply "supply the system with players capable of acceptably fulfilling their roles at the pragmatic posts required by its institutions."[60]

Accordingly, two categories of students will emerge more strongly, those who reproduce the technical and the professional intelligentsia. In addition to its professionalist function, the university will come also to improve the system's performance through an increasing role in the realms of job retraining and continuing education. There is a changing emphasis from transmitting knowledge *en bloc* to young people before they join the workforce to one that serves working adults, *à la carte*, to help them improve their skills and widen occupation horizons.

The general effect of the performativity principle is to subordinate the institutions of higher learning to the existing power, that is, in terms of legitimating myths, subordinating truth (as it figures in the emancipatory narrative) to efficiency and power. Lyotard writes:

The notion of "university franchise" now belongs to a bygone era. The "autonomy" granted the universities after the crisis of the late 1960's has very little meaning given the fact that practically nowhere do teachers' groups have the power to decide what the budget of their institution will be; all they can do is allocate the funds that are assigned to them, and only then as the last step in the process.[61]

New technologies will alter the medium of the transmission of knowledge—almost a truism in the postmodern age—and elementary training in informatics may become a compulsory requirement in the same way as a foreign language proficiency was/is a requirement in the *modern* university. Replacement of teachers by machines and technicians is only repugnant within the old master narrative of emancipationist humanism:

The question (overt or implied) now asked by the professional student, the State, or institutions of higher education is no longer "Is it true?" but "What use is it?" In the context of the mercantilisation of knowledge, more often than not this question is equivalent to: "Is it saleable?" And in the context of power-growth: "Is it efficient?"[62]

While Lyotard still has more to say in terms of the prospective vast market that exists in the postmodern era for competence in operational skills and the growth of "interdisciplinary" research teams that will further break down the traditional organization of knowledge according to Wilhelm Humboldt's model of the university, his message is plain, and his argument has run its course.

In a final essay, "Answering the Question: What Is Postmodernism?" (translated by Régis Durand), added to the English translation of his book, Lyotard returns once more to the opening themes. He addresses himself to Habermas's project of preserving the emancipatory impulse of the Enlightenment. If modernity has failed, according to Habermas it has done so by allowing the splintering of the totality of life or unity of experience into "a pluralisation of diverging universes of discourse" that has shattered the naive consensus. His answer to this "specifically modern experience" is to seek a relinking of modern culture with an everyday praxis through "clarifying a concept of communicative rationality that escapes the snares of Western logocentrism."[63]

Such a theory is his reconstructive theory of communication, which seeks this end through "the analysis of the *already* operative potential for rationality contained in everyday practices of communication."

Lyotard's question is to determine the nature of the unity sought by Habermas:

Is the aim of the project of modernity the constitution of sociocultural unity within which all the elements of daily life and of thought would take their places as in an organic whole? Or does the passage that has to be charted between hetero-geneous language games—those of cognition, of ethics, of politics—belong to a different order from that? . . . The first hypothesis, of a Hegelian inspiration, does not challenge the notion of a dialectically totalising *experience*; the second is closer to the spirit of Kant's *Critique of Judgement*, but must be submitted, like the *Critique*, to that severe reexamination which postmodernity imposes on the thought of the Enlightenment, on the idea of a unitary end of history and of a subject.[64]

NOTES

This is a slightly revised version of a paper previously published as "Techno-Science, Rationality, and the University: Lyotard on the 'Postmodern Condition,'" which appeared in *Educational Theory* 39, 2 (Spring 1989): 89–105. I wish to thank the editor of *Educational Theory* and the board of trustees of the University of Illinois for their kind permission to reproduce it here.

1. The text to which I refer is Jean-François Lyotard's *The Postmodern Condition: A Report on Knowledge*, first published in France in 1979. All references to this work in the text are to the English translation by Geoff Bennington and Brian Massumi (Minneapolis: University of Minnesota Press, 1984). (Henceforth referred to as *PMC*.)

2. *PMC*, p. 48.

3. Ibid., p. 3.

4. Ibid., p. xxv.

5. Matei Calinescu, *Faces of Modernity: Avant-Garde, Decadence, Kitsch* (Bloomington: Indiana University Press, 1977), p. 133.

6. See Andreas Huyssen, "The Search for Tradition: Avant-Garde and Postmodern-ism in the 1970s," *New German Critique* 22 (Winter 1981): 23–40; Hal Foster, ed., *Postmodern Culture* (London: Pluto Press, 1983), first published as *The Anti-Aesthetic*.

7. Irving Howe, "Mass Society and Postmodern Fiction," *Partisan Review* 26 (1959): 430–36.

8. Harry Levin, "What Was Modernism?" in *Refractions* (New York: Oxford University Press, 1966).

9. Boris Frankel, *The Post-Industrial Utopians* (Cambridge: Polity Press/Basil Blackwell, 1987), p. 2. Frankel critiques non-Marxist radical and alternative theories, arguing:

If the mainstream Left fails to listen to the eco-feminist and eco-pacifist critiques of existing societies, it will be condemning itself to a future of political conservatism and marginalisation. But without the political economic strength and experiences of the labour movement, the Green and alternative movements are equally doomed to snapping at the heels of those conservative political forces which threaten the future of the whole planet. (p. ix)

10. Krishan Kumar, *Prophecy and Progress* (Harmondsworth, England: Penguin, 1978), pp. 193–94.

11. Alan Touraine, *La Société Post-Industrielle* (Paris), trans. Leonard Mayhew (New York: Random House, 1971).

12. Peter Bürger, "The Decline of the Modern Age," *Telos* 62 (Winter 1985): 117.

13. Jürgen Habermas, "Modernity versus Postmodernity," *New German Critique* 22 (1981): 13.

14. Gérard Raulet, "Structuralism and Post-Structuralism: An Interview with Michel Foucault," *Telos* 53 (1983): 205.

15. Mark Poster, "The Future According to Foucault: The Archaeology of Knowledge and Intellectual History," in *Modern European Intellectual History: The Appraisais and New Perspectives*, ed. D. Lacapra and S. Kaplan (Ithaca, N.Y.: Cornell University Press, 1981), pp. 137–52.

16. Nancy Fraser, "Foucault on Modern Power: Empirical Insights and Normative Confusions," *Praxis International* 1 (1981): 272–87; "Foucault's Body-Language: A Post-Humanist Political Rhetoric?" *Salmagundi* 61 (1983): 55–70; and "Michel Foucault: A 'Young Conservative'?" *Ethics* 96 (1985): 165–84.

17. Poster, "The Future According to Foucault," p. 138.

18. Habermas, "Modernity vs. Postmodernity," p. 13.

19. Fraser, "Michel Foucault: A 'Young Conservative'?" p. 166.

20. Michel Foucault, "What Is Enlightenment?" in *Foucault Reader*, ed. Paul Rabinow (New York: Pantheon Books, 1984).

21. Foucault, "What Is Enlightenment?" p. 32.

22. Ibid., p. 38.

23. Ibid., p. 42.

24. Ibid., p. 43.

25. Richard Rorty, "Habermas and Lyotard on Postmodernity," in *Habermas and Modernity*, ed. Richard Bernstein (Cambridge: Polity Press, 1985).

26. Richard Rorty, *Philosophy and the Mirror of Nature* (Oxford: Basil Blackwell, 1980).

27. Richard Rorty, "Postmodern Bourgeois Liberalism," *Journal of Philosophy* 80 (1983): 585.

28. Ibid.

29. *PMC*, p. 4.

30. Ibid., p. 9.

31. Ibid., p. xxiii.

32. See Rorty, "Habermas and Lyotard on Postmodernity," p. 163.

33. *PMC*, p. xxiv.

34. Rorty, *Philosophy and the Mirror of Nature*.

35. *PMC*, pp. 9–10, p. 40.

36. Gregory L. Ulmer, "The Object of Post Criticism," in *Postmodern Culture*, p. 94.

37. Peter Munz, "Bloor's Wittgenstein or the Fly in the Bottle," *Philosophy of the Social Sciences* 17 (1987): 67–96.

38. See Peter Winch, *Trying to Make Sense* (Oxford: Basil Blackwell, 1987). In this new collection of essays Winch addresses himself to some old problems (such as those first canvased in "Understanding a Primitive Society") and applies Wittgensteinian insights to questions concerning our understanding of works of art (see "Text and Context").

39. Munz, "Bloor's Wittgenstein," p. 73.

40. Munz argues that followers of the "philosophy of closed circles"—or "paradig-matics"—are "thrown back upon a doctrine of spontaneity" (ibid., p. 73). Elsewhere, he shapes up a fundamental confrontation between Wittgenstein and Popper as the choice between two competing paradigms left in the wake of the demise of positivism: "the paradigm of epistemic authority of speech communities; and the paradigm of Evolution-ary Epistemology," see Peter Munz, *Our Knowledge of the Growth of Knowledge: Popper or Wittgenstein?* (London: Routledge & Kegan Paul, 1985), p. 8.

41. *PMC*, p. 10.

42. Ibid.

43. Frederic Jameson, "Foreword" to *PMC*, p. xi.

44. *PMC*.

45. Jean-François Lyotard, "Presentations," in *Philosophy in France Today*, ed. Alan Montefiore (Cambridge: Cambridge University Press, 1983), p. 122.

46. Ibid., p. 124.

47. *PMC*, p. 40.

48. Ibid., 41.

49. Ibid.

50. Jameson, "Foreword" to *PMC*, p. iv.

51. Rorty, "Habermas and Lyotard on Postmodernity."

52. Rorty, *Philosophy and the Mirror of Nature*, p. 359.

53. Ibid., p. 389.

54. *PMC*, p. 41.

55. The metalanguage used by logicians to describe a formal axiomatic system is "natural." It is also universal (in the sense that all other languages can be translated into it) but not consistent with respect to negation, for it allows the formation of paradoxes. See *PMC*, p. 43.

56. Ibid.

57. Ibid., p. 45.

58. Ibid., p. 58.

59. Ibid., p. 45.

60. Ibid., p. 48.

61. Ibid., p. 50.

62. Ibid., p. 51.

63. Jürgen Habermas, "Questions and Counterquestions," in *Habermas and Moder-nity*, p. 196.

64. Lyotard, "Answering the Question: What Is Postmodernism?" in *PMC*.

3 Lyotard and Rorty on the Role of the Professor

A. T. Nuyen

There has been for some time now a perception that education is in a crisis. Those of this opinion point, as evidence, to declining standards of literacy and numeracy, disciplinary problems in schools, conflicting educational theories and models, and so on. Some have claimed that the causes are external to the educational process, such as government policies concerning funding or the changing attitude toward education in general. Others contend that the main cause is internal, having to do with the nature of education itself. The latter group has interpreted the work of Jean-François Lyotard, particularly his *The Postmodern Condition*, as a vindication of its view.[1] In fact, the diagnosis of the internal problem was made long ago by Hannah Arendt: "The problem of education in the modern world lies in the fact that by its very nature it cannot forgo either authority or tradition, and yet must proceed in a world that is neither structured by authority nor held together by tradition."[2] According to many postmodernists, including Lyotard, the postmodern world has slipped further from the crutches of authority and tradition. If this is right then we cannot properly understand the crisis in education until we understand the postmodern condition. For this reason, philosophers of education have begun to examine the implications for education of the postmodernist discourse. The growing interest in postmodernism can be gauged from the frequency of articles appearing in journals devoted to the philosophy of education, such as *Educational Theory*, as well as from "the growing presence of this theme in educational conferences."[3]

In this chapter I am interested in one specific claim made by Lyotard, namely, that the postmodern condition means the death of the Professor. This claim contrasts sharply with Richard Rorty's view according to which the postmodern condition adds a special significance to the role of the Professor. Rorty's position on this issue appears to occupy the middle ground between the radical view proposed by Lyotard and the more traditional, more conservative view proposed by someone like Jürgen Habermas. At first sight, this topography makes sense because it matches the epistemological landscape where Lyotard occupies the radical, postmodern corner, Habermas the more conservative, rationalistic corner, and Rorty, by his own admission, "split(s) the difference between Lyotard and Habermas."[4] For those who believe that pedagogy reflects epistemology, this is as it should be. However, many writers reject the link between epistemology and pedagogy, calling it the "epistemological fallacy" (thus allowing the Professor to play a role even if one accepts Lyotard's epistemology).[5] Wishing neither to defend nor to reject the "epistemological fallacy," I want to argue here that in so far as epistemology determines pedagogy, Lyotard's postmodernist epistemology (as outlined in Section I) does not require the educational model he is advocating. I shall argue in Section II that Lyotard's postmodernism, far from leading to the death of the Professor, calls for a pedagogy in which the Professor has a crucial role to play. If I am right, my argument lends support to Rorty's case in his own polemics against Lyotard. In Section III I shall draw the parallel between my conclusion and those reached by Rorty.

I

How does Lyotard reach the conclusion that "the process of delegitimation and the predominance of the performance criterion are sounding the knell of the age of the Professor"? Clearly, there are for Lyotard two factors contributing to the death of the Professor: delegitimation and the performance criterion. As it turns out, both of these result from Lyotard's postmodernist epistemology. Let us look first at delegitimation.

In the introduction to *The Postmodern Condition*, Lyotard indicates that he "will use the term *modern* to designate any science that legitimates itself with reference to a metadiscourse . . . making explicit appeal to some grand narrative" and that he will "define *postmodern* as incredulity toward metanarratives."[6] By legitimation Lyotard means the process by which it is judged whether something, a statement, is science, or more generally knowledge. A narrative, in turn, is an account of some fundamental values, or an account of some metaphysical entities or ideals that are the sources of fundamental values. It is by virtue of such values that a statement is legitimated as science, or knowledge. Examples of legitimation by appealing to a grand narrative range from Plato's appeal to the immutable Forms, G. W. Hegel's appeal to Spirit, and the modernist appeal to the " 'people' (the nation, or even humanity)."[7] Thus for Plato only the Forms are *real* and only statements about those Forms can be *true* and form part of knowledge. Statements about *appearances* are excluded, and likewise statements made by poets. The *real* and the *true* are the fundamental values. For Hegel the only knowledge is the Spirit's self-knowledge, and something is knowledge only if it is perceived by the Spirit in the process of coming to know itself. The Spirit is the source of all fundamental values. Finally, it may be said that the advancement of "humanity" is the only fundamental value, and something is knowledge only in so far as it contributes to this value, for example, if it enhances the freedom and autonomy of the people.

According to Lyotard, there are two general ways of legitimating knowledge: the philosophical way, which employs the "speculative apparatus" (such as Plato's Forms, or Hegel's Spirit); and the political way, which employs the "emancipation apparatus" (such as the Enlightenment's freedom and autonomy of the people or the nation). However, both ways lead the process of legitimation into self-destruction. Consider first the "speculative apparatus," according to which "knowledge is only worthy of that name to the extent that it reduplicates itself . . . by citing its own statements in a second-level discourse (autonymy) that functions to legitimate them."[8] This "test" is a crucial premise in Lyotard's argument. Now apply the "test" to the following speculative statement: "A scientific statement is knowledge if and only if it can take its place in a universal process of engendering."[9] This statement defines what it is for a statement to be knowledge. If this very statement "can take its place in a universal process of engendering," then it is knowledge by its own definition. Given the Hegelian narrative of a self-engendering Spirit, this statement can be taken as an expression of that process of engendering, thus fulfilling the requirement it itself makes for it to be knowledge. However, any scientific statement will fail this test because the discourse of science is denotative; that is, it employs declarative sentences referring to some object, a referent, for example, "This piece of copper conducts electricity." When we refer to such a denotative sentence in an attempt to legitimate it, we are no longer within the scientific discourse. A scientific, denotative sentence cannot "reduplicate" itself in another discourse and remain scientific. We can paraphrase Lyotard by saying that scientific discourse is not *self-referential*. Any talk about science is itself not science. By contrast, any speculative, or philosophical, talk about philosophy is itself philosophy. This is why the attempt to legitimate science by the speculative apparatus ends up showing that "denotative discourse bearing on a certain referent (a living organism, a chemical property, a physical phenomenon, etc.) does not really know what it thinks it knows. Positive science is not a form of knowledge."[10] This process of legitimating science achieves the exact opposite, namely, delegitimating science.

The political process of legitimation employing the emancipation apparatus fares no better. The emancipation of the people through science has the consequence of rendering the people autonomous from science, which in turn renders their political, social, and ethical discourses also autonomous from science. Thus, instead of grounding science, the emancipation apparatus succeeds in making science just another discourse, another language game, "on par with the others."[11] Once again, the attempt to legitimate science achieves the opposite effect, namely, "to attack the legitimacy of the discourse of science . . . indirectly, by revealing that it is a language game with its own rules . . . and that it has no special calling to supervise the game of praxis."[12]

The self-destructive nature of the process of legitimation calls for a postmodernist response, namely, the abandonment of grand narratives and with it the delegitimation of knowledge. There is no longer any point in talking about God, Spirit, Form, humanity, *ego cogito* . . . , other than in an attempt to achieve some *local* effects, with values confined to a *localized* context (such as God in the context of worship or Spirit in the context of dialectics). Instead of a grand narrative that can legitimate other discourses, we are faced with a series of *petits récits*, of local "perspectives," of diverse language games, each with its own set of rules. Such is the postmodern condition as far as Lyotard is concerned.

Returning to science, it is clear that it has to legitimate itself by its own rules. But even here we cannot expect to have a set of rules that can legitimate all scientific statements. Not only that there is no grand narrative for all human intellectual activities, scientific as well as nonscientific—the breakdown of the grand narrative goes much deeper—there is no grand narrative governing scientific activities. Lyotard's argument for this phase of the breakdown of the grand narrative is as follows. A scientific statement has to be validated in a second-level discourse, an axiomatic metalanguage with logical rules linking the axioms to other statements. But there cannot be a universal axiomatic metalanguage capable of validating all branches of science due to the inevitable incompleteness of any such metalanguage (a theorem established by Kurt Gödel). As a result, there is a plurality of languages defining and legitimating a plurality of sciences. A scientist can progress by making a new move within the established rules or by inventing new rules that define a new game, a new science (a process described by Thomas Kuhn as a paradigm shift).

It is inevitable, then, that each scientific game, each branch of science, has to legitimate itself by its own rules. Yet despite the plurality of games, the process of legitimation seems to be common to all branches of science, providing a *proof* for a scientific claim. This observation allows Lyotard to conclude that the postmodern criterion of legitimation in science is *performativity*. His argument is as follows. The construction of a proof requires the description, or observation, of certain phenomena, which requires in turn the use of sophisticated instruments. A good instrument is one that performs this function well. Now the more access one has to "good" technology, the more information one can gather, which in turn enables one to prove more, hence better to legitimate one's activity. One's legitimated scientific activity in turn justifies greater expenditure on the technology that helped with the legitimation in the first place. Thus, technology in the scientific context is all about performance. This is how legitimation is reduced to performativity. Since the amount of information is the key (in the sense that more information means more can be proved, hence a greater degree of legitimation), the computerization of the society goes hand in hand with the process of legitimation in so far as the computer is the most efficient instrument for information processing.

Now that delegitimation and the performativity criterion have been explicated, we must consider how, for Lyotard, they contribute to the death of the Professor. Lyotard writes: "In the context of delegitimation, universities and the institutions of higher learning are called upon to create skills, and no longer ideals. . . . The transmission of knowledge is no longer designed to train an elite capable of guiding the nation towards its emancipation."[13] Nor, one might add, in case the speculative apparatus is considered in the process of legitimation, toward some metaphysical *terminus ad quem* (such as the Hegelian Absolute). I take it that Lyotard's argument is that among the functions of the Professor is to provide a theoretical (political or speculative) narrative capable of serving the legitimating function. In other words, Lyotard's assumption is that it takes a Professor to come up with a political, or speculative, theory and to transmit his or her theoretical views to the students who need them to see why something is, or is not, science, or knowledge. However, if there is no longer any need for any such narrative (as the argument for delegitimation above has shown), this function of the Professor disappears. Graduates trained in theoretical narratives will quickly find themselves unemployed. Here, the performativity criterion comes into effect: Either students will no longer be attracted to the prospect of being unemployable or funds will not be allocated to institutions that produce unemployable graduates. Thus, the training of graduates in theoretical matters, no matter how "desirable" such matters are on their own, will no longer take place, and no professors will be required to perform this function. Indeed, the university need not be the only place where knowledge, in the sense of skills, is transmitted. For "It does not seem necessary that the medium [of teaching] be a lecture delivered in person by a teacher in front of silent students."[14] The computer with its data banks can now perform this function. All that students need to be taught is "how to use terminals . . . , where should the question be addressed, in other words, what is the relevant memory bank for what needs to be known? How should the question be formulated to avoid misunderstanding?"[15]

In summary, Lyotard's argument is this: Any attempt to legitimate science, or knowledge, by grounding it in a grand narrative will achieve the exact opposite effect, namely, delegitimation. What we have is a plurality of branches of science, or fields of knowledge, functioning like language games, each with its own set of rules, and a statement has to be legitimated in the same way as a move is in a game, by the rules internal to the game. In science what matters is how much can be *proved*, which is the function of the speed and the amount of information processed. The Professor is no longer required to spin narratives to legitimate knowledge claims. Those narratives have zero performativity when it comes to proving knowledge claims. All the knowledge there is is contained in data banks, and education amounts to teaching students how to retrieve it. If Lyotard is right, the implications for education are immense. However, there are reasons to believe that Lyotard's pedagogy does not follow from his epistemology.

II

Lyotard's claims are so startling that one's initial reaction is to want to challenge them, and yet one feels powerless to challenge his description of the postmodern condition that gives him the initial set of premises, a description that has an undeniable initial plausibility. For instance, the claim that not only *truth* but *justice* as well is a function of information processing sounds so counterintuitive until one realizes that a greater access to legal precedents will lead to a greater success in proving a legal point, hence in winning a legal argument. Lyotard's claims present us with a mixture of plausibility and incredulity. However, once the effects of the initial plausibility have been absorbed, one feels inclined to ask a large number of questions. For instance: What about the old distinction between *techne* and *episteme*? What about fields of knowledge (such as abstract algebra) where "proof" is a theoretical process rather than an empirical one involving observations? What notion of truth does Lyotard have in mind when he separates the question, "Is it true?" from questions such as "What use is it?" "Is it saleable?" and "Is it efficient?" However, I want to set these issues aside to concentrate on the pedagogical implication of Lyotard's epistemology. The following points can be made.

The Demand for Narratives

Suppose we accept the following premises: (i) The role of the Professor is to educate students in the understanding of narratives. (ii) Narratives have zero performativity in proving scientific claims. How do they result in the death of the Professor? Lyotard seems to think that (i) and (ii) are sufficient for the elimination of demand for the Professor's services, and the Professor will go out of business as a result. However, there is no evidence for this. Narratives have a fascination of their own that continues to excite the curiosity of a large number of people. Rightly or wrongly, many people believe that one is not "educated" until one has an understanding of and appreciation for narratives. Many people just want to know what "great thinkers" through the ages—Plato, Aristotle through to Hegel, and indeed Lyotard—have had to say. It could well be true that those trained in theoretical matters will be unemployable, but they are unemployable only *as* persons trained in theoretical matters (ignoring the very small market for academics). The point is that the demand for understanding in narratives is not a market-related demand; hence it is unlikely to be affected by the performativity criterion. It is also true that there was a relative decline in enrollments in humanities in the 1970s and the 1980s. However, such a decline is hardly evidence for the claim that the Professor's death knell is sounding. Indeed, enrollments in the humanities have steadied, and in some institutions they have shown a significant increase. Given the fascination for narratives, one can predict that as working hours are reduced, or leisure time increased, and as Lyotard's performativity criterion bears fruit in increased prosperity, the demand for the teaching of narratives will increase, ensuring a bright future for the Professor.

The Logical Necessity for at Least One Narrative

Suppose that we accept all of Lyotard's epistemological premises as well as his accounts of delegitimation and performativity, that still leaves one question: Who is to spread the message about delegitimation itself? Who is to present the argument for the collapse of grand narratives? Not any technocrat or computer programmer: It will have to be a professor, someone like Lyotard himself. Since the collapse of grand narratives is itself a grand narrative, there is a logical necessity for at least one grand narrative. It follows that there is a necessity (though not a logical one) for at least one kind of professor, namely, the Lyotard kind. Lyotard has said that we should "wage a war on totality," in other words, a war on grand narratives.[16] Even if this is a war to end all wars, it still has to be fought, and by Lyotard's own account it cannot be fought with computers but, rather, with the resources possessed by the Professor. Unlike a conventional war, this intellectual war will be a never-ending one; and so if the Professor is dying, he or she had better be resuscitated to fight Lyotard's war. In other words, if Lyotard is right, we still need the Professor to teach students the reason why performativity is now the criterion rather than human emancipation or some other ideal, to reassure students that all they need to know is how to use computer terminals. If Lyotard is right, grand narratives are like stories about ghosts. There are no ghosts, but children still have to be reassured that it is so, and to be taught not to be afraid. The postmodernist framework has to be maintained because it does not maintain itself. This is the job for the Professor.

Who Is Dead?

The point above can be put in another way. If the Professor is dead, then Lyotard cannot be speaking as a professor, and if so then what is he speaking as? The logic of the question is as follows. Either Lyotard's account is a narrative about narratives or it is not. If it is not, then Lyotard must be speaking in another forum and in another idiom, in which what appears to be a narrative is in fact not so. But what forum and what idiom? While it is difficult to guess what the answer could be, we are not obliged to find out. For whatever it is, Lyotard's account is not supposed to tell anything we should *know* about narratives. That leaves the other alternative, namely, that his account is a narrative about narratives, in which case we are supposed to be *instructed* by it about narratives, about their roles and function. But if we are instructed by Lyotard's narrative, then he is by definition a professor. So either he is inconsistent in declaring the death of the Professor or his victim is not the real Professor, who is not dead after all, but someone else whose identity is confused by Lyotard's ruse. Given the more charitable interpretation, which saves Lyotard from inconsistency, the question that has to be asked is, "Who is dead?" "Who is Lyotard's victim?" It is plausible to suggest that Lyotard's victim is really the Hegelian Professor, the guardian of Truth, the one who knows about the Absolute and who can *profess* about the system that leads to it, that is, one who can tell us with absolute authority that such-and-such is legitimate knowledge and so-and-so is not.

If I am right in interpreting Lyotard charitably, and right about the real identity of his victim, then there is no mystery about the nature of Lyotard's narrative and no puzzle about his own role. But if I am wrong, not only will we have to live with the mystery and the puzzle, we also will have no way of knowing what to make of the faculty currently working in colleges and universities, how to treat *their* narratives (such as publications) or how to decide on hiring new ones and promoting existing ones. This point is meant to be a *reductio ad absurdum* of Lyotard's position, should my charitable interpretation be rejected. On balance, it seems preferable to be charitable, in which case there must be professors whose tasks include the championing of the canon by constructing narratives (*petits récits*) that are instructive about the canon. Lyotard himself is one such professor, there to champion the postmodernist narrative.

A Grand Narrative Could Cause the Death of the Professor

We can now turn Lyotard's argument on its head. In so far as the chief role of a grand narrative is legitimation, we can claim that it is precisely the predominance of grand narratives that corresponds to the diminution in the role of the Professor and that is is precisely the coming into dominance of one single grand narrative that sounds the knell of the Professor. Conversely, we can claim that the collapse of grand narratives, or the postmodern condition, means that the Professor's role is more crucial than ever. The first claim can be argued for from Lyotard's own premise that grand narratives tend to be terroristic and totalitarian. A grand narrative is meant to provide the grounding for, and thereby legitimate, other discourses. It does not allow for the questioning of its role and its nature, for to do so is to engage in another narrative. Thus, a grand narrative requires imposition and demands obedience, leaving no room for teaching and learning. To play a game, a player just has to know (in the sense of *absorb*) the rules of the game and play within them. What can be taught and learnt are the skills of the game, not the rules, as there is no room for questioning the rules. Of course, rules can be questioned, but that would be a different game. It follows that when a single grand narrative gained dominance, terrorism becomes extreme, and there will be no room for the Professor to teach and for the students to learn. This is dramatically demonstrated by that period in Chinese history known as the Cultural Revolution. In this period, there was only one grand narrative: the Maoist doctrine. As a result, teachers of all kinds were purged from the classroom and the Red Guards took over. Had the Chinese society been computerized, the "Red Computers" would have taken over. Notice that something like Maoism is not like Lyotard's grand narrative about the collapse of grand narratives. The latter is a negative narrative that is not terroristic; hence it can be taught and learnt as we saw above. Something like Maoism needs only an initial "professor," Mao himself, to propagate, and once propagated, it will be imposed rather than taught because it requires obedience rather than understanding.

Information and Understanding

According to Lyotard, the postmodern condition is characterized by the plurality of *petits récits*. However, in the postmodern age, the problem of legitimation has not been eliminated. Rather, each language game, each *petit récit*, legitimates itself. For this to happen, each language game must have two separate concerns: the playing of the game according to its rules, and the justification of moves made within the game. The question is whether the justificatory concern can be met by the computer and its data banks. Clearly, justification is itself a narrative, albeit a "small narrative" (*petit récit*). If, as Lyotard says, the "replacement of teachers by machines may seem inadequate or even intolerable" in "the context of the grand narratives of legitimation," I do not see why it can be adequate or tolerable in the context of the small narratives of justification.[17] If the Professor is needed in one case, he or she will be needed in the other case. In a game of sport, the coach is concerned with developing playing skills (and here performativity is important and technology crucial), but it is the umpire or the referee who is concerned with the legitimation of any move made. In the context of education, what students need to know is *why* a certain move, a statement, is legitimate within some field of knowledge. This is a problem of *understanding*. To know how to make a move is one thing, to understand why in terms of the governing rules is another. Each move, each statement, has to be placed in a context for it to be understood. It is here that the Professor is required because the computer cannot perform this task. The data banks only make the information available, they do not *make sense* of the information. As Heraclitus once said, "Information about many things does not teach understanding; if it did, it would have taught Hesiod and Pythagoras, and also Xenophanes and Hecataeus."[18] A postmodern Heraclitus would have said, "Information does not teach understanding; if it did, the computer would have replaced the Professor." As it does not, students have to be taught not just how to retrieve information but also what it *means*.

Imagination

Lyotard acknowledges that performativity requires more than just the retrieval of information. It is also a function of how bits of information are put together in a new way to create a new move. When a new move comes up against the rules of the game, what can be done is to create new rules and thereby define a new game. This is the way new sciences develop, the postmodern way of *progress*. The creation of new games and new moves within an existing game requires more than the transmission of information; it requires *imagination*. Strangely, Lyotard does not think that this aspect of his analysis affects his pedagogical model. The need for imagination, for Lyotard, does not justify the existence of a university and its professors: "It matters little whether [the conditions for "the promotion and 'stimulation' of 'imaginative' minds"] are officially a part of the university."[19] Lyotard offers no argument for this conclusion. I fail to see how it can be argued that machines are adequate to the task of promoting and stimulating imaginative minds. On the contrary, it seems clear that this is the Professor's job. To be sure, imagination cannot be taught. The role of the Professor is not so much to teach creative skills as to *set examples*, to inspire. Imagination needs inspiration, and the computer does not inspire.

Understanding, Imagination, and Teaching Machines

These points are not entirely new. Indeed, Lyotard's reference to the "replacement of teachers by machines" rekindles the 1960s debate about teaching machines.[20] There was then talk of the death of the teacher too. However, it is important to notice that in the earlier debate, teaching machines were thought by some to be the *cause* of the teacher's demise, whereas for Lyotard the Professor dies as a result of his epistemology and the teaching machines only happen to be there, conveniently filling the gap. Despite this difference, the various arguments raised in the earlier debate remain instructive. Many such arguments can be interpreted in such a way as to illustrate the nature and the role of understanding and imagination in pedagogy.

According to H. S. Broudy, the answer to the question, "Can or will the teaching machine displace the live teacher?" has to be yes because the idea of such a machine is to do "what a live teacher might be doing." Broudy adds, "There would be no profit in machines if they did not some how replace human labor."[21] This may sound as though Broudy agrees with the view that the teaching machine will replace the teacher. However, this is not his view. To begin with, notice that he says that the machine is expected to replace human *labor*, not human *intellect*. He then goes on to state:

In attitude formation human models and the value climate of the school as a whole are important, perhaps crucially so. Clearly the machine cannot serve as such a model, and if it displaces teachers who could serve as models, a serious gap in the educative experience of the learner could ensue. Or if the time for model and pupil to spend together is drastically reduced the effect would also be deplorable.[22]

The argument here is that we need the teacher as a "human model" for "attitude formation," which is an indispensable element in the "educative experience" of the learner. (Presumably the teacher, or the Professor, will benefit from the process too.) In a book written jointly with John R. Palmer, Broudy distinguishes four kinds of learning: (1) "learning how to do this or that (skill)," (2) "learning that this or that is the case (information)," (3) "learning why such and such is the case (explanation)," and (4) "learning to be a certain kind of person."[23] Teaching machines are eminently suited to (1) and (2), less suited to (3), and totally unsuitable as far as (4) is concerned.

It is interesting to note that in the debate in the 1960s, those most enthusiastic about teaching machines never argued for doing away with the teacher. Indeed, the strongest argument for machines is that they free the teacher from repetitive tasks, enabling him or her to do what he or she does best, namely, to assist in the learning of (3) and (4) in terms of the Broudy-Palmer account. Thus, Lee Sechrest and R. Wray Strowig argue that teaching machines allow the teacher to "become a valuable partner in the learning process."[24] They identify one factor in the learning process that machines cannot take into account: "concern for the identity and integrity of the individual."[25] This is similar to the fourth kind of learning identified by Broudy and Palmer, for which the teacher is indispensable as a "human model." It also illustrates the sense of my claim earlier that imagination needs inspiration, and the computer does not inspire.

III

Far from "sounding the knell of the age of the Professor," the post-modern condition as described by Lyotard defines a new and much more vigorous role for the Professor. Certainly there is a case for removing many functions presently performed by universities, particularly those associated with training in routine skills. This change would return the university to the model of the Academy in ancient Greece, where the Professor, from his (invariable "his" then) *chair*, inspired receptive minds to rise to ever-higher levels of creativity and imagination. In drawing these pedagogical implications, *contra* Lyotard, have I mis-interpreted the postmodern condition? Isn't the Professor sitting aloft in his chair the ultimate caricature of the Hegelian Professor whose role has been decisively deconstructed by Lyotard's postmodernism? This objection can be avoided if we carry the postmodern account beyond epistemology and into pedagogy itself. I want to argue in this section that this is what Richard Rorty has done, and in so doing he has drawn conclusions similar to those in Section II.

Rorty is a postmodernist by his own admission. His view on knowledge and truth is clearly expressed in his *Philosophy and the Mirror of Nature*.[26] Briefly, he rejects not only the notion of absolute truth but also truth as correspondence with the objective, real, world. Consequently, he rejects the view that education amounts to polishing the mind so that it reflects that world better. Indeed, Rorty urges philosophers to abandon the project of epistemology altogether and engage instead in a kind of hermeneutic conversation aimed at reaching agreements on matters of human progress and advancement (and what such matters are is also an agreement). Agreements are "what we get when we are no longer epistemological."[27] To those critics who claim that agreements yielded by hermeneutic con-versations do not amount to knowledge, Rorty replies that "the word *knowledge* would not seem worth fighting over."[28] To those who criticize him for having forsaken truth, he replies that compared to the pragmatic advantages of agreements, "the acquisition of truth dwindles in impor-tance."[29]

Rorty's view of epistemology is truly radical. Indeed, he speaks of the "demise of epistemology."[30] Now, if the Professor is the guardian of truth, charged with the responsibility of passing it on to the learner, then the "demise of epistemology," the "dwindling importance" of truth, necessarily leads to the demise of the Professor. On the surface, then, it would appear that Rorty's account of postmodern epistemology leads to the same conclusion as Lyotard's on the role of the Professor. In fact, there are reasons to believe that far from splitting the difference between Lyotard and Habermas, Rorty's epistemology is even more radical than that of the poststructuralists generally.[31] Thus there are reasons to expect Rorty to advocate a pedagogy more radical even than Lyotard's, one of anything goes. Yet this is far from the truth. On the role of the Professor, Rorty does in fact split the difference between Lyotard and Habermas, not advocating the death of the Professor, but at the same time taking away the Professor's traditional, or modernist, role. How is this possible?

One way of making Rorty's position possible is to break the link between epistemology and pedagogy, taking it to be an epistemological fallacy. However, there is another way: constructing a pedagogical model to fit. In more recent works, Rorty has undertaken the latter task. Given the traditional role of education as passing on the truth, or transferring knowledge, we are entitled to expect from Rorty a conclusion on the role of the Professor at least as radical as Lyotard's. However, Rorty rejects the traditional notion of education, claiming that "neither lower (primary and secondary) education nor higher education is primarily concerned with purveying truth."[32] What Rorty has in mind is a new pedagogical model—one that might be called postmodern pedagogy—in which there is a role for the Professor after all; indeed, an important role. At the lower level, what Rorty has in mind is a pedagogy that "should aim primarily at communicating enough of what is *held* to be true by the society to which the children belong so that they can function as citizens of that society."[33] At the higher level, and setting aside vocational training, the role of education is not to pass on the truth but *to edify*; it is not to give instructions but to build edification. This new model of pedagogy fits Rorty's idea of postmodern philosophy as "edifying philosophy" in contrast to the traditional view of it as "systematic philosophy." Let us remind ourselves of what Rorty has to say about edifying philosophy:

Great systematic philosophers are constructive and offer arguments. Great edifying philosophers are reactive and offer satires, parodies, aphorisms. . . . Great systematic philosophers, like great scientists, build for eternity. Great edifying philosophers destroy for the sake of their own generation. Systematic philosophers want to put their subject on the secure path of science. Edifying philosophers want to keep space open for the sense of wonder which poets can sometimes cause.[34]

In Rorty's model of pedagogy for higher education, we need a teacher who is able "to make students thrill to the same things they themselves thrill."[35] This matches Rorty's view of an edifying philosopher, in the quotation above, who wants "to keep space open for the sense of wonder." In an earlier paper Rorty argues that what is needed in education is someone who gives students opportunities to hero worship great thinkers, someone who "seduces" students into, rather than instructing them on, their own intellectual tradition.[36] What the new pedagogy requires is a teacher who can engage students in conversations not just with each other but with heroes of the tradition by emulating the latter's intellectual feats. This matches Rorty's advocacy of hermeneutic conversation as an alternative to traditional epistemology. In Rorty's postmodern pedagogy, what we need, clearly, is not a battery of computer terminals—their role is not denied in vocational training—but a whole range of Professors with different ideas, Professors who do not purvey truth, but who excite students' imagination.

According to Rorty's critics, his talk about seducing students into their own intellectal tradition seems narrow-minded. Indeed, J. M. Fritzman argues that Rorty's agreements can be "terroristic" in the sense that views not part of the tradition will be excluded.[37] On the other hand, Carol Nicholson argues that Rorty's pedagogy has to be supplemented with critical studies of society that examine its political, economic, racial, and sexual presuppositions and thus expose students to alternatives.[38] For Fritzman, Rorty is a little too conservative; for Nicholson, he is a little too radical. Such criticisms are a little unfair. *Pace* Nicholson, Rorty's educational program has many quite traditional elements, including the need to inculcate a critical attitude. As Rorty puts it in a reply to one critic, there is a need to "sort out the nut cases from the people to whom it pays to listen," as well as the need to open up to criticism from other points of view by appreciating the "attractiveness of those other points of view."[39] The latter point serves as a reply to Fritzman as well. Thus, far from being terroristic in excluding nontraditional views, Rorty's pedagogy calls for sensitizing students to various alternatives. Indeed, Rorty constantly speaks of "new alternatives," of "displacing" an intellectual world by considering a new one.[40] All this calls all the more loudly for a Professor who can think up new viewpoints, who can construct alternative intellectual worlds, who can transfigure tradition with "original and utopian" fantasies, like those of "Plato's and St. Paul's,"[41] who are "world-disclosing" thinkers rather than "problem-solving" thinkers.[42]

My arguments in Section II against Lyotard constitute an endorsement of Rorty's position as outlined in this section. It seems to me that one needs to carry the postmodern critique of epistemology into pedagogy as well. Lyotard's conclusion that the postmodern condition sounds the knell of the Professor follows only if we retain the traditional view of the Professor and the traditional view of his or her role. However, if we rethink pedagogy in the same way as we rethink epistemology, it will be clear that there is a new role for a new kind of Professor. The Professor is dead. Long live the Professor.

NOTES

The material in Sections I and II of this chapter have been previously published in A. T. Nuyen, "Lyotard on the Death of the Professor," *Educational Theory* 39 (1992). I wish to thank the editor of *Educational Theory* and the board of trustees of the University of Illinois for their kind permission to reproduce it here.

1. Jean-François Lyotard, *The Postmodern Condition: A Report on Knowledge*, trans. Geoff Bennington and Brian Massumi, Foreword by Fredric Jameson (Minneapolis: University of Minnesota Press, 1984). (Henceforth referred to as *PMC*.)

2. Hannah Arendt, "The Crisis in Education," in *Between Past and Future* (New York: Viking Press, 1961), p. 195.

3. Mustafa U. Kiziltan, William J. Bain, and Anita Canizares M., "Postmodern Condition: Rethinking Public Education," *Educational Theory* 40 (1990): 355.

4. Richard Rorty, "Habermas and Lyotard on Postmodernity," *Praxis International* 4 (1984): 42.

5. This term was coined by Jane Roland Martin, "Needed: A Paradigm for Liberal Education," in *Philosophy and Education*, Eightieth Yearbook of the National Society for Study of Education, Part 1 (Chicago: University of Chicago Press, 1981).

6. *PMC*, p. xxii and p. xxiv.

7. Ibid., p. 35.

8. Ibid., p. 38.

9. Ibid.

10. Ibid.

11. Ibid., p. 40.

12. Ibid.

13. Ibid., p. 48.

14. Ibid., p. 50.

15. Ibid., pp. 50–51.

16. Ibid., p. 82.

17. Ibid., p. 51.

18. The first sentence of this fragment is often translated as "much learning does not teach understanding." The key word is *polymathie*, which can be rendered as the learning of, or the gathering of information about, many things. The translation used here is Martha Nussbaum's, *The Fragility of Goodness* (Cambridge: Cambridge University Press, 1986).

19. *PMC*, p. 53.

20. See, for instance, E. Galanter, *Automatic Teaching: The State of the Art* (New York: John Wiley and Sons, 1959); and A. A. Lumsdaine and R. Glaser, *Teaching*

Machines and Programmed Learning (Washington, D.C.: National Education Association, 1960).

21. H. S. Broudy, "Teaching Machines: Threats and Promises," *Educational Theory* 12, 2 (1962): 152.

22. Ibid., p. 153.

23. H. S. Broudy and John R. Palmer, *Examples of Teaching Methods* (Chicago: Rand McNally, 1965), p. 5.

24. Lee Sechrest and R. Wray Strowig, "Teaching Machines and the Individual Learner," *Educational Theory* 12 (1962): 164.

25. Ibid., p. 167.

26. Richard Rorty, *Philosophy and the Mirror of Nature* (Princeton, N.J.: Princeton University Press, 1979).

27. Ibid., p. 325.

28. Ibid., p. 356.

29. Ibid., p. 365.

30. Ibid., p. 315.

31. A. T. Nuyen, "Rorty's Hermeneutics and the Problem of Relativism," *Man and World* 25 (1992).

32. Richard Rorty, "The Dangers of Over-Philosophication: Reply to Arcilla and Nicholson," *Educational Theory* 40 (1990): 42.

33. Ibid., p. 42.

34. Rorty, *Philosophy and the Mirror of Nature*, pp. 369–70.

35. Rorty, "The Dangers of Over-Philosophication," p. 42.

36. Richard Rorty, "Hermeneutics, General Studies and Teaching," *Selected Papers from the Synergos Seminar* 2 (1982).

37. J. M. Fritzman, "Lyotard's Paralogy and Rorty's Pluralism: Their Differences and Pedagogical Implications," *Educational Theory* 40 (1990).

38. Carol Nicholson, "Postmodernism, Feminism, and Education: The Need for Solidarity," *Educational Theory* 39 (1989).

39. Richard Rorty, "Truth and Freedom: A Reply to Thomas McCarthy," *Critical Inquiry* 16, 1990, p. 635.

40. Richard Rorty, "Is Derrida a Transcendental Philosopher?" in *Essays on Heidegger and Others* (Cambridge: Cambridge University Press, 1991), p. 121.

41. Ibid.

42. Ibid., p. 126.

4 From Pragmatism to the Differend

J. M. Fritzman

The pedagogical implications of Jean-François Lyotard's notion of the differend and Richard Rorty's pragmatism are distinct. Although there is no criterion that could decide between them, the differend overcomes the deficiencies of pragmatism. Moreover, Rorty now recognizes the possibility that some disputes cannot be resolved by criteria that are shared by the disputants, and so he implicitly recognizes the ineliminatable presence of differends. This chapter charts the places where the postmodern philosophies of Lyotard and Rorty approach each other and where they diverge.

I

I do not intend to stir up hatred, but to respect and make understood the differend.[1]

Lyotard opposes the legitimating of education through performativity, and on *this* point he agrees with the critical theorist Jürgen Habermas and disagrees with the systems theorist Niklas Luhmann. Lyotard writes:

The stronger the "move," the more likely it is to be denied the minimum consensus, precisely because it changes the rules of the game upon which consensus had been based. But when the institution of knowledge functions in this manner, it is acting like an ordinary power center whose behavior is governed by a principle of homeostasis. Such behavior is terrorist, as is the behavior of the system described by Luhmann. By terror I mean the efficiency gained by eliminating, or threatening to eliminate, a player from the language game one shares with him. He is silenced or consents, not because he has been refuted, but because his ability to participate has been threatened (there are many ways to prevent someone from playing). The decision makers' arrogance, which in principle has no equivalent in the sciences, consists in the exercise of terror. It says: "Adapt your aspirations to our ends—or else."[2]

According to Lyotard, those who advocate the legitimation of education through performativity call for abandoning the principle "that the acquisition of knowledge is indissociable from the training (*Bildung*) of minds, or even of individuals."[3] Indeed, Lyotard believes that the concept of education as *Bildung* has largely been abandoned. The friends of performativity urge that pedagogy should impart only the knowledge and skills necessary to preserve and enhance the operational efficiency of society. For these persons, operational efficiency is determined by the results of cost-benefit or input-output analyses. Society is conceived as an over-arching, totalizing system that is constituted through the interactions of its subsystems. These subsystems include the economy, the family, politics, and religion. The content of what is taught is determined by the technological requirements of the system, and educators are evaluated by how efficiently this content is conveyed. When education is legitimated through performativity, Lyotard notes, knowledge is not thought to have any intrinsic worth. Instead, knowledge is valued only as a commodity that can be sold; it no longer possesses "use value," but only "exchange value."[4]

Habermas also seeks to resist Luhmannian legitimation through performativity. In order to controvert Luhmann's performativity, Habermas hopes to discover—following certain suggestions made by Charles Sanders Peirce—the means to obtain universal consensus through *Diskurs*. Habermas understands *Diskurs* as a dialogue of argumentation where undistorted communication obtains. Lyotard supports Habermas's goal but not his strategy: "The cause is good, but the argument is not."[5] Although Lyotard recognizes the importance of consensus, he believes that paralogy is the goal of conversation: "As I have shown in the analysis of the pragmatics of science, consensus is only a particular state of discussion, not its end. Its end, on the contrary, is paralogy."[6]

Lyotard's discussions of "Postmodern Science as the Search for Instabilities" and "Legitimation by Paralogy" have as their primary purpose to show that postmodern education and science are legitimated neither by Luhmann's criterion of efficiency of performance nor by Habermas's search for universal consensus through *Diskurs*.[7] Rather, Lyotard believes that postmodern education and science are legitimated by paralogy, by the constant introduction of dissensus into consensus. That is, Lyotard urges that postmodern education and science flourish, instead of stagnating, through the search for new ideas and concepts that disrupt and destabilize previously existing consensuses. The goal of postmodern education and science is the discovery and invention of these new ideas and concepts: "Postmodern knowledge is not simply a tool of the authorities; it refines our sensitivity to differences and reinforces our ability to tolerate the incommensurable. Its principle is not the expert's homology, but the inventor's paralogy."[8]

Like Lyotard, Rorty rejects the notion of philosophy's discovering eternal truths and criteria by which to demarcate the boundaries of the various disciplines. Rather, Rorty believes that criteria exist historically; they emerge as the result of human practices. "There is nothing deep down inside us except what we have put there ourselves, no criterion that we have not created in the course of creating a practice, no standard of rationality that is not an appeal to such a criterion, no rigorous argument that is not obedience to our own conventions."[9] These criteria possess only heuristic usefulness. "On the pragmatist account, a criterion (what follows from the axioms, what the needle points to, what the statute says) is a criterion because some particular social practice needs to block the road of inquiry, halt the regress of interpretations, in order to get something done."[10] In short, Rorty hopes for a post-Philosophical culture.

This would be a culture in which neither the priests nor the physicists nor the poets nor the Party were thought of as more "rational," or more "scientific" or "deeper" than one another. No particular portion of culture would be singled out as exemplifying (or signally failing to exemplify) the condition to which the rest aspired. There would be no sense that, beyond the current intra-disciplinary criteria, which, for example, good priests or good physicists obeyed, there were other, transdisciplinary, transcultural, ahistorical criteria, which they also obeyed.[11]

Rorty recognizes the *logical* contingency of criteria. That is, he perceives that there is no contradiction in thinking that the criteria employed could have been otherwise. Rorty also sees that criteria are inherited as tradition, as the result of historical practices. Hence, he recognizes that had those practices been different, it is probable that the criteria would have been different as well. However, Rorty fails to emphasize that historical practices could have been otherwise, and so he insufficiently recognizes the *existential* contingency of practices and criteria. That is, not only is there no contradiction in thinking that social practices and criteria could have been different, but there also is no contradiction in thinking that the practices and criteria *can* be different and *should* be changed. Because practices and criteria could have been different, they still may be contested, and perhaps altered.

Because Rorty fails to note the existential contingency of practices and criteria, seeing only their logical contingency, he writes as though tradition were monolithic. He does not appreciate sufficiently that traditions often are in contradiction with one another, and also usually are subjected to severe internal tensions. Hence, it is frequently the case that one element of a tradition can be contested by appealing to another element within that tradition, or within another tradition. Further, it is possible to challenge a social practice, even if no tradition currently provides the resources for such contestation, by *imagining* a perspective from which to condemn the practice. Although it may be possible to appeal to tradition in order to justify some established social practice, such an appeal is never sufficient. In principle, practices—and the criteria that emerge as a result of the sedimentation of those practices—can always be called into question. The caveat "in principle" is necessary, since persons who benefit from certain practices frequently attempt to silence those who would contest such practices. No doubt Rorty would agree with Karl Marx when he writes, "Men make their own history, but they do not make it just as they please; they do not make it under circumstances chosen by themselves, but under circumstances directly encountered, given and transmitted from the past."[12] Due to Rorty's optimistic faith in the products of tradition, though, he would part company with Marx when he immediately adds, "The tradition of all the dead generations weighs like a nightmare on the brain of the living."[13]

Although Rorty allows that criteria emerge as the result of the congealment of human practices, he rejects the search for paralogies—new ideas and concepts that upset previously existing solidarities. Instead, he hopes to discover "a way to balance competing claims" in order to regulate conflicts. He thus applauds John Rawls,[14] whose understanding of the method of political theory he sees as "the attempt at reflective equilibrium."[15] Persons can agree, if not on substantive issues, then at least on the rules of procedure—the criteria—that will adjudicate conflicts and regulate differences. For Rorty these procedural rules can be challenged. They can be contested, though, only in accordance with other rules of procedure that are established in advance.

An example may clarify Rorty's understanding of how procedural rules may serve as criteria and in what ways they may be contested. Suppose that two persons disagree on which of them owns an apple tree, and so they take their disagreement to court. Legal rules of procedure will determine which moves are available to these persons in their litigation. In turn, there will be legislative procedural rules that prescribe mechanisms for altering laws. Presumably the court will rule that the apple tree belongs to the person who owns the property on which the tree grows. Who owns that property will be determined by deeds, and the boundaries of the property will be determined by surveying. These procedural rules can be changed. It may be that the individual who loses the litigation has picked apples from the tree for years. Perhaps this individual also has cared for the tree by watering it and spraying it to protect against disease and insects. The person whom the court declared the owner of the tree, though, has neither tended the tree nor gathered the apples. The individual who has lost the litigation may petition members of the legislature, urging that the existing law is unfair, and so persuade them to repeal the old law and to pass a new law. This new law might state that in cases where individuals consistently have used fruit trees and the property owners have not protested, the owners of the trees are those who have used them, regardless of who owns the property on which the trees grow. The members of the legislature will perform these actions according to established procedural rules for repealing and enacting laws.

Rorty believes that persons can obtain consensus on rules of procedure. In turn, these procedural rules will determine the "moves" that are permissible within a given "game." The procedural rules may be changed, thereby permitting different moves. However, different moves may be made only after the rules have been changed. Although Rorty does not support a *homeostatic* status quo, he does defend a *dynamic* status quo.

Lyotard differs from Rorty in seeing that rules of procedure can be called into question directly, without appealing to other procedural rules that have been established in advance. Rules, for Lyotard, "do not carry within themselves their own legitimation, but are the object of a contract, explicit or not, between players (which is not to say that players invent the rules)."[16] According to Lyotard, the criteria that Rorty would have regulate disputes can be contested directly and so themselves become embroiled in the dispute. Rules of procedure may become stakes in the game.

We know today that the limits the institution imposes on potential language "moves" are never established once and for all (even if they have been formally defined). Rather, the limits are themselves the stakes and provisional results of language strategies, within the institution and without. . . . Reciprocally, it can be said that the boundaries only stabilize when they cease to be stakes in the game. This, I think, is the appropriate approach to contemporary institutions of knowledge.[17]

Besides claiming that procedural rules can become stakes in the game, Lyotard also believes that the rules of a game collectively constitute that game, that the rules determine which moves are permitted, and that changing the rules changes the nature of the game. Lyotard would allow that persons may obtain consensus on rules of procedure, but he would add that it also is possible that they may not. He would agree with Rorty that procedural rules determine the moves that are permissible within a game, and that these rules may be changed, thereby constituting a different game that permits different moves. However, Lyotard would disagree with the claim that different moves can be made only once the established rules have been changed and new rules adopted. Rather, he would urge that an imaginative individual is one who discerns in a situation the possibility of a winning move that violates the existing rules of the game. Lyotard also would agree with Rorty in thinking that the contesting of rules follows rules. For Lyotard, however, the rules that are followed need not be established in advance. Rather, the rules themselves may emerge in the making of the move; they may be constituted in the moment of action. In this case, persons' actions might be *described* by appealing to rules, but it would be misleading to say that their actions are *governed* by rules.

The contrast between Lyotard and Rorty may be put in terms of Thomas Kuhn's distinction between normal and revolutionary science.[18] Lyotard believes that "consensus is only a particular state of discussion, not its end" and that the goal of science is the search for paralogies.[19] Hence, he would urge that science should seek to engender revolutions and that normal science is only a particular state of the discipline: "Consensus is a horizon that is never reached. Research that takes place under the aegis of a paradigm tends to stabilize; it is like the exploitation of a technological, economic, or artistic 'idea.' It cannot be discounted. But what is striking is that someone always comes along to disturb the order of 'reason.' "[20] Rorty would favor the conditions of normal science and would view revolutions as regrettable, although inevitable.

The example of a litigation to determine the ownership of an apple tree was employed above to clarify Rorty's view of the manner in which procedural rules serve as criteria and how these rules may be contested. This example can be modified so that it now illustrates Lyotard's belief that procedural rules can be called into question directly. Once again, suppose that two persons disagree on the ownership of an apple tree. The individual who has cared for the tree and gathered the apples recognizes that the existing laws grant ownership of the tree to the person who owns the property on which it grows. However, this individual may argue that these laws unfairly favor the rich and demand that the court nullify the laws by ruling in favor of those who actually tend and use fruit trees. Again, this individual may argue that this particular case is beyond the court's competence and so urge the court not to make any determination concerning the ownership of the tree. Or again, this individual may refuse to recognize the court's right to rule on the ownership of the apple tree and attempt to convince the neighbors to engage in nonviolent resistance so that agents of the state cannot bar access to the tree. In each case, the individual who has tended and used the apple tree makes moves that the existing rules disallow, and it is possible that these moves may be accepted; these arguments may persuade. Regardless of whether these moves are accepted, the individual will have contested the nature of the game by making the rules stakes in the game.

It might be useful to compare Rortyan players with Lyotardian players. Whereas Rortyans will follow rules and obey norms, Lyotardians will choose strategies.[21] Rortyans, recognizing only the logical contingency of the game and the rules that constitute that game, will play by the established rules of the game, will expect others also to observe these rules, and will cry foul when they are violated. Lyotardians, regarding the game and its rules as both logically and existentially contingent, will be prepared to violate the rules of the game, thereby constituting and beginning a new game. As Lyotard explains to Jean-Loup Thébaud in *Just Gaming*:

The point is not that one keeps the games, but that, in each of the existing games, one effects new moves, one opens up the possibility of new efficacies in the games with their present rules. And, in addition, one changes the rules: one can play a given game with other rules, and when one changes the rules, one has changed the game, because a game is primarily defined by its rules.[22]

From the perspective of the Rortyan players, Lyotardians are potentially—and often actually—cheaters. From the point of view of the Lyotardian players, Rortyans are unimaginative. The Lyotardian and Rortyan players cannot agree on what counts as properly playing a game, or even what counts as winning and losing. There is no criterion or procedural rule that would decide between the two types of players without constituting a wrong done to at least one of them. There is, then, a *differend* between the Lyotardian players and the Rortyan players.

As Lyotard uses these terms, litigations and damages are different from differends and wrongs. Litigations are disputes where all of the conflicting parties recognize that certain criteria obtain that allow for the adjudication of their disputes. Differends are disputes where such criteria do not exist. Litigations result from damages, whereas differends result from wrongs.

As distinguished from a litigation, a differend [*différend*] would be a case of conflict, between (at least) two parties, that cannot be equitably resolved for lack of a rule of judgment applicable to both arguments. One side's legitimacy does not imply the other's lack of legitimacy. However, applying a single rule of judgment to both in order to settle their differend as though it were merely a litigation would wrong (at least) one of them (and both of them if neither side admits this rule). Damages result from an injury which is inflicted upon the rules of a genre of discourse but which is reparable according to those rules. A wrong results from the fact that the rules of the genre of discourse by which one judges are not those of the judged genre or genres of discourse.[23]

A litigation would occur where two persons disagree on which of them owns an apple tree. A differend would occur where one person claims ownership of an apple tree, whereas the other individual does not admit that an apple tree can be owned—perhaps because this second individual is a member of a society that recognizes only usufructuary rights, but not rights to private property. In the case of a litigation, procedural rules will exist to determine ownership of the apple tree. In the case of a differend, no such procedural rules can obtain. Any such rule would have to presuppose that apple trees either are or are not things that can be owned. Judging in accordance with such a rule would constitute a wrong to one of the persons.

The difference between Lyotard and Rorty can be phrased within the language of *The Differend*. Rorty believes that all disputes either are litigations or can be transformed into such. In contrast to Rorty, Lyotard argues that there are disputes that cannot be regulated. Such disputes are differends rather than litigations. Further, not all differends can be transformed into litigations. To attempt to adjudicate a differend as though it were a litigation necessarily wrongs at least one of the parties.

Lyotard believes that differends are inevitable. To understand why he sees differends as arising inevitably, it is necessary to describe briefly

Lyotard's notions of phrases, phrase regimens, and genres of discourse developed in *The Differend*. Simplifying to the extreme, a phrase is the ultimate unit of analysis. Phrases are indubitable and immediately presupposed: "To doubt that one phrases is still to phrase, one's silence makes a phrase."[24] Neither was there a first phrase nor will there be a last phrase.[25] Each phrase must necessarily link onto a previous phrase and then be linked onto by the next succeeding phrase. The linkages that occur are not necessary; which phrases are actually linked together is a contingent matter. It is necessary that phrases link, but how they link is contingent.[26] Phrases linked together constitute phrase regimens, and each phrase belongs to some regimen, such as defining, describing, knowing, ordering, questioning, reasoning, recounting, and showing.[27] It is not always possible to determine the regimen to which a phrase belongs: "A linkage may reveal an equivocalness in the previous phrase."[28] Phrase regimens are heterogeneous; phrases belonging to one phrase regimen cannot be translated into another regimen. There is no metaregimen that would make commensurate phrase regimens. Further, since definition is itself a phrase regimen, it is impossible to define *phrase*.[29] Although phrases belonging to one phrase regimen cannot be translated into any other, phrases belonging to heterogeneous regimens can link together to constitute a given genre of discourse: "Genres of discourse supply rules for linking together heterogeneous phrases, rules that are proper for attaining certain goals: to know, to teach, to be just, to seduce, to justify, to evaluate, to rouse emotion, to oversee."[30] However, the rules for many genres—for example, philosophy—have not been determined: "There are many genres of discourse whose rules for linking are not stated."[31]

Somewhat misleadingly, it may be said that differends inevitably arise due to the "nature" of language. As has been seen, it is necessary that phrases link, but how they do so is contingent. Given an "actualized" phrase—for example, "What is the point of this?"—there are countless possible phrases that could link onto it. Yet only one of the possible phrases will actually be phrased next, and there are no criteria external to those of phrase regimens and genres of discourse to decide which of the possible phrases will actually be phrased. There is, then, a differend between the phrases that "wait" to be phrased.[32]

Because Lyotard believes that differends are inevitable, he understands politics as the pursuit, not of the good, but of the lesser evil.[33] *Pace* Rawls and Rorty, politics should not search for a reflective equilibrium that would regulate conflicts, thereby treating differends as litigations. Rather than pretending that differends can always be transformed into litigations, acting as though wrongs can be treated as damages without wronging one of the parties, politics should seek to preserve and bear witness to differends. A politics of the lesser evil would attempt to phrase wrongs so that they may be recognized as such, instead of being construed as damages. Of course, political decisions must be made, since not to decide is itself a decision that favors one set of options over others. Where there exists a differend between disputing parties, any decision will constitute a wrong done to at least one group. In light of this, what is to be done? A politics of the good would privilege a certain set of criteria and so would wrong at least one party. Instead of a politics of the good, Lyotard believes, a politics of the lesser evil must be developed. A politics of the lesser evil will not forget that there are differends that cannot be transformed into litigations and so will seek to make decisions that minimize the wrongs that necessarily occur. A politics of the lesser evil will attempt to leave open as wide a set of political options as possible.

II

I will have taught you only one thing, that there is no method in the first place. You are kindly told: that is called thinking.[34]

As was seen in Section I, Rorty believes that conflicts can be regulated, or balanced, in such a way that a reflective equilibrium is achieved; politics ought to seek for such an equilibrium. Complementary with his understanding of politics as the quest for reflective equilibrium, Rorty urges that the task of primary and secondary education is to communicate a sufficient quantity of what is accepted by society so that children will be able to function as citizens and their parents do not view the schools as subversive. Neither primary and secondary nor higher education should be concerned principally with purveying truth. The central purpose of primary and secondary education is socialization, although Rorty allows that social criticism is a component of the tradition that is to be conveyed.[35] Teachers must allow their doubts about the truth of what they teach to affect what is taught "only at the margins." Rorty maintains: "Whether it is true or not is none of the educator's business, in his or her professional capacity. . . . If a teacher thinks that the society is founded on a lie, then he had better find another profession."[36]

Lyotard would reject Rorty's position that primary and secondary education should principally be concerned with socializing children so that they can function as citizens and so that their parents do not view the schools as subversive. Rorty's position presupposes that specifying the nature of the social is unproblematic, and so he sees no difficulty in determining which tradition is to be communicated by primary and secondary education. Lyotard rejects this assumption.

The nature of the social—for example, its identification—by a definitional phrase, is immediately deferred. For, since it is given along with the universe of a phrase, since the finality (the direction of its sense, if you will) of this universe depends upon the phrase by which one links onto the preceding one, and since this linking is a matter for differends between genres of discourse, the nature of the social always remains to be judged. In this way, the social is the referent (the universe of a prior phrase taken as the referent of a subsequent phrase) of a judgment to be always done over again. It is a "case" pled contradictorily before a tribunal. And in this "case," the nature of the tribunal that must pronounce upon the case is itself the object of a differend.[37]

The ongoing controversies regarding whether children should be educated in their first language when that language is not English and whether all children should be taught a second language may serve to illustrate both the difficulty of determining the tradition to be conveyed by primary and secondary education, as well as Lyotard's claim that the nature of the social is immediately deferred. These controversies are differends because there is no common set of criteria accepted by all the parties that would allow their disputes to be adjudicated. Any attempt to adjudicate these controversies must presuppose a prior determination of what society is now and what it is to become in the future. Of course, such a determination would beg the question, since the disputing parties disagree on what society is and what it is to become.

What are the pedagogical implications of Lyotard's beliefs that postmodern education is legitimated by paralogy, that differends are inevitable, and that politics should be understood as the search for the lesser evil? As seen above, education should encourage students to develop new ideas and to challenge critically what passes as common knowledge and accepted wisdom. In addition, education should teach students to be sensitive to the inevitable presence of differends. For instance, children could be shown by examples drawn from current events that there are incommensurate beliefs concerning the meanings of *citizen* and *subversive*. Teaching children to be aware of differends would require enabling them to think critically, especially about what it means to think critically. In addition, students would be taught to recognize differends through learning that persons are constantly creating new literature, music, painting, and philosophy that do not confirm to existing definitions and descriptions.[38]

Perhaps students also would see that—as Lyotard observes in "Endurance and the Profession"[39]—the meaning and worth of learning and teaching are open to question. Further, children would learn about historical and cultural differences and so would see that all criteria are existentially contingent. They would become aware that criteria emerge from human practices, and that these practices and criteria can be challenged. Of course, there can be no question of a method here; there is no formula that would prescribe how this is to be done. Any application of a method or formula would generate differends.

The discussion of Rortyan pragmatism and Lyotardian paralogy may still be somewhat abstract. Perhaps it will become concretized if an illustration is constructed. Rorty believes that higher education, insofar as it is not vocational education, should be concerned mainly with edification.[40] Hence, he stresses the need for educational pluralism at the university: "There, within the sanctuary of a kind of academic freedom which cannot be extended to the secondary schools, doubts about the society may become central rather than marginal to education."[41] Knowledge may be thought of as a bag of tricks, and the range of options available at the university should resemble those of bazaars or flea markets.[42] Rorty believes that university faculties should "exert themselves to take in representatives of every conceivable movement—deconstructionists, Marxists, Habermasians, Catholics, Straussians"—and he would have academic decisions, for example, determining the contents of the university's core curriculum, made as a result of free and open debates between professors.[43] However, what of those movements that are not conceivable, that is, those positions not now recognized as either minority views or legitimate, or what of those persons expressing unpopular thoughts who are not representatives of any recognized movement? On Rorty's account, it would seem that they are out of luck and will be excluded. At best they may continue to advance their perspectives until the time, if ever, that they persuade the faculty members that their positions should be granted recognition. Further, such persons are caught in a double bind: They must be recognized as legitimate in order to put forward their views, but they must also be able to put forward their views in order to be recognized as legitimate. Until they do persuade, though, they will be excluded.

It is not sufficient, then, to agree with Carol Nicholson that "no serious voice" should be "left out of the great conversation that shapes our curriculum and our civilization."[44] Persons left out of conversations are always said to be insufficiently *serious* by those who would exclude them. As Rorty notes, the universalist and realist philosophers assert that pragmatists are "essentially frivolous."[45] Listening "to those who are telling stories about what it means to be excluded from a conversation or a community because their 'heroes' or 'heroines' are different from those of the dominant group" includes listening to voices not now recognized as serious by anyone, including the speakers.[46] Rorty writes:

Assumptions become visible *as* assumptions only if we can make the contradictories of those assumptions sound plausible. So injustices may not be perceived as injustices, even by those who suffer them, until somebody invents a previously unplayed role. Only if somebody has a dream, and a voice to describe that dream, does what looked like nature begin to look like culture, what looked like fate begin to look like a moral abomination. For until then only the language of the oppressor is available, and most oppressors have had the wit to teach the oppressed a language in which the oppressed will sound crazy—*even to themselves*—if they describe themselves *as* oppressed.[47]

For individuals to recognize themselves *as* oppressed or excluded, and to be recognized as such by others, is itself a major achievement. It is not a thing that happens as a matter of course! The recent histories and struggles of lesbians and gay men illustrate the processes whereby a class of persons develops a self-description—and is seen by others—as excluded. Put otherwise, the oppressed must persevere in creating new self-descriptions, even when these sound absurd to them too.

Lyotard would recognize that besides attempting to persuade professors and administrators to recognize positions, frequently there are other options to be employed in obtaining a hearing for unpopular opinions and gaining legitimation. It is the role of the imagination to create and discover these options. Such options might include creating interdisciplinary academic journals; founding alternative educational institutes; writing letters of protest to trustees, legislators, state and national accreditation boards, and newspapers; occupying the administration building; seizing the library; and pseudonymously submitting papers to reputable journals.[48]

It may be objected that Lyotard's paralogy is dangerous, since it allows imaginative moves that directly contest the procedural rules that claim to regulate and adjudicate conflicts. If it is claimed that there are always established criteria available to regulate and adjudicate conflicts, that such procedural rules should always be employed, and that these rules can only be contested by appealing to other criteria established in advance, then Lyotardian paralogy is dangerous. There are, however, no arguments to support such assertions that do not presuppose the conclusions they are intended to demonstrate. Paralogy can be suppressed only through what Lyotard refers to as terror—that is, treating differends as though they were litigations, imposing rules that claim to regulate disputes, and refusing to allow these rules to be challenged directly. It may be that paralogy is dangerous, but terror has its dangers as well.

III

"The philosopher" did not come to teach you philosophy (impossible, says Kant), he came to make what he believed he had thought bend under the requirements of other regimes of thought. *Exerciti*: we tested ourselves.[49]

It was claimed above that victims of oppression must persevere in constituting their new self-descriptions, even when these sound absurd. In "Feminism and Pragmatism," Rorty recognizes that once an oppressed group invents a new language, its terms and categories may be commensurable neither with that group's previous self-descriptions nor with those of its oppressors. In light of this, Rorty believes that "we have to give up the comforting belief that competing groups will always be able to reason together on the basis of plausible and neutral premises."[50] In adopting this position, Rorty allows that conflicts may not be resolvable through litigation. Here Rorty's pragmatism approaches, indeed touches, Lyotard's notion of the differend. So conceived, politics no longer seeks the good but, rather, the least bad. The task is not only to resist recognized oppressions but also to invent new self-descriptions, to bear witness to those oppressions that are not now recognized as such, and to testify to the possibility of still unimagined new languages that would call into question currently accepted practices and institutions.

NOTES

1. Jean-François Lyotard, *Heidegger and "the Jews,"* trans. Andreas Michel and Mark Roberts (Minneapolis: University of Minnesota Press, 1990), p. 39.
2. Jean-François Lyotard, *The Postmodern Condition: A Report on Knowledge*, trans. G. Bennington and B. Massumi (Minneapolis: University of Minnesota Press, 1984), pp. 63–64. (Henceforth referred to as *PMC*.)
3. *PMC*, p. 4.
4. Ibid., pp. 4–5.
5. Ibid., p. 66.
6. Ibid., pp. 65–66.
7. Ibid., pp. 53–67.
8. Ibid., p. xxv.

9. Richard Rorty, *Consequences of Pragmatism: Essays, 1972–1980* (Minneapolis: University of Minnesota Press, 1982), p. xlii.

10. Ibid., p. xli.

11. Ibid., p. xxxviii.

12. Karl Marx, *The Eighteenth Brumaire of Louis Bonaparte* (New York: International Publishers, 1963), p. 15.

13. Ibid.

14. John Rawls, *A Theory of Justice* (Cambridge, Mass.: Harvard University Press, 1971).

15. Richard Rorty, "The Old-Time Philosophy: The Case against Allan Bloom on Philosophy and Democracy," *The New Republic* 198, 14 (1988): 28–33.

16. *PMC*, p. 10.

17. Ibid., p. 17.

18. Thomas S. Kuhn, *The Structure of Scientific Revolutions*, 2nd ed., enlarged (Chicago: University of Chicago Press, 1970).

19. *PMC*, p. 61.

20. Ibid.

21. See Martin Hollis, *The Cunning of Reason* (Cambridge: Cambridge University Press, 1987).

22. Jean-François Lyotard and Jean-Loup Thébaud, *Just Gaming*, trans. Wlad Godzich (Minneapolis: University of Minnesota Press, 1985), p. 62.

23. Jean-François Lyotard, *The Differend: Phrases in Dispute*, trans. Georges Van Den Abbeele (Minneapolis: University of Minnesota Press, 1988), p. xi.

24. Ibid., pp. xi–xii.

25. Ibid., pp. 59–60.

26. Ibid., p. 66.

27. Ibid., p. xii.

28. Ibid., p. 81.

29. Ibid., pp. 68–69.

30. Ibid., p. xii.

31. Ibid., p. 80.

32. Ibid., p. 140.

33. Ibid.

34. Jean-François Lyotard, *Political Writings*, trans. Bill Readings and Kevin Paul Geiman (Minneapolis: University of Minnesota Press, 1993), p. 78.

35. Richard Rorty, "The Dangers of Over-Philosophication: Reply to Arcilla and Nicholson," *Educational Theory* 40, 1 (1990): 40–44.

36. Ibid., p. 42.

37. Lyotard, *The Differend*, p. 140.

38. Ibid., p. 139.

39. Lyotard, *Political Writings*, pp. 70–76.

40. Rorty, "The Dangers of Over-Philosophication," p. 42.

41. Ibid.

42. Rorty, "The Old-Time Philosophy," p. 32.

43. Ibid.

44. Carol Nicholson, "Postmodernism, Feminism, and Education: The Need for Solidarity," *Educational Theory* 39, 3 (1989): 204.

45. Rorty, *Consequences of Pragmatism*, p. 172.

46. Nicholson, "Postmodernism, Feminism, and Education," p. 204.

47. Richard Rorty, "Feminism and Pragmatism," *Michigan Quarterly Review* 30, 2 (1991): 231–32.

48. Richard Levins and Richard Lewontin, *The Dialectical Biologist* (Cambridge, Mass.: Harvard University Press, 1985), pp. 122–31.

49. Lyotard, *Political Writings*, p. 81.

50. Rorty, "Feminism and Pragmatism," p. 234.

5 Postmodern Feminisms

Carol Nicholson

The purpose of this chapter is to explore some of the pedagogical implications of the relationship between feminism and postmodernism. Since both feminism and postmodernism are heterogeneous movements containing diverse and sometimes incompatible perspectives, such a study will necessarily be selective and incomplete. I do not intend to consider all of the aspects of postmodernism as a cultural, political, and economic phenomenon but will focus primarily on Jean-François Lyotard's characterization of postmodernism as an attitude of epistemological skepticism. Similarly, I do not discuss feminism broadly construed as a movement for social changes in the position of women but will focus on feminist theory and its various efforts to rethink the principles of philosophy on the basis of women's equality.

Feminist philosophers and critics have responded in a variety of different ways to postmodern challenges to the intellectual tradition of the Enlightenment. Some regard postmodern philosophy as an ally of feminism because both are engaged in questioning traditional ways of theorizing about knowledge, language, and the self. It has also been argued that feminism and postmodernism are complementary intellectual movements, each of which can correct the weaknesses of the other when their insights are integrated. Feminist critics of postmodernism, on the other hand, fear that its skepticism about historical metanarratives and rejection of universal principles will destroy any possible basis for political action. A different response, represented by the work of Camille Paglia, is that postmodern cultural trends reveal serious problems in feminism itself, which must be reformed from within to remain viable and relevant. I shall discuss the strengths and weaknesses of each of these feminist approaches with particular attention to their pedagogical implications, suggesting that in order to avoid the pitfalls of "political correctness" on the one hand and cynical nihilism on the other, an interdisciplinary and multicultural approach to education is needed that would integrate feminist perspectives throughout the curriculum.

HISTORICAL BACKGROUND OF MODERNISM-POSTMODERNISM

The debate between modernism and postmodernism emerged in the latter half of the twentieth century during an era when both the theoretical framework and the political hegemony of the Western European tradition began to be challenged. Modernists defend traditional ideals of freedom and reason, whereas postmodernists question the existence of universal truths or disinterested knowledge apart from relations of power.

René Descartes is said to have initiated modern philosophy by searching for a secure foundation for all knowledge through the method of universal doubt. After subjecting all of his beliefs—those derived from authority, religious tradition, custom, common sense, sense perception, and even mathematics—to radical questioning, Descartes discovered one idea that resisted all attempts to doubt it, "*Cogito ergo sum*" (I think, therefore I am). The impossibility of doubting the existence of his own thinking self led Descartes to conclude that all knowledge is grounded in the clear and distinct ideas of the individual rational mind, which, if not obscured by tradition, superstition, imagination, or emotion, can accurately represent universal truths about objective reality.

Throughout the seventeenth and eighteenth centuries, rationalist and empiricist philosophers debated about the methods by which these clear and distinct ideas can be discovered and about the way in which human knowledge is related to the Truth as seen in the mind of God, but they all assumed that the individual rational mind is capable of understanding universal principles and that freedom is the ultimate reward of the quest for truth. These beliefs, combined with a philosophy of history as the progressive realization of freedom, inspired the revolutionary movements of the Enlightenment period and continued to be the dominant presuppositions of Hegelian and Marxist philosophies during the nineteenth century. The unprecedented violence and barbarism of the twentieth century, however, led to skepticism about the power of speculative reason to grasp truth and about history as the story of inevitable progress.

Critics of the modern tradition have attacked it on epistemological, political, and pedagogical grounds. Richard Rorty attempts to deconstruct the tradition of modern epistemology by criticizing its central metaphor—the image of the mind as a kind of mirror—and its notion of truth as correspondence between thought or language and the world.[1] Following the American pragmatists, Rorty argues that language and thought are more like tools for coping with experience than pictures of reality. He advocates the end of epistemology and the beginning of a new kind of "edifying" philosophy, or "hermeneutics," which would not seek to represent an independent reality but would simply try to keep the conversation going in the broadest possible sense. Rather than be defined as specialists in a particular field or method, philosophers would be redefined as "all-purpose intellectuals" or "culture critics." From this point of view, education should be seen as helping students to get in touch with their own potentialities, not with something nonhuman called Truth or Reality. This can best be accomplished, says Rorty, by initiating them into an intellectual community through conversation with teachers who define themselves in terms of books and ideas that have influenced their lives. Human solidarity replaces objectivity as the educational ideal.

Jean-François Lyotard's *The Postmodern Condition* presents a different view of the implications of postmodernism for education.[2] Lyotard defines modernism as the attempt to legitimate science by appealing to "metanarratives," that is, philosophical accounts of the progress of history in which the hero of knowledge struggles toward a great goal such as freedom, equality, or the creation of wealth. Postmodernism, defined as skepticism about all the grand narratives of legitimation, represents a radical break with the tradition that has played an important role in the development of Western educational institutions. Lyotard warns that the criterion of efficiency of performance is rapidly replacing legitimation through metanarratives, and as a consequence education has been transformed into the production of skilled experts to fill slots in the economy. He thinks that the "Age of the Professor" is coming to an end, since computers can perform all the traditional tasks of the teacher once grand narratives disappear. While recognizing that the computerization of society may lead to totalitarian control, Lyotard holds out the hope that it could also lead to free public access to all available information, which would encourage radical freedom and innovation rather than conformity. Lyotard's vision of the educational ideal in a postmodern society, in contrast to Rorty's, emphasizes individual autonomy rather than solidarity with one's community.

POLITICAL IMPLICATIONS OF POSTMODERNISM

There has been a great deal of controversy about the political implications of the deconstruction of modern philosophy. Some postmodernists identify the universal claims of modernism with the experience of a dominant elite (mainly white European males), connecting epistemological privilege with sexual, racial, political, and economic privilege. Jacques Derrida attacks "logocentrism," the tyranny of the Western philosophical perspective, which he argues, has suppressed, excluded, or marginalized all otherness and difference in the modern tradition. His proposal of a "logic of *différance*" celebrating plurality, contingency, and diversity has encouraged some feminists and minority groups to ally themselves with the deconstructionists in their struggle for equal rights.

On the other hand, it has been argued that postmodernism's emphasis on differences and opposition to universality can easily degenerate into cynical relativism if not balanced by a search for common theoretical ground as a rational basis for action. Jürgen Habermas defends modernism redefined as a still unfinished project that keeps alive the Enlightenment hope for a more just, equal, and rational society, grounded in the ideal of free and open communication, rather than in absolutes or totalizing theories.[3]

PEDAGOGICAL IMPLICATIONS OF POSTMODERNISM

The debate between modernism and postmodernism has resulted in bitter conflicts in education about the core curriculum and "political correctness." Postmodern advocates of diversity argue that all students should be exposed to the perspectives and contributions of many cultures other than their own, both temporally and geographically. They should also become aware of the heterogeneity of their own societies and learn not just to tolerate but also to value differences of race, ethnicity, class, gender, and sexual preference. The ideal of "multicultural literacy" challenges the modernist assumption that the perspective of historically dominant groups is superior or objectively true. It is also viewed as an important counterweight to the natural human tendency to fear differences, given that students must learn to live and work in a rapidly changing world. In addition to demanding curricular reform, some postmodernists defend campus speech codes restricting the use of racial slurs or other expressions offensive to certain groups on the grounds that this language creates a climate that interferes with equality of educational opportunity.

Critics of postmodernism are outraged at what they see to be the politicization of education. Alan Bloom argues that women's studies, African-American studies, and other attempts to diversify the mainstream curriculum have resulted in the lowering of standards and the corruption of the ideal of objective Truth.[4] E. D. Hirsch insists that students need to master basic concepts in their own tradition before being exposed to other cultures.[5] Dinesh D'Souza attacks the politics of race and gender as a new form of totalitarianism in which freedom of thought and expression are stifled in the name of tolerance of diversity.[6] Defenders of multiculturalism reply to the charge that they are making education too political by saying that educators have always had to make controversial decisions about what to include in the curriculum and what kind of speech and behavior to tolerate. Whether or not this fact is acknowledged, they maintain, education is and always will be political.[7]

It is likely that the debate between modernism and postmodernism will continue for some time to come. Modernists defend the existence of objective standards of quality that ideally would guide choices about course requirements and ethics, but they have not succeeded in developing educational principles or programs that command universal agreement. Postmodernists argue that students should be taught not to depend upon fictional ideals of objectivity, but no comprehensive postmodern philosophy of education has yet been produced. Perhaps this is not surprising in a movement that defines itself in terms of the critique of tradition. It remains to be seen whether a constructive phase of postmodernism will emerge out of the attempt to deconstruct modern philosophy and culture.

FEMINIST RESPONSES TO POSTMODERNISM

It has often been noted that feminism and postmodernism overlap at many points in their analyses, since both challenge the neutrality, objectivity, and universality of traditional knowledge claims. While postmodernists question the theoretical possibility of universal principles, feminists argue that truths alleged to be universal are in fact valid only for men of a particular race, class, and culture. Jane Flax regards feminism and postmodernism as natural allies. In "Postmodernism and Gender Relations in Feminist Theory," she argues that there are three kinds of thinking—psychoanalysis, feminist theory, and postmodern philosophy—that best fulfill the true function of philosophy as defined by G. W. Hegel, to apprehend our time in thought.[8] Each tries to understand the self, gender, knowledge, and culture "without resorting to linear, teleological, hierarchical, holistic, or binary ways of thinking and being."[9] Flax interprets feminist theory as a species of the genus of postmodern philosophy because while challenging the current system of gender relations, it is also engaged in the larger project of deconstructing modern presuppositions of reason and selfhood.

The emergence of postmodern themes within feminism has resulted not only from the influence of such figures as Lyotard, Rorty, Derrida, Jacques Lacan, and Michel Foucault but also from a new sensitivity to differences among feminists themselves. Women of color, working-class women, and women in other cultures have insisted that their experiences are quite unlike those of the white, middle-class, educated women who have tended to dominate feminist politics. Feminist theorists are by no means in agreement even about such basic issues as how to define and analyze the concept of gender, and some are skeptical about the very possibility of arriving at a "true" feminist perspective. As Flax points out, "We cannot simultaneously claim (1) that the mind, the self, and knowledge are socially constituted and that what we can know depends upon our social practices and contexts *and* (2) that feminist theory can uncover the Truth of the whole once and for all."[10] Perhaps the assumption that reality has a single structure, which has perpetuated much inconclusive debate about whether gender, race, or class is *the* primary factor in social organization, involves falsely universalizing modes of thinking which are affected by the very forces of domination that feminists are trying to understand and uproot. According to Flax, the close relationship between feminism and postmodernism means that no feminist theory will ever be final or complete. Like all forms of postmodernism, feminist theories should encourage tolerance of ambivalence, ambiguity, and multiplicity in interpretation.

On the other hand, some feminists regard postmodernism as their natural enemy and maintain that the Enlightenment ideals of truth and freedom are still the best foundation for the feminist project. Christine Di Stefano locates feminism firmly within the modern tradition, arguing that central to the women's movement are unified concepts of gender and of the self, ideas that are necessary not only for theoretical coherence but also to provide a basis for political action. She echoes Nancy Hartsock's question, "Why is it, just as the moment in Western history when previously silenced populations have begun to speak for themselves and on behalf of their subjectivities, that the concept of the subject and the possibility of dis-covering/creating a liberating 'truth' become suspect?"[11] Rather than noting the structural similarities between the postmodern and feminist critiques of totalizing and universalizing theory, these feminists question the motives of postmodern authors, mainly privileged white men of the

European tradition, who have already had their Enlightenment and tend to be insensitive to issues of gender. They emphasize the subversive tendency toward relativism in postmodernism, which has the potential to undermine feminist theory altogether.

A third view of the relation between feminism and postmodernism holds that a synthesis of the two movements can build a new and powerful form of social criticism. Nancy Fraser and Linda Nicholson argue that feminism is neither a species of postmodernism nor its enemy; the two movements are complementary, each having weaknesses that the other can correct and strengths from which the other can benefit.[12] Both movements have developed new paradigms of social criticism without traditional philosophical foundations, but from different directions; postmodernism is strong in the area of metatheory, feminism in the area of social critique. "Postmodernists offer sophisticated and persuasive criticisms of foundationalism and essentialism, but their conceptions of social criticism tend to be anemic. Feminists offer robust conceptions of social criticism, but they tend at times to lapse into foundationalism and essentialism."[13] A robust postmodern feminism would not abandon theorizing on a grand scale but would aim to be pragmatic, fallibilistic, and cross-cultural rather than universal. Gender would be treated as "one relevant strand among others, attending also to class, race, ethnicity, age and sexual orientation."[14] Multiple categories, methods, and epistemologies would be employed in a framework of "feminisms," much like a tapestry composed of multicolored threads. The main political advantage of such an alliance between postmodernism and feminist theory would be its ability to encourage solidarity while recognizing the diversity of women's experiences and needs.

PAGLIA'S CHALLENGE TO CONTEMPORARY FEMINISM

A quite different view of the relationship between postmodernism and feminism is found in Camille Paglia's *Sex, Art, and American Culture*.[15] Although she does not identify herself with either contemporary feminism or postmodern theory, Paglia is important to consider in this context. She takes a stance associated with postmodernism in attacking the gap between the high culture of academia and the mass media, she writes as a feminist criticizing feminism from within, and she relates these ideas to the need for educational reform. Paglia argues that feminism has taken a wrong turn toward moralism and prudery and that a new kind of feminism is needed for future generations. The new feminism she envisions would be open to the mysteries of art and sex and would stress personal responsibility rather than the victimization of women. She believes that the failure of feminism is related to its inability to appreciate the appeal of popular idols (like Madonna) as well as to serious intellectual weaknesses—a narrow view of history, a perverse aesthetics, an incomplete psychology, and a naive politics.

Paglia argues that women's studies programs focus too much on contemporary issues and texts and fail to instill a broad historical perspective. According to the "politically correct" agenda of many feminists, white male imperialism is responsible for most of the evils of the world; an understanding of history reveals, however, that Egypt, Persia, China, and Japan were imperialist long before Europe and the United States. Students should learn that the love of beauty is not the invention of Madison Avenue advertisers, but is as old as civilization itself. Women's studies courses, according to Paglia, are also deficient in psychology. They censor Freud on the grounds that he was a sexist, neglecting the fact that no psychologist worth reading can be understood without a prior knowledge of Freudian theory. In feminist discourse, language is abused to the point where "sexual harrassment" includes all sexually explicit language, whether or not any intimidation is involved, and "homophobic" applies to anyone who doesn't like gays. The current furor over date-rape indicates to Paglia that women are treated as victims rather than being encouraged to take full responsibility for their own sexuality.

Paglia's critique of contemporary education is interesting in that it does not fit the stereotypes of either left- or right-wing politics. Like postmodernists and feminists on the left, she defends multiculturalism, but she argues that most of the current programs designed by the academic avant-garde are not nearly multicultural enough. Not only does a curriculum based upon Derrida, Foucault, and Lacan fail to give the historical and cultural breadth needed for a well-rounded education, but it is absurd to assign these authors to students who have never read Plato, René Descartes, and Sigmund Freud. At the same time, like many conservative critics of education, she argues that the great classical texts should be central to the core and that the "quota" method of adding token women and minority authors to reading lists has resulted in a lowering of standards. Contemporary studies in sex and gender lack the sophistication of high-level intellectual history, so students in women's studies programs would be better off reading Hegel, in spite of the fact that he was male.

Unlike such conservatives as Alan Bloom, Paglia does not insist that education should consist exclusively of traditional works of high culture. She believes that the split between academe and the mass media has been disastrous for both and must be healed by free-flowing communication between the university and the larger society. Professors have little knowledge of American life and even less impact on public policy. She writes, "The American intellectual should mediate between academe and media, the past and the present. Language should be lucid, concrete, direct, with the brash candor of the American people and the brusque, can-do rhythms of American life."[16] Paglia herself exemplifies the intellectual as mediator; she writes about movies, rock music, pornography, and popular culture heroes as well as fine art, literature, and philosophy, and her style of writing captures the easy, straightforward, jargonfree voice of the vernacular. She cuts across traditional schools of thought to point the way toward a new synthesis that is radically multicultural, historical, and interdisciplinary.

Paglia's program for educational reform would involve "true multiculturalism," as opposed to simply adding a few novels or articles by women or minority authors. She thinks all undergraduate teachers should be generalists who are knowledgeable about many cultures and capable of teaching in several fields outside their area of specialization. Undergraduates should be required to take a two-year sequence of core courses beginning in prehistory and covering the archaeology of all the great traditions as well as sacred texts from every world religion. The humanities curriculum would be arts based, focusing on music (including jazz and blues) and dance, and every humanities teacher should be conversant in all the arts. She calls for an end to the "ghettoization" of women's studies, which should be replaced by "sex studies," a new field integrating not only heterosexual men's and women's issues but also literature on homosexuality, with which everyone (not just gays) should be familiar. The key concept in this program for educational reform is the integration of diverse modes of experience and thought—Eastern and Western, scientific and aesthetic, intellectual and sensual, Apollonian and Dionysian.

PEDAGOGICAL IMPLICATIONS OF POSTMODERN FEMINISMS

Each of the feminist approaches that we have examined has significant and useful applications to education. Postmodern feminism encourages sensitivity to differences and to a plurality of interpretations of human experience. It also teaches a critical eye for unfounded claims to universal truth. Feminist critics of postmodernism, on the other hand, stress the danger that too much tolerance of differences can lead to relativism, and extreme skepticism about universal truths can lead to nihilism. Because it is a short step from doubting grand narratives to denying the possibility of theorizing at all, it has been charged that postmodernism in education entails neoconservatism in politics. Students who are taught that there is no rational way to justify political change are in effect being told to accept the status quo, an attitude that is ultimately stultifying to thought. Feminists opposed to postmodernism emphasize the need to give students ideals to live for, principles to live by, and a vision of a better future that they can help to achieve.

The synthesis of postmodern and feminist themes that Nicholson and Fraser call "social criticism without philosophy" is able to answer many of the standard objections to postmodernism in education. While recognizing that feminist theories, like the Western tradition in general, have sometimes been guilty of overgeneralization and insensitivity to differences of race, class, and culture among women, they do not succumb to extreme skepticism toward all grand narratives. They argue for a kind of thinking that is particular, pragmatic, and fallibilistic. Theories developed with this attitude would be historically based and explicitly attuned to specific differences of societies, groups, and periods. The virtue of this type of social criticism is that it overcomes the naivete of some feminisms and avoids the nihilistic tendencies of postmodernism. The main drawback of this approach from a pedagogical standpoint is its isolation from nonacademic culture. As Paglia puts it, "Most of the absurdities of women's studies and French theory would have been prevented by close observation of ordinary life outside the university."[17] Even those academics who find value in postmodern and feminist theory must admit that the issues involved are remote from the interests of the average undergraduate. Most students do not identify themselves as feminists, although they believe in equal rights and equal pay for women. Postmodern texts are so full of technical jargon that they are impossible for undergraduates to understand. Ideally, postmodern feminist education would aim to instill sensitivity to diversity and a sense of social responsibility to participate in the struggle toward a more just and equal world. Realistically, however, if students cannot relate the theoretical framework of this educational program to their everyday lives, it is unlikely that these aims will be achieved.

Paglia argues for a radical restructuring of the curriculum on the basis of students' needs rather than theoretical considerations.

We have a generation of latchkey children, the product of divorce and absentee working parents. Many were raised by permissive Sixties parents loath to impose repressive religion on the children. Consequently, our students are anxious, adrift, often self-destructive. They are desperately searching for meaning. We need reconstruction, not deconstruction.[18]

If it is true that the most important task for teachers in the postmodern era is to help students reconstruct their experience in ways that are meaningful, then we should look seriously at Paglia's proposal for educational reform and work on integrating the insights of feminism and postmodernism with the concerns of the larger society.

NOTES

1. Richard Rorty, *Philosophy and the Mirror of Nature* (Princeton, N.J.: Princeton University Press, 1979).

2. Jean-François Lyotard, *The Postmodern Condition: A Report on Knowledge*, trans. Geoff Bennington and Brian Massumi, Foreword by Fredric Jameson (Minneapolis: University of Minnesota Press, 1984).

3. Jürgen Habermas, *The Philosophical Discourse of Modernity*, trans. F. Lawrence (Cambridge, Mass.: MIT Press, 1987). See also Richard J. Bernstein, *The New Constellation: The Ethical-Political Horizons of Modernity/Postmodernity* (Cambridge, Mass.: MIT Press, 1992).

4. Alan Bloom, *The Closing of the American Mind* (New York: Simon & Schuster, 1987).

5. E. D. Hirsch, *Cultural Literacy* (Boston: Houghton Mifflin, 1987).

6. Dinesh D'Souza, *Illiberal Education: The Politics of Race and Sex on Campus* (New York: Macmillan, 1991).

7. See, for instance, Stanley Aronowitz and Henry A. Giroux, *Postmodern Education: Politics, Culture, and Social Criticism* (Minneapolis: University of Minnesota Press, 1991); and Darryl J. Gless and Barbara Herrnstein Smith, eds., *The Politics of Liberal Education* (Durham, N.C.: Duke University Press, 1992).

8. Jane Flax, "Postmodernism and Gender Relations in Feminist Theory," in *Feminism/Postmodernism*, ed. Linda J. Nicholson (New York: Routledge, 1990).

9. Ibid., p. 39.

10. Ibid., p. 48.

11. Christine Di Stefano, "Dilemmas of Difference: Feminism, Modernity, and Postmodernism," in *Feminism/Postmodernism*, ed. Linda J. Nicholson (New York: Routledge, 1990), p. 75.

12. Nancy Fraser and Linda J. Nicholson, "Social Criticism without Philosophy: An Encounter between Feminism and Postmodernism," in *Feminism/Postmodernism*, ed. Linda J. Nicholson (New York: Routledge, 1990).

13. Ibid., p. 20.

14. Ibid.

15. Camille Paglia, *Sex, Art, and American Culture* (New York: Vintage Books, 1992).

16. Ibid., p. ix.

17. Ibid., p. 236.

18. Ibid., p. 234.

6 Critical Pedagogy and the Pragmatics of Justice

Peter McLaren

CRITICAL PEDAGOGY AND THE POLITICS OF MEANING

The economic collapse of the Soviet Union and its eventual disintegration has become the star witness for Cold War hawks in their gleeful claim that capitalism has defeated socialism due in part to the immanent democratic nature of the free market. The orgy of smug self-congratulation that has surrounded the rhetoric of conservatives and liberals in the United States has led many to proclaim that history is on the side of international capitalism and political leadership of the United States. The cultural apparatuses of the West have represented the dismantling of the Soviet bloc as the triumph of individualism over the hegemony of the totalitarian state. The image of the communist has been hypertrophied into that of a global *ideologue troleur* living off the detritus of capitalism in the back alleys of the crumbling Eastern marketplace. In fact, what has been described as the autonomous logic of the free market has been accorded a sacerdotal status despite the misprision surrounding such claims and the proliferation of corruption scandals involving business and government leaders. Although capitalism produces its own limits and creates conditions that work immanently against its success, its socially reproductive effects on schooling show little sign of abatement at this present historical conjuncture. Successful as a *trompe-l'oeil* for the great social equalizer,

Chapter 6 is dedicated to the Ejercito Zapatistas de Liberación Nacional.

schools still serve as vigorous mechanisms for the reproduction of dominant race, class, and gender relations and the imperial values of the dominant sociopolitical order.

Although I acknowledge the importance of recognizing the conceptual limits of Marxian analysis for reading certain aspects of the postmodern condition, such as the nonsynchronous production of race, class, and gender inequalities, I believe that the main pillars of Marxian analysis remain intact: the primacy of economics and the identification of contradictions and antagonisms that follow the changing forces of capitalism, including new regimes of capital accumulation that reflect an expansion of the informal economy and service sectors. I also believe, along with Jean-François Lyotard, that information will become a major component in global struggles for power and competitive advantage. It is important that critical educators not lose sight of these foci in their move to incorporate into their curricula and policy deliberations insights from continental social theorists who write under the sign of postmodernism.

This chapter will focus mainly on the work of Lyotard and its potential for rethinking some aspects of the project that has come to be known as "critical pedagogy"—a nascent disciplinary trajectory within education that has its roots in Marxian analyses of class but has recently made efforts at appropriating deconstructive readings of discursive formations and certain strands of poststructuralist thinking.

I do not have the space to rehearse all the features of critical pedagogy. I merely wish to summarize some of its most generally accepted principles. Although there are now many different articulations of critical pedagogy (i.e., Freirean pedagogy, feminist pedagogies, ludic and resistance postmodernist pedagogies), most of them endorse to a greater or lesser extent the following axioms: Pedagogies should constitute a form of social and cultural criticism; all knowledge is fundamentally mediated by linguistic relations that inescapably are socially and historically constituted; individuals are synechochically related to the wider society through traditions of mediation (family, friends, religion, formal schooling, popular culture, etc.); social facts can never be isolated from the domain of values or removed from forms of ideological production as inscription; the relationship between concept and object, and signifier and signified, is neither inherently stable nor transcendentally fixed and is often mediated by circuits of capitalist production, consumption, and social relations; language is central to the formation of subjectivity (unconscious and conscious awareness); certain groups in any society are unnecessarily and often unjustly privileged over others, and although the reason for this privileging may vary widely, the oppression that characterizes contemporary societies is most forcefully secured when subordinates accept their social status as natural, necessary, inevitable, or bequeathed to them as an exercise of historical chance; oppression has many faces, and focusing on only one at the expense of others (e.g., class oppression vs. racism) often elides or occults the interconnection among them; an unforeseen world of social relations awaits us in which power and oppression cannot be understood simply in terms of an irrefutable calculus of meaning linked to cause-and-effect conditions; domination and oppression are implicated in the radical contingency of social development and our responses to it; mainstream research practices are generally and unwittingly implicated in the reproduction of systems of class, race, and gender oppression.[1]

For the criticalist in the classroom, meaning is not self-generated; it is not, in other words, wholly available to the active consciousness of autonomous agents. Nor does it reside in some preontological nether world of Orphic harmony and bliss where power circulates in a self-contained, self-referencing universe. Power is viewed by the criticalist as partaking of relations among persons who are differentially enabled to act by virtue of the opportunities afforded them on the basis of their race, ethnicity, class, gender, and sexual orientation. Mainstream pedagogy simply produces those forms of subjectivity preferred by the dominant culture. Such an approach to pedagogy domesticates, pacifies, deracinates agency, harmonizes a world of disjuncture and incongruity, and smoothes the unruly features of daily existence. At the same time, student subjectivities are rationalized and accommodated to existing regimes of truth. To see the classroom as a contestatory, agnostic site of competing discourses that structure what is questioned and what is taken for granted is not easily recoverable within a pedagogy that views knowledge as something external to the discourses in which such knowledge is located. Critical pedagogy, on the other hand, brings into the arena of schooling practices insurgent, resistant, and insurrectional modes of interpretation that set out to imperil the familiar, to contest the legitimating norms of mainstream social life, and to render problematic the common discursive frames and regimes within which "proper" behavior, comportment, and social interactions are premised.

Critical pedagogy attempts to analyze and unsettle extant power configurations, to defamiliarize and make remarkable what is often passed off as the ordinary, the mundane, the routine, the banal. In other words, critical pedagogy ambiguates the complacency of teaching under the sign of modernity, that is, under a sign in which knowledge is approached as ahistorical and neutral and separated from value and power.

For the criticalist educator, agency is structurally located and socially inscribed; and although every formation of agency is an arbitrary imposition of meaning and value and not a transparent reflection of universal selfhood, it cannot be denied that subjectivities are shaped overwhelmingly by articulatory practices that include the social relations of production and consumption, as well as the social construction of race, gender, and sexuality. The overall project of critical pedagogy is directed toward inviting students and teachers to analyze the relation among their own quotidian experiences, classroom pedagogical practices, the knowledges they produce, and the social, cultural, and economic arrangements of the larger social order.[2] Critical pedagogy is engaged in assisting students to interrogate the formation of their subjectivities in the context of advanced capitalist formations with the intention of generating pedagogical practices that are nonracist, nonsexist, nonhomophobic and directed toward the transformation of the larger social order in the interests of greater racial, gender, and economic justice.

Critical pedagogy reveals how omnipotent mainstream approaches to meaning in school settings instantiate the formalistic and formulaic repetition of sameness and essay a world that ontologizes its own representation, valorizing its iteration as natural and commonsensical. It prevents liberating instruction with the injunction to accept what is inevitable, to posture intellectual scarcity as plenitude. Possibility is denied in the act of turning the inert present into a social fate. The result is the demarginalization of the political in pedagogy.

Not only is it impossible to disinvest pedagogy of its relationship to politics, it is theoretically dishonest. The belief that knowledge is removed from history, above politics, and that it is immune from the realm of the ethical is a belief that has had the political effect of disqualifying and disauthorizing the voices of criticalists who work in schools of education. Classrooms are complex cultural sites ripe neither for revolution nor for mindless complicity with oppression; rather, they possess the potential for occupying liminal zones of transgressive practices where identities are constantly negotiated, a place of counterpressures and counternarratives. Critical educators occupy the borderlands-liminal zones, between places of hybrid possibilities, sites of cultural struggle and of crossing that mix meaning and knowledge, aesthetics and politics, fact and value. Outside the borderlands, these characteristics or qualities remain highly demarcated, separated out and kept apart by the unified, predictive logic of identity of scientific empiricism and the will to totality in modern science—all of which rationalizes difference through its forms of domination.

In the borderlands of the criticalists, authenticity ceases to exist because all knowledge, all awareness, is contaminated by prior knowledge that has "officially" disappeared but whose traces remain in the tangled arcs of prior meanings. All knowledge contains the afterglow of lost worlds. All sign systems are populated by silent interlocutors. Criticalists work against the traditional role of teachers as museum curators of the mind. They criticize the museumization of classrooms as places where knowledge is salvaged from its "primitive" beginnings, admired in its "advanced" stages, and mounted as display: on chalk-boards, in reading centers and language laboratories, as visual catechism. Only what can be seen can be evaluated. Even the most liberal variants of mainstream pedagogy only reproduce aporetically through their practices their own relations of subordination with respect to dominant social and cultural relations. Only the finished form counts. Critical pedagogy, on the other hand, tries to make thematic its own situatedness, its own contingency, its own enmeshedness in moral and political positions and practices.

PERVERSITY AND SCHOOLING

From my own position as a criticalist I want to argue that capitalist schooling is generally perverse. It is perverse precisely in that it "solicits desire not with the purpose of obtaining its consent but instead with the intention of hiding from us the yawning gap through the play of an object/answer/disavowal that, from this point of view at least, bears all the characteristics of a perverse object."[3] What schooling hides in its solicitation of desire is the field of difference and alterity. Perverts cannot tolerate difference, so they "invent, in its place, a quasi-delirious image of a nonlack."[4] Under the sign of capitalism, an image of common culture is cultivated in order to "avoid what is intolerable about desire."[5] In other words, culture in its commodified forms becomes "half-truths that seem intolerable not to perceive as absolute."[6] That is, culture is turned into an idealized relationship to an imaginary other. In this light I am aware of the similarity between teaching as a form of advertising and the role of propaganda:

The object advertising offers to us is not the object of desire, but an alibi for no longer desiring the object. The place where it consolidates collective thought is the conviction it propagates that this world of free circulation of goods contains all of the objects necessary to satisfy us. Thanks to advertising, therefore, it is no longer necessary to desire.[7]

In the sense that it is premised on the perverse advertisement for a common culture populated by an enforced tolerance for difference, schooling too often becomes an alibi for not exploring otherness, for not engaging in a politics of difference. It becomes an alibi not to desire. Contemporary schooling dares students to become productive, loyal citizens. Whilst students are exhorted to "be all they can be," such a transgressive challenge—of saying no to drugs and yes to books, for instance—is always already situated within a total obedience to normative codes of conduct and standardized regimes of valuing. This, in my view, is not empowering education but a perverse form of prohibition in which desire as human agency is not permitted to explore its own constitutive possibilities. Students are treated as objects of consumption as they are simultaneously taught the value of becoming consuming subjects. In this way, schooling transforms itself into a perverse ritual in which students disavow the enablement of their own destiny in order to remain subjectively compatible with the commodity form.

DISSOLUTION IN THE WORKPLACE

According to Lyotard, the very act of work takes place within a libidinal economy in which slavery is invested with a strange form of pleasure experienced in the destruction of the inorganic bodies imposed by capital on workers. According to Lyotard:

And if one does *this* [work], if one becomes a slave of the machine, the machine of the machine, the screwer screwed by it, eight hours a day, twelve in the last century, is it because one is forced to do it, constrained because one clings to life? Death is not an alternative to *that*, it is part of it, it attests that there is a *jouissance* in it. The workless English did not become workers in order to survive, they were—buckle up tightly and spit on me later—delighted [*joui*] by the hysterical exhaustion, masochism, who knows, of *staying* in the mines, in the foundries and workshops, in hell. They were delighted in and by the insane destruction of their inorganic body which was of course imposed on them, delighted by the decomposition of their personal identity which the peasant tradition had constructed for them, delighted by the dissolution of families and villages and delighted by the new and monstrous anonymity of the suburbs and the pubs in the morning and evening.[8]

Julian Pefanis describes the "prostitutive relationship imposed by capital" that although perverse, changes nothing "because, according to Lyotard, it was always so."[9] For Lyotard, to start a revolution that was simply a reverse of the sphere of economic and political power only gives ultimate validity to capital and serves to maintain that very sphere responsible for domination and oppression. He notes that in its attempt to universalize exchangeability, capitalism "creates a differend for the specific, the unexchangeable, and so on."[10] Simon During captures Lyotard's perspective on capitalism as follows:

Capitalism itself works to undo the force of the order of discourse. In capitalism, money, rather than language, installs exchangeability as the dominant relation between objects in the world. But money is also stored time and security—one might add, stored pleasure. Thus capitalism disburdens itself from notions such as humanity and progress which underpin high-cultural imperialism. But it also discounts the formations which resist these ideas: in particular, nationalism and philosophical deliberation. Ultimately, for Lyotard, capitalism even implies the end of effective political institutions. The play of exchange, the production of money as security, will delegitimate the discursive presuppositions of institutions too.[11]

Lyotard sees the laws of exchange—the exchangeability of all values—as capitalism's only universal law. According to the law of "indifferent exchange," profits exchange lost "labor" time for "real" time and value becomes equivalent to the rate of transaction rather than the objects of transaction. For Lyotard, capitalism levels singularity through the logic of exchangeability and equivalence. Peter Dews captures Lyotard's criticism of capitalism as follows:

The world of capitalism . . . is not an alienated world. Rather, the cynicism and polymorphous perversity of an economy which can absorb any object, any capacity, any experience into the circuit of commodity exchange parallels the aimless voyage of intensities on the libidinal band, indeed—because forms of order are now themselves seen as merely stases of energy—is indistinguishable from the great ephemeral pellicule itself. Admittedly, in this respect capitalism, like every system of signification and exchange, dissimulates. The capitalist is concerned not with the product as such, but only with the constant augmentation of production, so that capital as a whole functions as a "great totalizing Zero" which neutralizes the singularity of the object into indifferently exchangeable sign of a value.[12]

I believe that critical pedagogy must enable a sustained criticism of the effects of global capitalism. Further, it must renounce and contest the production of race, class, and gender injustices through capitalism's terroristic logic of production and consumption linked to the commodity form. The conceptual advances of continental thinkers such as Lyotard have added significantly to the seriousness and urgency of this and other challenges posed by critical pedagogy. One pressing question I believe Lyotard's work raises for critical educators is: How do we move away from current strategies of liberation in order to give pedagogy a tactical centrality? This chapter attempts to evaluate Lyotard's potential contribution to a pedagogy of liberation in light of this question.

THE QUESTION OF AGENCY

The central challenge posed by critical education has been an analysis of the conceptual ground upon which subjectivity rests in what is becoming known as the era of global capitalism. While the terrain of postmodern social theory is admittedly abyssal and heteronomous, and reads like an itinerary of unpredictable epistemological excursions, ruptured genres of criticism, and of dramatic discursive inflections, it has shed exciting new light on the constitution of subjectivity. Few criticalists in education still ascribe to the notion of the freestanding autonomous subject self-fashioned through free will and good intentions. Subjectivity is now recognized as bearing a constitutive relationship to social power and the relationships to which it gives rise. One issue concerns the extent to which subjectivity as it is manufactured socially must be articulated in a totalizing opposition to otherness (i.e., male versus female; African-American versus white; First World versus Third World) or whether it can be self-reflexive with respect to its own constitutive elements. Another important issue that stems from this debate involves identifying and examining the social relations, cultural contradictions, and antagonisms that inform (organize and shape) the constitution of difference with respect to personal, local, and situated knowledges and experiences. These issues center themselves around the question of agency—a question that is one of Lyotard's central concerns in that "he sees it as underlying the historical epoch we call modernity."[13]

I am sympathetic to the conjunctural view of agency set forth by Judith Butler:

Agency belongs to a way of thinking about persons as instrumental actors who confront an external political field. But if we agree that politics and power exist already at the level at which the subject and its agency are articulated and made possible, then agency can be presumed only at the cost of refusing to inquire into its construction. Consider that "agency" has no formal existence or, if it does, it has no bearing on the question at hand. In a sense, the epistemological model that offers us a pregiven subject or agent is one that refuses to acknowledge that agency is always and only a political prerogative. As such, it seems crucial to question the conditions of its possibility, not to take it for granted as an a priori guarantee.[14]

Butler poses a number of questions related to agency that speak to the possibility of agency as both collective and historical and potentially transformative of existing relations of power and privilege. She asks:

What possibilities of mobilization are produced on the basis of existing configurations of discourse and power? Where are the possibilities of reworking that very matrix of power by which we are constituted, of reconstituting the legacy of that constitution, and of working against each other those processes of regulation that can destabilize existing power regimes?[15]

I should emphasize that agency is never complete, as subjects are continually being produced within and by relations of power and systematic structures of exclusion, disempowerment, abjection, deauthorization, and erasure. According to Butler, subjects are produced to a considerable extent *in advance* of the political field in which they are engaged. She writes, in fact, that "agency can never be understood as a controlling or original authorship over that signifying chain, and it cannot be the power, once installed and constituted in and by that chain, to set a sure course for its future."[16] In other words, a political signifier is always resignified in that it derives from the sedimentation of prior signifiers, of a repetitive citation of prior instances of itself. For Butler, then, agency is located in the performativity of signifiers that are repeated or cited. To be constituted by a discourse is not the same thing as being determined by it.

Paradoxically, according to Butler, identity seeks to foreclose the very contingency upon which it depends. Butler notes that "agency is the hiatus in iterability, the compulsion to install an identity through repetition, which requires the very contingency, the undetermined interval, that identity insistently seeks to foreclose."[17] To claim that the subject is constituted as such is not to claim that agency is determined or that the subject is dead; rather, it is to understand that the belief in an autonomous subject is induced—the notion of subjectivity must be approached as a problematic—and to suggest that its constitution within discursive formations is the very precondition of its agency. Lyotard's concept of the self as a constellation of language games in constant collision subverts settled assumptions with respect to agency and generally affirms the politics of contingency articulated by Butler and other poststructuralists. The self

is viewed as fragmented and lives at the unstable intersection of a series
of language games that become absorbed into the ever-expanding commodity form. Lyotard applies the presumption of incommensurability of
language games relentlessly to the concept of subjectivity and in doing so
debunks imperial signifiers and pushes the practice of judgment against
the frayed limits of reason. However, Lyotard's privileging of quasi-theory
over theory, his location of *jouissance* as an unmediated site of sensational
self-reading or auto-intelligibility and of a "post-political bodily ecstasy"
or "corporeal subjectivity" tends to deflect an interrogation of those
capitalist relations of production and consumption that are complicitous
in the formation of experience.[18]

PERSONS, INDIVIDUALS, AND SUBJECTS

It is important that we situate the problematic of agency and our own
discussion of Lyotard's challenges to critical pedagogy within a larger
discussion of historical agency. Recently, Wlad Godzich has provided a
tentative frame for considering agency in his discussion of premodern,
modern, and postmodern structures of identity.[19] In doing so Godzich
traces different forms of sociopolitical regulation. According to Godzich,
premodern or oral cultures produced *persons* rather than *individuals* who,
generally speaking, were discursively constituted in preestablished roles.
Persons may be described as those occupying the subject positions of a
particular hegemonic discourse or a discursive regime. Here emphasis is
placed on the primacy of the group and its collective well-being. Whereas
premodern persons tended not to view themselves as autonomous entities
who possessed the power or the right to associate freely, modern individuals consider themselves to be the coherent bearers of a unified,
universal consciousness.

There exists within modernity a rationalization of the social sphere
anchored in a politics of individualism in which individuals are seen as
reflections and constitutive elements of civil and political society. Within
Godzich's conceptualization, the individual is not so much defined culturally as politically—as, for instance, a normative, abstract, and universal
subject. This form of individualism is referred to by Godzich as principled
individualism and requires the submission of individuals to specifiable
social regulations and forms of socialization, marked by a steady encroachment of the state into the civil sphere. Modern individuals are also
submitted to preferred forms of socialization.

Postmodern identity formations are different still. They are formed
through new modalities of social regulation that do not construct in-

dividuals but rather *subjects*. Abstract individualism is replaced by concrete, empirical subjects that have differentiated needs and desires produced through "new machines of production and consumption."[20] The genesis of this form of agency can be traced to the eighteenth century and to development of the idea that the economy is an autonomous sphere separated from the public sphere. The public sphere (the sphere of intellectual deliberation) came into being as a symptom of, and as a corrective to, the alienation and "rejectionary forces" brought on by the autonomization of the economy. We inhabit a new world of postmodern modalities of social regulation that work not from a premodern collectivist cultural paradigm of human agency or a modernist individualist political paradigm but, rather, from a paradigm centered on new forms of global capitalism grounded in new global technocratic machineries of production and consumption. Here, individual subjectivity is exploited not for collective ends but for private rituals of self-fashioning.

Godzich's typology raises numerous implications for educational criticalists that may be summarized in the following questions: What does it mean to educate students who are no longer individuals in the modernist sense of being coextensive with the sphere of civil politics but, rather, subjects produced by an autonomous economy? To what extent can the school, as a public sphere, serve as a "site in which what is felt to be in common is defined and where a nonalienated form of society comes into being and delineates its own course of action?"[21] If in a global economy there can be only subjects and no society, only subjects permanently confined to their subjection, are schools then simply destined to continue serving as compensatory and ultimately reproductive mechanisms for new forms of subjectivity based on a merging of identity and the fetishized consumer object?

LYOTARD'S SUBALTERN

Lyotard's work on subjectivity and distance gives supportive emphasis to the typology outlined by Godzich. With Lyotard, Immanuel Kant's transcendental subject has been hijacked and brought from the firmament to the terra firma where it is constructed within a politics of incongruences, incommensurables, and impossible possibilities. Lyotard's pagan subject is not grounded in a metaphysics of presence; rather, it deictically anchors itself in a political pragmatics of reading. Godzich summarizes Lyotard's position on agency as follows: "Lyotard challenges the idea of the autonomy of the subject as enunciator of the law by showing that such an act of enunciation always presupposes a chain of prior enunciations and enunciators, none of which can claim originary status except as a character in a mythic discourse that needs to be enunciated in any case."[22]

Lyotard's perspectives on agency generally affirm the poststructuralist critique of autonomous subjectivity offered by Butler (cited above) and others and share a certain limited affinity with a number of the more "postcolonialist" approaches within critical pedagogy. Postcolonial educationalists remain sympathetic to the position on the subaltern Other taken by Rey Chow, Gayatri Spivak, and other postcolonial critics in the sense that they agree that the "speaking self [of the subaltern] belongs to an already well-defined structure of history and domination."[23] Drawing upon Lyotard's notion of the *differend*, Chow maintains that "a radical alternative can be conceived only when we recognize the essential untranslatability from the subaltern discourse to imperialist discourse."[24] She further recognizes that "the 'identity' of the native is inimitable, beyond the resemblance of the image."[25] Efforts to situate the subaltern in new and specific contexts in an attempt to resurrect the native's victimized voice/self too often makes those who would read the native visible while simultaneously neutralizing "the untranslatability of the native's experience and the history of that untranslatability."[26] The problem of modernity, notes Chow, is

the confrontation between what are now called the "first" and "third" worlds in the form of the differend, that is, the untranslatability of "third world" experiences into the "first world." This is because, in order for her experience to become translatable, the "native" cannot simply "speak" but must also provide the justice/justification that has been destroyed in the encounter with the imperialist. The native's victimization consists in the fact that the active evidence— the original witness—of her victimization may no longer exist in any intelligible, coherent shape. Rather than saying that the native has already spoken because the dominant hegemonic discourse is split/hybrid/different from itself, and rather than restoring her to her "authentic" context, we should argue that it is the native's silence which is the most important clue to her displacement. That silence is at once the evidence of imperialist oppression (the naked body, the defiled image) and what, in the absence of the original witness to that oppression, must act in its place by performing or feigning as the pre-imperialist gaze.[27]

I take a position similar to Chow with respect to the concept of cultural hybridity—a concept gaining a great deal of currency in cultural studies. Chow warns of the danger that the idea of cultural hybridity will be limited to the idea that cultural texts are invariably split or resistant; that the native's voice is *always already* present in the ambivalence of the discourse of the dominator. Too often this position unwittingly

revives, in the masquerade of deconstruction, anti-imperialism, and "difficult" theory . . . an old functionalist notion of what a dominant culture permits in the interest of maintaining its own equilibrium. Such functionalism informs the investigatory methods of classical anthropology and sociology as much as it does the colonial policies of the British Empire. The kind of subject-constitution firmly inscribed in Anglo-American liberal humanism, is the other side of the process of image-identification, in which we try to make the native more like us by giving her a "voice."[28]

Faye Harrison underscores Chow's observation in her recent discussion of postmodern experiments in ethnographic writing. She argues that

although postmodernist experiments in ethnographic writing highlight difference, Otherness, power and authority—issues originally foregrounded by Third World and feminist thinkers—many of these experiments inadvertently reinscribe neocolonial domination, wherein the Other is objectified and appropriated. Textual and representational strategies and literary techniques tend to privilege the force of rhetoric over substantive concern with concrete/institutional relations of power. . . . For example, the concern with dispersing authority and engaging in dialogue is often reduced to a polyphonic style whereby a form of narrative ventriloquism is performed, creating the magical illusion of the Other's coming to voice.[29]

MULTICULTURALISM MATTERS

Lyotard's notion of justice built on the regulatory principle of the differend, his effort to become more appreciative of and alert to the modernist illusion of perfecting subjectivity, and his attempt to lay bare the swindle of the modernist dream of self-mastery and his probing of the dissonance of the self have given us conceptual tools to reexamine established frames for making judgments. Bill Readings has attempted to capture Lyotard's pragmatics of justice in the context of examining the untranslatability of subaltern discourses into majority discourses.[30] He has done this through a discussion of Werner Herzog's film *Where the Green Ants Dream*. Herzog's film focuses on a small mining station in Australia in which a young white mining engineer is conducting blasting tests for mineral deposits. Local Aborigines believe these blasts will disturb the "dreaming" of the green ants and will hasten the end of the "universe world." The Australian Supreme Court rules on the dispute in favor of the mining company. Readings follows Lyotard's paralogical approach to postmodern aesthetic experience to analyze the film. According to Readings the film accommodates a Lyotardian approach to the *incommensurability of language games* in the way it chooses not to represent the Aborigines but to foreground the differend in the act of representation itself. Readings is able to make some important observations about Lyotard's approach to the subaltern through his analysis of this film. For instance, Readings claims that the film illustrates Lyotard's insistence on doing justice rather than representing the truth by bearing witness to an otherness without attempting to represent the truth of such otherness. Readings further claims that it is the filmmaker's intent to displace the governing frames of reference with which such otherness is normally understood. A comparison can be made between the filmmaker's techniques and Lyotard's paganism consisting of quasi-aesthetic experiments. In general sympathy with the filmmaker, he notes that there is an incommensurability of the landscape with green ants and the rational discourse that seeks to represent it, the latter referring to a republican discourse founded on the Idea of Man. The film captures "the heterogeneity of Aboriginal to western argument,"[31] and it "refuses to identify the Aborigines as simply the inchoate or primitive opposite of the rationality of technological man."[32] The Aborigines are irrepresentable. Readings makes an effective case against the idea of common humanity and Western liberal democratic tolerance. Differences arising from cultural diversity must, in this view, be overcome. Common law will arbitrate in the name of liberation what counts as human freedom. Readings notes that the claimants in the dispute are each "right in their own terms."[33] According to Readings:

Injustice in the proceedings of translation comes not from the fact of simply speaking a different language but from the fact that the language of the Aborigines is untranslatable into the language of the court, heterogeneous to the language of common law, of common humanity. An encounter takes place, it happens, but no language is available to phrase it, for the Aboriginal language is insistently local, rooted in the land from which it comes; it cannot become multinational. It cannot, that is, become modern: no one can immigrate into Aboriginal culture.[34]

Lyotard's stress on the incommensurability of phrase regimes or language games can certainly be applied to the struggle over multiculturalism, especially as this struggle has been defined in the context of the United States. Lyotard's work can be appropriated as a means of guarding against the translation of otherness into the discourse of Western imperialism. Similarly, Lyotard's call for diversity could effectively serve to challenge the restoration and recuperation of sameness in the attempt by conservative multiculturalists to foster a common humanity or culture. This perspective of conservative multiculturalism assumes that justice already exists and needs only to be evenly apportioned. It also assumes that the major historical agreements between groups are in the past. Further, it assumes that difference is commensurable with democratic citizenship in the sense that citizenship is capable of welding diverse voices into a unity within differences. It ignores that agency is constructed within differentially constituted relations of power. The common culture argument locates culture as largely a forum of consensus with different minority viewpoints simply accretively added on. Differences become important in liberal pluralistic approaches to multiculturalism in that they can all be equally shed in order to reveal a common humanity—a relation of pure exchange-ability that, of course, universalizes white culture as having privileged status. In Lyotard's politics of incommensurables, there is an implicit appeal for dissensus rather than harmony.

Lyotard's position on cultural difference would appear to support Trinh T. Minh-ha's statement that "multiculturalism is not, therefore, to suggest the juxtaposition of several cultures whose frontiers remain intact, nor is it to subscribe to a bland 'melting-pot' type of attitude that would level all difference. It lies instead, in the intercultural acceptance of risks, unexpected detours, and complexities of relation between break and closure."[35]

However, Lyotard's celebration of multiplicity and plurality and his call for a radical tolerance of incommensurability can fall prey to the very liberal pluralist stance he is criticizing. For instance, an uncritical celebration of multiplicity and heterogeneity can be used in the politics of multiculturalism as an alibi to exoticize "otherness" in a nativistic retreat that locates difference in a primeval past of cultural authenticity. Russell Berman describes such a retreat as "returning to some of the ancient pleasures of narration freed from an obligatory legitimation."[36] It is an attempt to recover "the untroubled coherence of the prelapsarian community."[37] We see a tendency in Lyotard to romanticize the pagan theater of the subversive and the unknown in which the elimination of grand narratives would lead to the dissolution of power and confrontation. It is a dream of the prepolitical arena, the artistic and the literary over the theoretical, experimentation over determinate concepts, the decadent over the transcendent, local validity over official standards of judgment, the mythic over the narratological, the aesthetics of the sublime over practical reason, figural narrativity over discursive efficiency, and radical singularity over heterogeneity. Berman describes this situation as "winning the postmodern game" by "hitting a homer, breaking a record, and getting back to the communal dugout where it all began, where no wise-guy umpire or rational lawgiver would dare tread with his fixation on rigid rules or abstract notions of justice."[38] There seems to be a presumption on the part of Lyotard that conflicts over differences will somehow eventually cancel themselves out if the horizon of possibility for new forms of subjectivities and social practices is kept open. On this note, Peter Dews remarks that Lyotard is dangerously wrong in his assumption that once the aspiration to cognitive or moral universality is abandoned, "a harmonious plurality of unmediated perspectives" will result. The danger carried by this assumption lies in the inability of Lyotard's position to "prevent the perspective of one minority from including its right to dominate others: the Empire which Lyotard so vehemently denounces is simply the minority which has fought its way to the top."[39]

What is ultimately troubling in Lyotard's view of the subaltern subject is that it refuses all attempts to name such a subject, even provisionally, on the grounds that any form of naming is an act of appropriation and ultimately an act of violence. Antidialecticians such as Lyotard effectively expel the other, often in a well-intentioned attempt to protect the singularity of the Other. This position can ultimately lead to both political and pedagogical paralysis as the subaltern is continually exiled into the realm of the uncodifiable, the nonhuman, the undecidable.

Lyotard is correct in arguing that the eventhood that is being repressed in every act of representation betrays the utter impossibility of representation. Such a position warns against constructing an underlying unity among incommensurable regimes of representation that can be politically abused. For instance, the notion that "we are all alike under the skin" offers white culture the alibi it needs to define oppressed groups against the invisible legitimating norms of whiteness. Yet there is a sense in which Lyotard's activation of the differences recuperates a neoliberal move toward unity and consensus under the cover of agonistics and dissensus. Lyotard's refusal to name otherness suggests a tolerance of difference rather than an engagement with it, and intractable difference becomes something to be endured rather than activated as a common ground of struggle against structures of domination.

Although it is true that African-Americans, Latinos, and Anglos may speak incommensurable idiolects, Lyotard's idea of incommensurability does not take into account the cultural production of intersubjectivity—the fact that First World cities such as Los Angeles are inhabited by groups who, unlike Herzog's Aborigines, have influenced each other historically for generations (which is not to deny the overdetermination of structures of difference within capitalist imperialism, the reality of domination, and the violence of hegemonic social relations). Steven Best and Douglas Kellner speak to this deficit in Lyotard's work in the following passage:

Postmodern theories of language often omit or downplay concrete communication practices and while Lyotard—unlike other postmodern theorists—does stress the importance of a pragmatic dimension of language analysis, his stress on agonistics covers over the problem of how understanding is produced in language, how language helps produce intersubjectivity and mutual understanding.[40]

We regard Lyotard's refusal to represent the other as exceedingly noble in that he is sensitively trying to avoid the imposition of colonial or neocolonial idioms on the voice of the other, and the terrorism that is implied in all forms of identification with the other. Yet Lyotard's position betrays a discomfiting silence with respect to understanding how agency can be linked to a pedagogical project of social justice that must include some prescriptive components, even if on a provisional and contingent basis. I agree with Lyotard that there is no true or just way of representing the Other and that to argue otherwise could lead to a prescription for fascism. Yet I feel that there must be some sense in which the self must acknowledge the movement of nonidentity in its own identity. In other words, critical self-reflexivity is a necessary but certainly not sufficient component of critical pedagogy—a position that brushes against the grain of Lyotard's intellectual trajectory that rejects reason as a form of imperialism.

A critical pedagogy dedicated to a critical multiculturalism needs to be formulated within a goal-oriented social praxis. Lyotard's u-topos, wherein "differences may converge without fusing,"[41] needs to be grounded in a riposte to the totalizing narratives of modernity that refuse to admit a politics of doubt. This demands a project of political praxis in which every group is encouraged to distrust its own certainties yet strive to solve the conflict of needs among competing groups situated asymmetrically in relations of power. This demands a theory of agency that not only forswears and terminates representations, or forfeits all purchase on their historical meaning, but vigorously transforms existing representations in the interests of the dispossessed. I believe critical pedagogy must have a preferential option for the poor, the marginalized, and the disenfranchised. Lyotard's project helps us to guard against dogmatism but lacks the substantive elements necessary for guiding our choices toward these ends.

I find problematic as well Lyotard's implosion of the self into the social. Lyotard's imploded subject is one constructed out of the ruins of modernity, out of an entrapment in the machine logic of speed technology. The dissolution of individuals in the so-called consumer society should, in Lyotard's view, be affirmed.[42] This parallels Theodor Adorno's view of postliberal capitalism as the progressive liquidation of the distinction between the unconscious and the ego, resulting in the narcissistic personality type.[43] Agency at times appears to be reduced in Lyotard's work to unbridled subjectivity, to the sundered realms of the self crashing through the gates of identity and official knowledge, to difference left unfettered in an aesthetic field. I am asked to invigilate this terrain to make sure nobody claims a greater purchase on the truth than anybody else. As I shall explore later, this becomes a highly daunting task.

WHAT A DIFFERENCE JUSTICE MAKES

It is a mark neither of exaggeration nor of romanticization to consider Lyotard's work as a type of taboo, a transgression of sorts. According to Julian Pefanis:

Transgression, and the thought for which it was a rhetorical figure, would ultimately come to replace the dialectical thought of contradiction. Transgression is the game of limits: a play at the conventional frames of language, at the border of disciplines, and across the line of taboo. . . . Transgression maintains the taboo since without it would lose its fundamental violence. A society without taboos would be outside human society. And the taboo also maintains transgression, since the concept of a limit, such as a taboo, is only possible on the condition of its infringement: an unpassable limit would require no social constraint to prevent its crossing.[44]

Pefanis's phrase "lurching at the abyss of *unreason*" is, in my estimation, an appropriate description of the way in which Lyotard is able to position his work outside any existing genres of criticism and in a position of radical incredulity toward reason and the critique.

Lyotard moves us beyond a flirtation with abstract negation to face militantly the question of ethics in a world that betrays an attitude of skepticism toward all grand narratives. Through his incredulity toward emancipatory metanarratives and his dismissal of rational metadiscourses of legitimation, Lyotard challenges the very politics of the political in that he refuses to be concerned with who or what is represented; rather, he chooses to concern himself with the violence inherent in the very act of representation (i.e., the function of representation in the West since Plato). To critically interrogate the act of representation is, for Lyotard, yet another form of representation (and in this sense his work cannot avoid recuperating that which it attempts to critique). Consequently, Lyotard calls for a politics of the irrepresentable. Bill Readings argues that for Lyotard,

the political is not the final meaning of representations, but one kind of apparatus, along with others (such as visual perspective, realist narrative, theoretical discourse) for the reduction of heterogeneous singularities to a unifying rule of representability within which all is recognizable. Politics, then, is not simply a question of who is represented, since the exercise of domination is the effect of the representational apparati that have governed the understanding of cultural experience. For example, under capitalism the function of commodification is to submit all events to the rule of capital by reducing them to representations of value within a system of exchange. Existence is thus determined as an effect of representation. The politics that seeks to "represent legitimate aspirations" is itself the subjection of desire to the rule of capitalist commodification and exchange. Theoretical "critique" is itself merely the nihilistic inversion of this movement, either the simple attempt to make commodities circulate in the opposite direction within a system itself functioning in terms of binary oppositions, or the ultimate capitalization whereby the system may know itself as commodity. According to Lyotard any politics that remains within the realm of representation is necessarily complicit with the exclusionary politics that have oppressed women, workers, ethnic and sexual minorities, and others as yet unrecognizable.[45]

According to Lyotard, all representation, including images representing metalinguistic prescriptive commands, inhabits discourse as a radical alterity to any meaning assigned to it. Lyotard calls for a transgression of the very order of the concept and the cognitive idiom itself. Lyotard effectively and at times capriciously pulls the ethicocognitive safety net from under the ontological readings of the metanarratives (emancipation of humanity, liberation through science, self-autonomy, etc.) within a modernism dominated by the logic of identity manifested in the exchange principle. His work serves to dispossess us of the representational ground upon which we negotiate the real. Lyotard calls for the "suspension of symbolicity"[46] through a type of exteriorization in which privileged representations are frustrated. This amounts on Lyotard's part to provoking "symbolic 'indifference' toward every type of official culture."[47] Lyotard stops at nothing short of trying to radically unsettle the social bond of official culture—"the social bond that is reasserted in the face of the difficulty of communication."[48] Following the writings of Lyotard's libidinal economy phase, Lyotard no longer sought to find the ground of unintelligibility in transgressive desire; rather, he could discover them instead in the incommensurability of language games.[49] Lyotard would argue that "the ethical language game, that of prescriptives based on the command from the other, could never be reconciled with the language game of description based on the visible presence of ontological reality."[50]

Resistance to capitalism involves not political organization but the temporality of ethics—he wants to disrupt the synthesis of sense impressions into knowledge by means of concepts. Lyotard seeks, in other words, a temporal alterity. This is the basis of materiality for Lyotard, the insertion of resistant time into the system. Time must be inserted that capitalism can not account for or make accountable. Reading must be given the status of an event, an experiment. Reading is ethical in that it always encounters laws that are indeterminate, are yet to be determined, and can never be determined in advance. According to Readings, "Lyotard is not advocating simply an oppositional wasting of time; rather, he proposes an opening of historical or sociological (modernist) time to a temporal otherness that displaces its accounting, that is untamable, irreconcilable."[51]

Abandoning a concern with agency as materially constitutive of social relations of production and the new social physics of consumption brought on by a post-Fordist variety of flexible specializations, agency for Lyotard is to be found in the fissures and faultlines of language games or phrase regimes. Society as a totality slips from the focus of investigation to be replaced by an emphasis on language and discourse. Lyotard is correct in arguing that it is both impossible and undesirable to give specific or universal content to the category of the subject, since agency demands a continual openness and resignifiability. All normative foundations for building a politics of social justice and transformative agency must necessarily be contingent and provisional. Here Lyotard evokes a palpably diminished faith in critical self-reflexivity and transformative praxis.

Lyotard's rhetorical moves are made within a philosophy of language and not a philosophy of consciousness. However, within his pragmatics of discourse, rules are viewed as unable to provide any advance criteria for judgment of any language game. Rules only apply to games that have already been played. Only the rules germane to a particular language game have any legitimacy (not within themselves but as part of an implicit contract among players), yet ironically all judgments precede their own rules. Lyotard's sentiment here is aptly captured by Wlad Godzich:

It is the games that turn us into their players and not we who constitute the games. Players are immanent to the games they play; as a result they cannot extricate themselves from these games and cannot produce a metadiscourse that could dominate this plurality. The only option that remains is that of an indefinite experimenting with language games, somewhat on the order of the scientific inventiveness that operates by rupture rather than continuous derivation.[52]

Lyotard's preference for small narratives as distinct from master narratives privileges a society of micro-events over one resulting from a master plan. In a very profound sense Lyotard's position is radically important precisely because the modern claim of autonomy has wreaked so much havoc in the name of universal social justice. This idea is worth exploring further.

According to Lyotard, it is reading that is our mode of constitution of subject, and this yields the structure of the postmodern.[53] However, during the act of reading the notion of the freestanding subject is induced. Lyotard advocates a notion of agency in which the subject relearns the practice of reading so as to understand the constitutive moment of subjecthood in the act of reading itself. According to Godzich:

Reading is not actualizing something that lies there; it is deictically to anchor ourselves in relation to that which is around us, and such a deictic anchoring requires that to the phrase we voice we counterpose another phrase, that is, we become the link in the concatenation of these phrases, with all this implies in terms of selection, organization, and ruse. It is not the transcendental positions of meaning that matter; it is how we deictically anchor such meaning as obtains around us.[54]

The type of justice that is advocated by Lyotard is the justice of heteronomy, of irreducible difference. This is a justice that is not lawless but does not legislate. It results in an "unresolvable dissensus" in which no individual is subjected to a law that is alien to him or her. This is the justice of the *différend*, in which the Kantian Ideal of Reason is invoked only to serve as a regulatory mechanism that maintains the preservation of the idea of incommensurability of language games or phrase regimes. It means recognizing a world of pluralized logics and heterogeneous value systems and engaging in a politics with no criteria or normativity, a politics of indeterminate or experimental judgment in which agonistics becomes the founding principle. This may seem odd for a man whose early writings had stressed political action and a revolutionary praxis—"Man is the work of his works."[55] It is equally strange for someone who "had long been torn between the life of writing and the life of militant political action," who had been one of the founding members of the neo-Trotskyist left-wing group *Socialisme ou Barbarie* (a tradition of non–PCF French Marxism and socialism that included such members as Claude Lefort and Cornelius Castoriadis), who worked on behalf of Algerian freedom fighters in the 1950s, who was active in Mouvement du 22 Mars, and who took part in storming the administration building that ensconced Dean Paul Ricoeur at Nanterre in May 1968.[56]

LYOTARD'S WAR ON TOTALITY

Lyotard's "war on totality," his activation of the differences, has led to a serious problem that we are now facing in many current articulations of postmodern discourses, articulations that have taken us from the realm of abstract negation to a more determinate form of negation in order to attempt to destabilize and unsettle the *archai* of modernism. This problem may be described as the privileging of an entirely new set of fixed binary oppositions—an antimetaphysical move in name only. Have we not witnessed in Lyotard's work the metaphysical endorsement of a new set of reified binarisms, a valorization of otherness over sameness, of contingency over necessity, of singularity and particularity over universality, of fragmentation over wholeness?[57]

Lyotard's search for a theory of political judgment is premised on a semiurgical grammar: specifically, the rhetorical moves of language games. His call for a multiplication of justices is, on the one hand, admirable given his attempt to recover a minority discourse by rescuing the social pluralities that have been "suppressed in the West by the commodity terrorism of capitalist hegemony and in the East by the 'rational terrorism' of bureaucratic Communism."[58] Underlying such a project is Lyotard's important recognition that justice is plural. Justices must be understood as contextually specific and in relation to the many different spheres of society in which they need to be seen in their incommensurability. However, there is a problem in Lyotard's refusal not to privilege any of these justices, subjects, or positions. Best and Kellner write:

In a sense, Lyotard's celebration of plurality replays the moves of liberal pluralism and empiricism. His "justice of multiplicities" is similar to traditional liberal pluralism which posits a plurality of political subjects with multiple interests and organizations. He replays tropes of liberal tolerance by valorizing diverse modes of multiplicity, refusing to privilege any subjects or positions, or to offer a standpoint from which one can choose between opposing political positions. Thus he comes close to falling into a political relativism, which robs him of the possibility of making political discriminations and choosing between substantively different political positions.[59]

What regulates the idea of politics in the arena of the Lyotardian post-modern is not the "piety" of a transformative praxis but, rather, the idea of multiplicity and the plurality of language games. Minority discourses would prevail; that is, no one language game would prevail. The problem with this perceptive, notes Peter Murphy, is Lyotard's repudiation of the idea of totality.[60] Lyotard believes that there should be no Mother of All Games, only the maintenance of all known games regulated by the idea of minority. Every discourse would remain a minority discourse such that none of the *petits récits* would be situated in a conceptual hierarchy or prevail as the majority. The metaphysical claim of identity subjugating difference is therefore ruptured and in its place would be a "multifold history of narrative clusters"—a narrative imagination purged of injustices.[61] Lyotard writes:

Destroy all monopolies of narrative, destroy the exclusivist themes of parties and markets. Remove from the Narrator the privilege he gives himself and show there is just as much power in narrative listening and narrative action (in the socially narrated world). . . . Struggle for the inclusion of all Master Narratives, of theories and doctrines, particularly political ones, within the (little) narratives. So that the intelligentsia may see its task not to proclaim the truth or save the world, but to seek the power of playing out, listening to, and telling stories. A power that is so common that peoples will never be deprived of it without riposte. And if you want an authority—that power is authority. Justice is wanting it.[62]

Murphy asks if there is "a discourse that draws together all the other discourses or system of knowledges without destroying them, without imposing a reign of tyranny over them."[63] In answering his own question he affirms that "the discourse of rights or freedom" is such a discourse because it is always in need of being supplemented with other stories, other narratives. Such a discourse recognizes the importance of understanding how domination can be eliminated "in the relations between the pluralistic cultures of modernity."[64] Murphy criticizes Lyotard's antagonism toward totality as follows:

Lyotardian postmodernism is scandalized by the idea of totality. Yet, in totality, we see the fragments of modernity *in relation to each other*: confronting, avoiding, colliding, remonstrating, debating, accommodating, outwitting, and judging each other. It is this—the drama of modernity and its mediations—that a Lyotardian postmodernism cannot convey. . . .

The Lyotardian postmodernist may honor divergence. But there is divergence and divergence. Whatever their differences, the pluralistic cultures of modernity *need* to "hang together." They need each other. And, in fact and in deed, these fragments *can* "hang together," *only* insofar as they participate in the idea of freedom. A metadiscourse is *a reflection which, moreover,* judges these relations—relations which are sometimes domineering, sometimes tragic, sometimes mutually enriching. But to judge we must have a *criterion of judgment*—a criterion that will justify us not only in refusing colonizing relations between the plural cultures of modernity, but will also allow those cultures to speak to, to argue with, and to understand each other, however gropingly. This criterion is the idea of freedom. Freedom is the common measure of all the discourses of modernity.[65]

According to Norman K. Denzin, Lyotard "promotes a kind of neo-liberal pluralism,"[66] a pluralism that "ignores the very structures of oppression other metanarratives, including feminism, make problematic."[67] He concludes that "Lyotard's is an *existential pragmatism* which by making no appeal to a grand narrative, only personal conscience and local narratives, always leaves open the potential of the very reign of terror he (and Sartre, Merleau-Ponty, and Rorty) so vehemently opposes."[68] Murphy's answer to Lyotard's existential pragmatism is the construction of a metadiscourse of freedom. This means, in Murphy's view, that we need to distinguish between a master discourse and a metadiscourse. He claims that

a master discourse wants to impose itself on all other discourses—it is progressive, they are reactionary; it is right, they are wrong. A metadiscourse, on the other hand, seeks to understand society as a totality. By this I mean, it sets out to portray the contradictory nature of society and the complex interactions between the different spheres of society—their dramatic collisions and their dialogues, their tensions and reconciliations, their conflicts and accommodations.[69]

The problem in Lyotard's work of reconciling "a multiplicity of justice with a justice of multiplicity"[70] is a formidable one. To judge without criteria, as Lyotard urges, affirms the imagination as the grounds for making ethical decisions. Yet ethical decisions presuppose, in our view, the construction of an ethical imagination. Although the "scruple of undecidability" set forth by Lyotard and other poststructuralist thinkers offers us an important means of resisting metaphysical absolutes stored in the narrative archives of the nation-state and helps us to unsettle the dominant tropes and schematizing power of the sovereign imagination responsible for the standards that have historically terrorized our judgments (witness Auschwitz), it does little to help us construct the criteria for what constitutes an ethical imagination. Critical education must move beyond simply affirming a proliferation of language games, or effecting new moves, new efficacies, and new intensities. Critical pedagogy calls for an ethical imagination that, following Richard Kearney, "suffers the other to be other while suffering with (*com-patire*) the other as other."[71] Kearney writes:

One must ask, at some point, what guides our evaluation of conflicting interpretations? What standards form or inform our judgments? And a post-modern ethic of dissemination which dismisses such questions as "futile and wrong-headed" is itself futile and wrong-headed. If it is true that we cannot possess knowledge of what is good in any absolute sense, it is equally true that we have an ethical duty to decide between what is better and what is worse.[72]

The problem with Lyotardian analysis of difference is that it tends to unwittingly support a notion of difference reduced to its particularity such that concepts such as class, capital, and patriarchy are seen as totalizing master concepts and unhelpful in its understanding. From this perspective, overall social organization, notes Himani Bannerji, becomes unnamable. She writes that attempts at viewing society as an overall social organization

are dismissed as totalizing and detrimental to individuality, uniqueness of experience and expression. Concepts such as capital, class, imperialism, etc., are thus considered as totalizing, abstract "master narratives," and untenable bases for political subjectivity since they are arrived at rationally and analytically, moving beyond the concreteness of immediate experience. And the master narrative of "patriarchy" . . . fractured through experience and locked into identity circles, also can not offer a general basis for common action for social change, without sinking into a fear of "essentialism" or "totalization."[73]

Critical pedagogy needs what Seyla Benhabib calls "a regulative principle of hope" without which a radical transformation of morality and social transformation is unthinkable. Benhabib writes:

What scares the opponents of utopia, like Lyotard, for example, is that in the name of such a future utopia the present in its multiple ambiguity, plurality, and contradiction will be reduced to a flat grand narrative. I share some of Lyotard's concerns insofar as utopian thinking becomes an excuse either for the crassest instrumentalism in the present—the end justifies the means—or to the extent that the coming utopia exempts the undemocratic and authoritarian practices of the present from critique. Yet we cannot deal with these political concerns by rejecting the ethical impulse of utopia but only by articulating the normative principles of democratic action and organization in the present. Will the post-modernists join us in this task or will they be content with singing the swan-song of normative thinking in general?[74]

CONCLUSION: TOWARD A RADICAL IMAGINARY AND EXPERIMENTAL PRAXIS

Bannerji echoes the concern of critical educationalists in her call for the creation of "an actively revolutionary knowledge" that will lead to the transformation of the conditions and social relations that give rise to our experience. She writes that "this new theorization must challenge binary or oppositional relations of concepts such as general and particular, subject and object, and display a mediational, integrative, formative or constitutive relation between them which negates such polarization."[75] Drawing on Karl Marx's concept of mediation, Bannerji notes that the purpose of the concept of mediation is

to capture the dynamic, showing how social relations and forms come into being in and through each other, to show how a mode of production is an historically and socially concrete formation. This approach ensures that the integrative actuality of social existence is neither conceptually ruptured and present fragmentarily nor abstracted into an empty universalism. Neither is there an extrapolation of a single aspect—a part standing in for the whole—nor the whole erasing the parts. Within this framework the knowledge of the social arises in the deconstruction of the concrete into its multiple mediations of social relations and forms which displays "the convergence of many determinations."[76]

The important objective here is to show "how the social and the historical always exist *as* and *in* concrete forms of social being and knowing. Bannerji is able to express a notion of self and agency in which everything that is local and immediate and concrete is "specific" rather than "particular." Agency that is "specific" is spaciotemporally present yet it is also the product of history and the politics of social relations. It is both singular and general. In this sense, experience becomes the starting point for politics, since experience must then be read critically through a recounting of experience "within a broader socio-political and cultural framework that signals the larger social organization and forms which contain and shape our lives."[77]

Bannerji advocates cutting through the "false polarity posited between the personal/the private/the individual and the mental, and the social/collective/the public and the political, and find a formative mediation between the two."[78] Here one can see the emergency of an "interconstitutive relation between the mental and the social."[79] Experience, then, becomes a point of departure for critical knowledge. It becomes a form of interpretation, "a relational sense-making" that has the potential to both create and transform. Bannerji notes that "experience, therefore, is that crucible in which the self and the world enter into a creative union called "social subjectivity."[80]

Bannerji's position is not unfamiliar to many criticalists engaged in the project of transformative pedagogy, especially those who work from a Freirean perspective that invites the critical interrogation of experience as the starting point for developing a transformative praxis. Read against this critical interrogation and transformation of experience, there is something troubling in the way Lyotard's subject luxuriates in its inevitable and intractable cultural contradictions and the singularity of its own production. Further, there is something unsettling in Lyotard's attempt to marshal a respect for difference as an antidote to the normalizing conventions of formulaic commodity narratives and fetishized self-identity. Difference tends to self-destruct if it is not linked to some constitutive outside. For Lyotard, experience constitutes an irreducible complexity that can never be grasped, since the sublime always occupies the gap between the experiential and the conceptual. This makes it exceedingly difficult to mount a pedagogy of critical self-reflexivity.

The underlying political project that informs the production of meaning constitutes the fundamental characteristics of knowledge production. If the construction of meaning is always already undergirded by ethicopolitical imperatives, which could also be read as motivated "absences," it is possible that teaching can be informed by a project of social transformation such that the forms of knowledge produced will be radically more liberating than those that result from a pedagogy designed simply to promote membership in certain sanctioned communities of discourse predicated on the joint task achievement of assuming monolithic executive identities in order to produce entrepreneurial agents of capital and modernity's colonial and neocolonial situation. It is possible to a priori stipulate ethically yet still advance relationally and contingently a pedagogical project that cautions against rationalizing the social sphere based on the idea of individualism or taking as its normative subject the obedient, hard-working, and creative citizen whose goal is to preserve existing relations of social privilege that have been produced out of the blood and mortar of official history. In making such a claim, I fully acknowledge with Lyotard that individuals engaged in such a project unconsciously accept roles they did not write and submit unwittingly to certain forms of social regulation that they consciously decry. Our motivations and actions are never fully transparent to our reason.

I am with Lyotard when I maintain that transformative pedagogy begins with the local, concrete, and situated knowledges of the students themselves—an approach that validates the construction of their historical agency. But I diverge from Lyotard when, as a criticalist, I seek to move beyond the specificity of experience—beyond local narratives—as the central referent for political action. Critical pedagogy seeks to uncover the social relations that organize experience and as such must seek to interrogate the social as a totality while simultaneously avoiding the terrorism that totalization often entails. Ernesto Laclau has suggested a way to understand the relationship between particularism and universalism that we find instructive. Arguing that "there is no real alternative between Spinoza and Hegel," Laclau remarks that "if a particularity asserts itself as a mere particularity, in a purely differential relation with other particularities, it is sanctioning the status quo in power relations between the groups."[81] For instance, the identity of an ethnic minority group can be fully achieved only within a nation or state context. If that minority succeeds in establishing a complete identity within such a context, then it becomes integrated into that context. If identity does not become fully achieved, then this is due to unsatisfied demands within such a context (equal access to education, employment, etc.). Laclau notes that such demands cannot be made in terms of difference but "on the basis of some universal principles that the ethnic minority shares with the rest of the community."[82] Consequently, the universal is part of the identity of this ethnic minority group insofar as their differential identity has failed in the process of constituting itself—that is, insofar as such an identity is "penetrated by a constitutive lack."[83] This means that the universal "emerges out of the particular not as some principle underlying and explaining it, but as an incomplete horizon suturing a dislocated particular identity."[84] Here, the universal is not an imposed metanarrative but "the symbol of a missing fullness." Consequently, "the particular exists only in the contradictory movement of asserting a differential identity and simultaneously concealing it through its subsumption into a nondifferential medium."[85] This perspective offers us a way of contesting Western Eurocentrism insofar as Eurocentrism is the result of universalistic values being imposed on concrete social actors whose incommensurability with such values is not taken into consideration. In other words, "if the social struggles of new social actors show that the concrete practices of our society restrict the universalism of our political ideals to limited sectors of the population, it becomes possible to retain the universal by widening the spheres of its application—which, in turn, will redefine the concrete contents of such a universality."[86]

Laclau points to an apparent paradox in his formulation of the relationship between particularism and universalism, namely, "that universalism is incommensurable with any particularity yet cannot exist apart from the particular."[87] Such a condition represents not a terminal paradox but, as Laclau puts it, "the very precondition of democracy." "If democracy *is* possible," writes Laclau, "it is because the universal does not have any necessary body, any necessary content. Instead, different groups compete to give their particular aims a temporary function of universal representation."[88]

I have tried to make the case that for the purposes of constructing a critical pedagogy, Lyotard does not adequately stipulate the need to make critical discriminations among incommensurable discourses. So long as claims of substantiation remain unredeemable and criteria of obligation for making judgments remain absent, it is difficult to develop a transformative praxis.[89] I believe, following Selya Benhabib,[90] that there are more conceptual and normative options to the death of Man, History, and Metaphysics than allowed by Lyotard, and as such a fallibilistic and procedural concept of rationality needs to be developed in order that a certain "reasonable and ethical conversation" be made available, that is, in order for the admission of certain normative options that are necessary for an emancipatory educative praxis. In other words, "the agonistics of language" and a "polytheism of values" are not the only options following the end of metanarratives and the demise of the episteme of representation.

There may be no foundational criteria of truth transcending local discourses, no commensurability of language games or discursive means that can derive an "ought" from an "is," but this need not rule out provisionally normative human coexistence and the construction of warranted assertions about what constitutes oppression and liberation. Ethics and epistemology speak of standards of justification, and such standards are always imbricated in politics. Ethics and epistemology have political effects as discursive interventions, and we need to be able to stipulate which effects are oppressive and which are productive of social transformation.

To this end I appeal to what Benhabib calls the standpoint of "interactive universalism," which allows us to recognize "the dignity of the generalized other through an acknowledgment of the moral identity of the concrete other."[91] This is not a prescriptive moral theory that sets out to unqualifiedly defend the standpoint of the concrete other. Rather, its purpose is to recognize the reversibility of perspectives between the concrete and generalized other. It is important to distinguish this position from "substitutionalist universalism," which "dismisses the concrete other behind the facade of a definitional identity of all as rational beings."[92]

As a criticalist, I believe that to defend the value of emancipation means more than simply speaking differently. It means, rather, to understand difference *relationally*. This is a different position than Lyotard's search for a socially undifferentiated community in which "every naratee may become a narrator in an eternal present untarnished by a linear conceptualization of time."[93] Although Lyotard's articulation of the differend as a principle of justice in which minority and subaltern voices are allowed to speak is an important corrective to totalitarian narratives that silence the other, we must make certain that not all voices are celebrated for the simple sake that they remain unfettered by *a priori* rules of judgment. Here, practice is reduced to "the eternal return of an agonistics of power."[94]

What is necessary according to Benhabib is to examine the radical situatedness and contextualization of the subject. This is a project that we believe Bannerji has engaged with considerable success. Such a project entails the proposition that the subject is more than the sum total of its signifying practices, more than an unstable ensemble of shifting subject positions. What is important here is that subjects are invited to explore the constitutive possibilities of their own desiring such that they are able to disavow the foreclosure of their own destinies. This is not a call for transforming students into versions of postmodern refusniks who simply "zone out" when confronted with normative political, ethical, and social demands but a call for a conjunctural politics in which agents, while refusing assigned roles produced by fixed determinations, are able to act in oppositional ways. Lyotard's call to think liberation otherwise, to tell another story, demands a self-reflexive agent who is able to make sure that the *other stories* we tell ourselves about ourselves have less painful historical consequences for those generally left out of such stories or who are generally unwittingly narrativized as the victims. It also suggests the importance of constructing pedagogical tactics as opposed to strategies.

Strategies, notes Rey Chow (after Michel De Certeau), deals with subjects who wish to solidify a place or barricade a field of interest. Tactics, on the other hand, deal with calculated actions outside of specific sites. Strategic solidarities only repeat "what they seek to overthrow."[95] Michael

Shapiro (following De Certeau) describes strategies as belonging "to those (e.g., the police) who occupy legitimate or what is recognized as proper space within the social order."[96] Further, he describes them as "part of a centralized surveillance network for controlling the population." Tactics, on the other hand, are described as belonging "to those who do not occupy a legitimate place space and depend instead on time, on whatever opportunities present themselves." Describing tactics as "weapons of the weak," De Certeau is worth quoting at length:

A tactic is a calculated action determined by the absence of a proper locus. . . . The space of a tactic is the space of the other. Thus it must play on and with a terrain imposed on it and organized by the law of a foreign power. It does not have the means to keep to itself, at a distance, in a position of withdrawal, foresight, and self-collection: it is a maneuver "within the enemy's field of vision," . . . and within enemy territory. It does not, therefore, have the option of planning, general strategy. . . . It operates in isolated actions, blow by blow. It takes advantage of opportunities and depends on them, being without any base where it could stockpile its winnings, build up its own position, and plan raids. . . . This nowhere gives tactic mobility, to be sure, but a mobility that must accept the chance offerings of the moment, and seize on the wing the possibilities that offer themselves at any given moment. It must vigilantly make use of the cracks that particular conjunctions open in the surveillance of proprietary powers. It poaches them. It creates surprises in them. . . . It is a guileful ruse.[97]

Lyotard's pragmatics of justice uncannily embodies many of the characteristics of De Certeau's tactics. Lyotard makes use of the zones of uncertainty, creating the possibility for tactical maneuvers that work like the shock effect of Dada. Here, the constitutive space of resistance is realized in the rootlessness of the temporal and the contingent, the realm of atopia, of some other realm that is not here and now but cannot be defined or represented. As the self implodes under the impact of multiple stories on route to the circuit of commodification, new spaces of possibilities are seized, powers are poached. The methodological provocation advanced by Lyotard helps to remind us that all representations as forms of violence must be ceaselessly interrogated and continually reinvented outside the totalizing logic of grand narratives. Our postmodern imaginary must be put into the service of dreaming beyond the acceptance of such violence and seek new forms of social, political, and ethical relations: in short, new forms of human community hitherto unimaginable. Yet because Lyotard has renounced a general theory of politics, we need to turn to elsewhere in order to fulfill the challenge he has put before us.

NOTES

1. Joe Kincheloe and Peter McLaren, "Rethinking Critical Theory and Qualitative Research," in *Handbook of Qualitative Research*, ed. Yvonna Lincoln and Norman Denzin (Beverley Hills, Calif.: Sage Press, in press).

2. See Henry Giroux, *Theory and Resistance in Education* (South Hadley, Mass.: Bergin and Garvey, 1985) and *Border Crossings* (New York: Routledge, 1992); Peter McLaren, "Border Disputes: Multicultural Narrative, Identity Formation, and Critical Pedagogy in Postmodern America," in *Naming Silenced Lives*, ed. Daniel McLaughlin and William Teirney (London: Routledge, 1993), and "Multiculturalism and the Postmodern Critique: Towards a Pedagogy of Resistance and Transformation," in *Between Borders*, ed. Henry Giroux and Peter McLaren (London: Routledge, 1994); Colin Lankshear and Peter McLaren, eds., *Critical Literacy: Politics, Praxis, and the Postmodern* (Albany, N.Y.: Suny Press, 1992).

3. Doris-Louise Haineault and Roy Jean-Yves, *Unconscious for Sale* (Minneapolis: University of Minnesota Press, 1993), p. 184.

4. Ibid.

5. Ibid., p. 186.

6. Ibid., p. 187.

7. Ibid., p. 193.

8. Cited in Julian Pefanis, *Heterology and the Postmodern* (Durham, N.C.: Duke University Press, 1991), p. 98.

9. Ibid.

10. Simon During, "Postmodernism or Post-Colonialism Today," in *Postmodern Conditions*, ed. Andrew Milner, Phillip Thomson, and Chris Worth (Oxford: Berg, 1990), p. 123.

11. Ibid., p. 124.

12. Peter Dews, *Logics of Disintegration* (London: Verso, 1987), p. 137.

13. Wlad Godzich, "Afterword," in Jean-François Lyotard, *The Postmodern Explained to Children* (Minneapolis: University of Minnesota Press, 1992), p. 112.

14. Judith Butler, "Contingent Foundations: Feminism and the Question of 'Postmodernism,'" in *Feminists Theorize the Political*, ed. Judith Butler and Joan W. Scott (New York: Routledge, 1992), p. 13.

15. Ibid.

16. Judith Butler, *Bodies That Matter* (New York: Routledge, 1993), p. 219.

17. Ibid., p. 220.

18. Mas'ud Zavarzadeh and Donald Morton, *Theory, (Post)Modernity, Opposition* (Washington, D.C.: Maisonneuve Press, 1991), p. 157.

19. Wlad Godzich, "Introduction" to Haineault and Jean-Yves, *Unconscious for Sale*.

20. Ibid., p. xvii.

21. Ibid., p. xviii.

22. Godzich, "Afterword," p. 126.

23. Rey Chow, *Writing Diaspora* (Bloomington: Indiana University Press, 1993), p. 36.

24. Ibid., p. 35.

25. Ibid., p. 36.

26. Ibid., p. 38.

27. Ibid.

28. Ibid., p. 35.

29. Faye Harrison, "Writing against the Grain," *Critique of Anthropology* 13, 4 (1993): 407.

30. Bill Readings, "Pagans, Perverts or Primitives? Experimental Justice in the Empire of Capital," in *Judging Lyotard*, ed. Andrew Benjamin (London: Routledge, 1992).

31. Ibid., p. 179.

32. Ibid.

33. Ibid., p. 183.

34. Ibid.

35. Trinh T. Minh-ha, *When the Moon Waxes Red* (New York: Routledge, 1991), p. 232.

36. Russell A. Berman, *Modern Culture and Critical Theory* (Madison: University of Wisconsin Press, 1989), p. 9.

37. Ibid.

38. Ibid., p. 7.

39. Dews, *Logics of Disintegration*, p. 218.

40. Steven Best and Douglas Kellner, *Postmodern Theory: Critical Interrogations* (New York: Guilford Press, 1991), p. 171.

41. Richard Kearney, *Poetics of Imagining* (London: Harper Collins Academic, 1991), p. 219.

42. Dews, *Logics of Disintegration*.

43. Ibid.

44. Pefanis, *Heterology and the Postmodern*, pp. 85–86.

45. Bill Readings, *Introducing Lyotard* (London: Routledge, 1991), pp. xxvii–xxviii.

46. Sande Cohen, *Academia and the Luster of Capital* (Minneapolis: University of Minnesota Press, 1993), p. 142.

47. Ibid., p. 145.

48. Ibid.

49. Martin Jay, *Downcast Eyes: The Denigration of Vision in Twentieth-Century French Thought* (Berkeley: University of California Press, 1993), p. 580.

50. Ibid.

51. Readings, *Introducing Lyotard*, p. 133.

52. Godzich, "Afterword," p. 127.

53. Ibid.

54. Ibid., p. 133.

55. Pefanis, *Heterology and the Postmodern*, p. 87.

56. Godzich, "Afterword," p. 110.

57. Richard Bernstein, *The New Constellation* (Cambridge, Mass.: MIT Press, 1992), p. 310.

58. Arthur Kroker, *The Possessed Individual: Technology and the French Postmodern* (Montreal: New World Perspectives, Culture Texts Series, 1992).

59. Best and Kellner, *Postmodern Theory*, pp. 174–75.

60. Peter Murphy, "Postmodern Perspectives and Justice," *Thesis Eleven* 30 (1991).

61. Kearney, *Poetics of Imagining*, p. 200.

62. Cited in ibid., p. 201.

63. Murphy, "Postmodern Perspectives and Justice," p. 126.

64. Ibid.

65. Ibid., p. 127.

66. Norman Denzin, *Images of Postmodern Society* (London: Sage Publications, 1991), p. 39.

67. Ibid., p. 44.

68. Ibid., p. 41.

69. Murphy, "Postmodern Perspectives and Justice," p. 126.

70. Kearney, *Poetics of Imagining*, p. 196.

71. Ibid., p. 225.

72. Ibid., p. 221.

73. Himani Bannerji, "But Who Speaks for Us? Experience and Agency in Conventional Feminist Paradigms," in *Unsettling Relations*, ed. Himani Bannerji, Linda Carty, Kari Dehli, Susan Heald, and Kate McKenna (Toronto: Women's Press, 1991), p. 84.

74. Seyla Benhabib, *Situating the Self* (London: Routledge, 1992), p. 229.

75. Bannerji, "But Who Speaks for Us?" p. 93.

76. Ibid.

77. Ibid., p. 94.

78. Ibid., p. 96.

79. Ibid.

80. Ibid., p. 97.

81. Ernesto Laclau, "Universalism, Particularism, and the Question of Identity," *October* 61 (Summer 1992): 88.

82. Ibid., p. 89.

83. Ibid.

84. Ibid.

85. Ibid.

86. Ibid., p. 90.

87. Ibid.

88. Ibid.

89. Willem van Reijen, "Philosophical-Political Polythesim: Habermas versus Lyotard," *Theory, Culture and Society* 7, 4 (1990).

90. Benhabib, *Situating the Self*.

91. Ibid., p. 164.

92. Ibid., pp. 164–65.

93. Berman, *Modern Culture and Critical Theory*, p. 7.

94. Ibid., p. 6.

95. Chow, *Writing Diaspora*, p. 17.

96. Michael J. Shapiro, *Reading the Postmodern Polity* (Minneapolis: University of Minnesota Press, 1992), p. 103.

97. Cited in Dwight Conquerwood, "Ethnography, Rhetoric, and Performance," *Quarterly Journal of Speech* 78 (1992): 82.

7   Lyotard, Postmodernity, and Education: A Critical Evaluation

John Hinkson

RETHINKING THEORIES OF POSTMODERNITY

Postmodernist thought is often embraced as an approach that allows us to discard tired conceptual and practical perspectives. This positive enthusiasm, however, needs to be contrasted with an opposing reaction: a profound wariness toward what is seen as an iconoclastic orientation that appears to be thoroughly unworked out.[1] These responses are made in a great variety of settings including educational ones. The argument of this chapter will seek a way past such reactions. It will take postmodern thought as a *sign* of profound change—in education as well as in broad social settings. This allows a recognition that many of our familiar methods and conceptual schemes are under strain and that this is related to the emergence of a transformed social reality, while the particular ways in which that reality is to be represented is open to critical evaluation. There *is* a social reality outside of postmodernism, and it is an important point of reference—and a source of possible critique—for thinking about the standpoints popularized by postmodernism.[2]

This argument will take up two aspects from this general approach. First, it will examine the distinction just introduced between postmodernity as idea and postmodernity as social reality in order to make some critical comments on Jean-François Lyotard and other theorists who are typically influential in this debate. Second, it will draw these comments into some basic debates within education in order to demonstrate their potential for generating insight into educational practice and interpretation.

Postmodernism is a cultural movement that is not easy to characterize. It has had a rich and diverse elaboration in a wide variety of fields. Nevertheless, it is important to evoke some sort of overview of postmodernist concern if an orientation is to be explicit in this chapter, and one major and highly generalized theme it takes up has considerable significance: the emergence of a new conception of space and time. Globalization of social settings—a new space—and the radical juxtaposition of many historical styles within the one postmodern setting—nonlinear time—are powerful and recurring themes. This is not merely a question of the reduced significance of any particular place. For internationalization is being generalized as a feature of postmodern culture in a very special way. In particular, the "space" of globalization has characteristics that allow it to overcome linear conceptions of time. The way in which one might spell out the nature of this space *socially* is a critical issue in this chapter. It is one way to evaluate postmodernity and postmodern education.

There is also the theme of aestheticization, certainly a postmodern preoccupation, one closely related to the new significance of technologized forms of the image constituting a cultural medium of a new type.[3] Indeed, the image begins to displace the printed word in the production and transmission of culture, thus transforming that value hierarchy taken for granted within Western forms of education centered around the written word. Postmodernism is thoroughly immersed in the emergence of these forms and actively criticizes the value assumptions of a modernist movement, grounded in the printed word, for its defense of a high culture differentiated from popular culture (itself significantly reshaped by the new forms of the image). If modernism and modernity can be shown to be irretrievably tied to certain notions of hierarchy and bureaucratic forms, postmodernism and postmodernity are inseparable from notions of flow and "democratization."[4] All these master themes weigh heavily upon any educational perspective or curriculum theory.

These issues are themselves interwoven with themes taken from poststructuralist and deconstructionist method. Modern philosophy is grounded in notions of a stable foundation for the self, what is referred to as the unified self, and poststructuralism quite rightly characterizes this as essentialist. Thus modern philosophy deals with a static essentialist or given self such that it seems to make sense to refer not only to a "self" but also to a "social whole." It is, the argument goes, as though society can be mapped out in terms of its total set of social relations. Poststructuralists regard this notion of the unified self as an illusion. There are no universal human qualities; they are all social constructions. Social relations are in constant motion. Not only is the self fractured along contradictory lines but, given the constant movement of social relations and the self, it is also impossible to characterize a society as a whole. One can refer only to a process of constant movement or of many societies; any attempt to grasp "it" in its wholistic form will lead to a new tyranny, an attempt to render reality along the lines of a prior conception held by an intellectual of a certain type—the modern, serious, print-based intellectual who is an ecclesiastic in secular clothing.[5]

These few themes from the postmodernist debate put on the table some key notions that have strong points of reference within education. Some writers are content to simply try to map them onto educational practice. However, here I prefer to attempt what seems to me to be a more reflexive approach, one that does not assume a conversion by the educational practitioner. I mean by this that people in education need to hear the arguments about why new approaches in education should displace old ones. They also need to be placed in a situation to be able to evaluate the various recommendations made from a postmodernist standpoint, choosing some, rejecting others as unconvincing. A simple process of postmodernist mapping does not work very well from this point of view.

A different method is possible, however, if one can identify processes that are arguably significant for the unfolding of postmodernist perspective, processes that give a point of reference distinct from postmodernist themes themselves and can simultaneously be seen to be influential within the field of education. In this way one can hope to generate debate and critical perspectives on these developments and not simply speak the "pure truth." It does make my argument more complex and, I'm sure, less accessible; this is unfortunate, but given such unfamiliar materials there would seem to be no alternative. In any case it is an approach that allows the argument to be set firmly within the reflexive side of the educational tradition, and this seems desirable given the contemporary tendency to reduce education to economic rationalist terms.

As a beginning let me make one simple noncontroversial observation: that the communications revolution is crucial for both postmodernism and any conception of a postmodernity. This is to refer not merely to new means of communication but to that general development that increasingly frames the sciences, the information revolution. It is the medium of image, abstracted from its historic embeddedness within social relations, and technologized, that is the first level in which one can speak of a support for the postmodern view. But it is not merely image that is critical here. For this revolution makes materially possible both the flow of technologized image *and information more broadly* and this is the basis for a material break with modernity. The reason for its centrality within postmodern concerns is, first, the sheer power of the information revolution to take "nature" apart as it was known within modernity; second, its capacity to redefine in international terms the setting of communication; and, finally, the ability of the medium of image to engage in self-formative processes, as seen with television generally, including advertising, which lead to more fluid conceptions of the self or subject.

It is possible in this chapter to deal only a little with a few of the issues that this development brings into contention, and these will bear especially on education. Arguably there are two broad sorts of issues that need to be explored. First is the range of transformed relations between institutional spheres and the transformations within institutions that seem to be stimulated into being by the communications revolution. As long as any account is kept within clear limits, one might expect to gain something close to a consensus about the way these processes work. Second is the question of what these developments mean. Postmodernists take the first level for granted and proceed to make arguments about the multiplicity of meanings that that changed setting generates. This is the level where most disagreements can occur and where I want to argue one must go beyond the constraints of poststructuralism and postmodernism for educational research.

At what is being called the first level—that is, the emergence of observable institutional practices and interrelations—one issue is highly significant for education: At the center of these changes is the emergence of the technologized image and information as a medium of communication. Educators have largely taken for granted their relation to the print medium, the medium of the book, for the development of their practices. This is not just a question of educators now having to take into account image communication in their syllabuses. They certainly have to do that, but the shifts are much more profound than that. For there is a sense in which the main institutions that are the carriers of image, the mass media, *transform and take over functions long associated with education*. Here one can speak of how that crucial aspect of education which introduces young people to the wider society and makes that wider society comprehensible to them—that makes it possible for young people to enter society and find their way around it, with some significant points of orientation including a moral direction and sense of alternative possibility—is increasingly a task "handled"[6] by the media.[7] The means of what has often been called *social integration* from modernity, based in the printed word, are now experienced as marginal and often enough not relevant to contemporary experience. This can be seen as an observable struggle between two significant institutions with education increasingly losing out. One has only to take note of the conflicts over general curriculum, especially the tendency for any notion of a general curriculum to lose form and any sense of consensus, and put this in the context of a new form of media knowledge that is broadly "accepted," with controversy around its margins, to see what is being suggested here.[8]

On the other hand, that other aspect of modern education, the transmission of a variety of skills, now comes into the foreground in a transformed state. Under the influence of the information revolution, the nature of skills change. Just as the information revolution introduces more general and abstract processes into productive settings in the form of high tech, so too does it call out the need for more general skills. These are not the familiar vocational skills of the industrial era because such skills now have greater generality and in fact are associated with claims about a new form of general curriculum, implicit in the notions *flexible skills* and *generic skills*. As a consequence education is projected more strongly toward the economy. For the first time with any generality education has a practice that is able to be sold. As the older form of social integration necessary for the constitution of the self and society, often described as education for education's sake, is displaced by the media, education is stage by stage pushed toward the market.[9]

But, it may well be asked, what place is there for human agency in this analysis? Certainly it is true that the argument to this point has referred only to objective transformations that place us in a situation of a new kind. This is not to suggest that these changes are sealed off from human agency, but they do answer to long-term historical tendencies that are affirmed by our cultural assumptions. It is certainly not my belief that a transformation as basic as the information revolution can be reversed. But if that can be put aside, there are still quite basic practices that require human agency within education as well as society more generally. Thus if it is agreed that these structural transformations are real, there is still the question of what such developments *mean*? Through this question a whole range of issues arise that allow us to explore different possible directions for the information revolution. This is to turn to what were called earlier a second-level of issues, ones that are predictably more controversial. If we can say that the first level gives one kind of justification for speaking of a postmodernity, how are we to approach this second level? How are we to interpret this shift to the medium of image? What is the significance of the information revolution? What does it mean for how we are to live and educate?

When Lyotard took up many of the above themes in *The Postmodern Condition*, he did not attempt to differentiate the observable structural transformations associated with the information revolution from arguments about what they meant.[10] When, for example, he argues that in the future, education will be concerned with the facilitation of access to the data bank and that there will be no need for the teacher as a repository of knowledge who teaches, he engages a deep logic of the new medium, but he does much more than that. For he accepts this reality as *the* reality, as a process that is *the* model of social relations in education after the information revolution. It is precisely this that needs to be problematized in arguments about postmodernity and postmodern education, and to do so one must differentiate the transformations from what role they may play within our practices. The latter is not a closed question. It is a crucial question of human agency, and it will be argued that this lack of differentiation in Lyotard and other postmodern theorists leads to deep biases that inscribe an emergent form of intellectuality at a center of power in the society that is emerging.

Thus the emergence of a deep logic in social or educational practice does not necessarily mean that such practices need to be reduced to this form. Although it is no doubt true that social practices will be significantly affected by such a development, there still remain significant choices to be formed and made here.

Lyotard's account of the implications of the information revolution for education is, of course, inseparable from other themes he has promoted, especially those that announce the demise of grand narratives.[11] One cannot emphasize too much how this is a crucial question for education because the disciplines and subjects long associated with educational practice gain their structure from the more general structure of the print-based grand narrative that addresses and integrates a fragile yet relatively stable society. In a sense the data bank, which is outside of a narrative able to be internalized by the self, is one of the mediums that, for Lyotard, stands in for the grand narrative. It provides a substitute form of organization that no longer relies on a substantial self and processes of internalization of knowledge. Although not Lyotard's direct concern, it can be argued that in related ways the media, or technologized image, also stands in for grand narrative. Narratives that could be said at one time to have supported a unified self, or have helped to integrate our diverse and contradictory experiences of the self, are increasingly displaced by mediums that seem to work through fragmented narratives supporting diverse expression and an aestheticized self-creation. Crucially for education, the principle of social integration of these image-based mediums is not available to those subjected to them because the older grand narratives from modernity are unable to address the novelty of the emerging image-based settings.

What is to be our relation to these developments is the critical question here. But it is precisely this question that much postmodern theory tends to close off. This is certainly not a problem that can be attributed to Lyotard alone. But in his work, his wish to convey the profound nature of the shifts associated with the information revolution flows over to a reductive specification of what it means for postmodern practice. If the information revolution generates databases that reinscribe the teacher as a facilitator to the skills of access, he tends to write of such developments as though they are the only sustainable reality within education. If image-based mediums support apparent diversity and a more mobile self with no obvious form of unity, is this to become that reality which supports what Lyotard calls "the temporary contract" in social relations? Or can one ask whether such mediums can play a different role within a larger conception of self and society, one, for example, where the process of self-constitution is more available to us than was possible in earlier societies? If the information revolution can validly be said to bring into contention modern grand narratives, why should this be taken as the end of general perspectives that argue for certain forms of unity, as well as diversity, in self and society? Even to speak of an information revolution or of globalization is to suggest general qualities at work, a certain form of universality that at least in the postmodern case allows us to experience diversity. How is this to be characterized, and how does it relate to other aspects of our social constitution?

Thus although there is in Lyotard a recognition of a major social development that can reasonably be signified by the term *postmodern*, with fundamental implications for education, the further and more difficult task is to contest the meanings attributed to such a development. That is, postmodernity can be argued to have different possibilities with major implications for education. To open these up for consideration it is necessary to see how Lyotard is much too closely tied to that model of social and educational practice found in the commodity-oriented form that has been our experience to date of the information revolution,[12] as, indeed, are the usual accounts of generic skills in education. We should resist the idea that this setting can give us a useful perspective for educational thought and practice.

There are ironies here because there is no doubt that Lyotard, like many postmodernists, is critical of the commodity and technoscience. The problem lies with his theoretical and practical attempts to avoid a social form defined by the universalizing commodity, in particular his tendency, like that of many theorists writing out of poststructuralist method, to see the solution to the systemic possibilities (and tyrannies) of the information revolution in a gravitation toward the concrete and the marginal. That local narratives might be profoundly reconstituted by the information revolution is certainly recognized, but it cannot be acted upon because of a problem within Lyotard's mode of theorizing. Consequently, the information revolution gains an implicit positive account for him when he speaks of local narrative and a negative account when he refers to grand and systemic narratives and state practices. This not only leaves us at the mercy of one expression of high technology but also ignores how the reconstituted local narratives might call out systemic expressions of high technology. At bottom the problem lies in the lack of social space for relations constituted outside of those generated by high-tech means.[13]

This indeed is a real limit of the linguistic turn, one that finds expression in an inability to adequately differentiate and flesh out the meanings of one kind of practice from another—say, the teacher working with the technology of the book compared to the teacher oriented to image and information, or the worker with the technology of the lathe compared to the worker after the lathe has been computerized—because all such practices can be described (universally) within terms that demonstrate their constitution through language.

If *this* postmodern direction is not going to be fully accepted, how can a reconceptualization that is not simply dismissive of the new developments take place? Is it possible to give full recognition to the significance of the image and information revolution while defending a reflexivity that is threatened by most forms of expression of that revolution? The contention is that the cultural and political issues of personhood and of the social form in postmodernity need a method that can differentiate social relations constituted in ordinary language from those constituted in writing and from those constituted in technologized image and information.

To seek another way through postmodern developments and the communications revolution, a turn will now be made toward Michel Foucault, initially for support, and then through critique. This is possible because all of the postmodern writers are preoccupied in one way or another with the new technologies but also because Foucault is quite clear on the relation between technology and new forms of intellectuality.[14] His novel contribution to the theory of power lies precisely in his identification of technologies of power that grow out of the human sciences and engage in processes of subject formation. It is this power/knowledge, this power as a positive constituting force, that is the man way in which we have known Foucault's theory of intellectuality and power, an emphasis that leads one *not* to associate him with reflections on the communications revolution. Yet this is demonstrably a false view of Foucault's contribution, although his historical interests did not give him much opportunity to be directly expansive on such an upheaval.

In "Truth and Power" Foucault outlines what has become a fairly familiar thesis about a shift from the "universal" intellectual to what he calls the "specific" intellectual.[15] The universal intellectual roughly corresponds to what Lyotard calls grand narrative, that is, an intellectual who speaks for us all and is the conscience of our culture. The specific intellectual is, rather, one who works "within specific sectors, at the precise points where their own conditions of life or work situate them (housing, the hospital, the asylum, the laboratory, the university, family, and sexual relations)."[16] And, one could certainly add, the schools. This specific intellectual is for this reason much closer to material reality, the world of the everyday. Foucault then goes on:

It seems to me that this figure of the "specific" intellectual has emerged since the Second World War. Perhaps it was the atomic scientist (in a word, or rather a name: Oppenheimer) who acted as the point of transition between the universal and the specific intellectual. It's because he had a direct and localized relation to scientific knowledge and institutions that the atomic scientist could make his intervention; but, since the nuclear threat affected the whole human race and the fate of the world, his discourse could at the same time be the discourse of the universal. . . . The "universal" intellectual derives from the jurist or notable, and finds his fullest manifestation in the writer, the bearer of values and significations in which all can recognize themselves. The "specific" intellectual derives from quite another figure, not the jurist or notable, but the savant or expert.[17]

A number of points need to be made about these observations. First, Foucault is making a distinction between his work on the specific intellectual in the nineteenth century, whether one speaks of the psychologist, the psychoanalyst, or whatever, and the specific intellectual in the late twentieth century. A process has emerged in the interim, which Foucault makes no attempt to outline, that generates a profusion of specific intellectuals. Second, the specific intellectual gains his or her name because of the specific institutional setting that is the site of the intellectual's power. And third, the nuclear scientist is a "point of transition," for he or she holds together the specific and the universal, the latter because "the nuclear threat affected the whole human race and the fate of the world."

Foucault offers no theory of these processes. His method is here grounded in intuitive observation.[18] But this is not to question the significance of the specific intellectual. For he or she is actually an expression of practical intellect inseparable from what has been termed above, the information revolution. Lacking a theory of these processes, however, Foucault makes an error that may seem insignificant but actually prevents a recognition of how profound this development is to be judged. For in attributing to the nuclear scientist an ambiguous role—a point of transition where specificity and universality are simultaneously present—he demonstrates the limits of his intuitive method. This universality of the nuclear scientist, which leads to a threat against the whole human race, is taken to be a hangover from the past, a residual orientation from the era of the universal intellectual.[19]

These observations made by Foucault based on the contrast of universality and specificity correspond to the categories of Lyotard in the contrast of grand and local narratives. The contrasting categories are not innocent ones: They serve a wider role in the general antipathy of French social theory toward system and totalities they associate with modernity. Whatever insight this categorical ethical imperative of poststructuralist thought may generate, it also produces a significant blindness toward the meaning of the specific intellectual and, as a consequence, gives us insufficient insight into the nature of postmodernity. They give us a feel for it, as does Lyotard's notion of all social relations becoming temporary contracts, but these are mere expressions of a new reality: a phenomenal working with it that implies acceptance rather than a critical interpretation.

To go beyond what Foucault achieves by his distinction between the universal and the specific intellectual, one must be able to speak of what makes intellectual practices distinctive. To do this it is necessary to bypass the familiar forms of social interpretation and theorize the social relations of intellectuals.[20]

This could hardly be done by speaking of this theory or that content. Intellectuals have to know some particular things, and they have particularized relations with others, but content is not what makes them distinctive. The specific intellectual is no different in this regard. It is more fruitful to see intellectual relations as primarily formal, as social relations of a special type defined by their abstraction. That is, these relations have an abstract form that makes them difficult to experience *as* relations as such, and this comes about through the way in which they are inseparable from technological extension. For the intellectual, relations to the *other* are primarily extended through space and time via technology—the book in one era, the book supplemented by electronic communication networks in ours. The implications for how such cultures work and form the self are actually quite profound. It can nevertheless be put in a deceptively simple way: for relations mediated by technology in this way, the physical presence of the other is not structurally required. It is precisely this characteristic that lends intellectual practices their universalizing qualities, for they are not restricted to the particularities of time and place.

This is to say that universalizing practice is especially distinctive to intellectuals. This is a quality that does not exclude Foucault from its effects; but if we are to avoid an essentialist view of this process, it is important to take hold of the different mediums and social relations that allow us to differentiate the modern from the postmodern intellectual. The universal intellectual described by Foucault is the intellectual formed through the extended mediums of print typical of modernity. This intellectual is the intellectual of the book. What he calls the specific intellectual is actually one formed in an emergent medium that marks him or her off from modernity—the extended mediums of image and information. For although Foucault sees the emergent abilities of the specific intellectual to take up positions in the social structure, he does not see that the *reason* for this is the nature of the technique of the specific intellectual. The universality of an Oppenheimer is not a residual hangover to be cast aside by history. It lies at the very heart of what the specific intellectual means, allowing us to see why specific intellectuals—or what I prefer to call the intellectually trained—come to emerge as a powerful social stratum within postmodernity. For the universality of the medium of information and image—contrary to the medium of print—has the capacity to remake the settings of everyday life and the institutions of the social structure *in terms of the technologically mediated social relation*. As this revolution unfolds, the presence of the other in *all* social settings becomes more and more incidental.[21] The specific intellectual is both at the center of this unfolding process and able to move easily into the social spaces within the social structure created by the revolution.

So if we are to ask what these postmodern processes mean, it becomes clear that we need an answer that has broad horizons with a critical perspective in a new mode. We see some of the effects directly in education in the sense that the work process, production, and the skills one needs to engage in production are remade along the lines of information. In terms of the social relations involved, the system of production is increasingly framed by those trained in higher education, the intellectually trained. These are the carriers of what are now called generic skills, certain abstract and formal processes of thought supported by the intellectual culture.

Developments in education that tie it to the economy, and the generation of flexible skills, typically do so while—sometimes consciously, sometimes through ignorance—not allowing too much insight into the new divisions implicit in the development. All of this is to not even mention those who are increasingly not able to get a foot into the new productive methods and thus join the ranks of the permanently unemployed, a development that brings to earth many of the basic principles of emancipation that were the justification of a modern liberal education. That is, a liberal education in modernity assumes one role for intellectuality that includes the emancipatory possibilities of gaining new insights and sensibilities, but what are we to say about an education system that lies at the center of a practical transformation in life-ways that excludes many and leaves us dominated by the intellectually trained? Can we not see the seeds of Los Angeles in these developments?

The other aspect of this transformation of the social structure by the technologically mediated social relation relates to the poststructuralist critique of essentialist conceptions of the self. That is, abstracted from the social relations within which it has been historically embedded and then technologized, image becomes the basis for new processes of self-constitution. If the printed word always allowed a certain intervention in self-formation beyond the relations of family and local community—Friedrich Nietzsche would speak of the priest, Foucault would speak of new technologies of power at work in the nineteenth century— in our momentus times technologized image enters into the very core of processes of primary formation. The self is, as it were, set in motion. It is formed increasingly through relations of self to other, where the Other is the fleeting image. It is no longer predominantly formed through relations where the tangible other is available to the self. This is what Lyotard glibly refers to as the temporary contract, a reference colored much too strongly by an implicit positive evaluation. Within these formal relations all kinds of diverse contents are possible, but arguably the critical thing is not the varied contents. Rather, it is the nature of the form and the identity crises—crises of meaning—that such a form can hardly avoid.

POSTMODERN EDUCATION

Some Implications for Educational Research

If we are to speak of a changed context that in some significant sense can be described as postmodern, this poses some novel problems for the educational researcher. The previous section explored ways to conceive of postmodernity with a critical standpoint. Here that question will be taken up with a broad concern for the role of the researcher seeking to conceptualize the student as a postmodern subject.

The central issue here is the relation of the researcher to the phenomenon of postmodernity where the postmodern is not diffusely conceived as a general emergence but one in the first instance that is grasped as a class-divided social form unique in the way in which intellectual technique inscribes a new form of power. If this is our conception of postmodernity, all the while holding it open to new or potential social directions, any conception of the student as a postmodern subject that ignores social division and social choice is overgeneralized and paralyzed by that method which proclaims the victory of difference. It ignores the substantial intersubjective issues of choice that face educators and students in post-modernity.

Education in postmodernity can entail heightened processes of value and critical social choice, or it can be passive and quietist. We can ask how the "postmodern subject" reconstructs the practice of education, hoping for a new benchmark to tell us what to do; or the project of education can become multileveled and entail a valued advocacy that is one aspect of educational renewal after economic rationalism. What direction is taken hinges around one central question: What is the relation of the various publics, and those who study them, to this postmodernity? A unique and especially unattractive form of quietism emerges from a conception of postmodernity where it just happens to students and teachers and publics while *we* study it.

The passivity implicit in this relationship needs to be spelled out because there are some crucial issues of pedagogy here as well as research attitudes and practices. There are at least two aspects to this: first, the relation of researcher to researched; second, the whole issue of choice in postmodernity.

Let me first address the view that postmodernity happens while intel-lectuals study it. One could complain that such a relationship of intellectual to publics is a mere continuation of a typical relation within the history of the West, especially that of modernity. That is, the social structure is *there*, the intellectual is *here*; the latter studies the former.

This may indeed seem a strange issue to raise given the typical concerns of postmodern theory. Indeed, it is this proto-modern relation of intellec-tuals to the social structure that many postmodern theorists wish to critique. This is both implicit and explicit in the critique of intellectuals made by Foucault and Derrida. One common object of critique here is high modernism, with its hierarchy of evaluative principles; high modernism is contrasted with the more "democratic" flow of popular culture carried in the contemporary media. It would seem, then, that postmodern theory is well prepared to avoid the implications of a radical division between researchers and researched.

But *that* kind of critique of the modern relation of intellectual and public—the differentiation between the two—is not really the problem of the postmodern intellectual.[22] Formulated in that way the issue of intellectuality in postmodernity is normalized and thereby reduced in significance. That is, the typical postmodern critique of the intellectual can serve as an ideological screen that prevents insight into the profound role the intellectual now plays in postmodern settings.

The critique of the modern intellectual gives no insight whatsoever into the profound change in the relation between intellectual culture and social practice that marks off postmodernity from modernity. It is the emergent relation between intellectual practice and social context that is constitutive of the very nature of the social processes that we refer to as postmodern. As earlier argued, the information revolution or the communications revolution is, at its heart, an expression of intellectual practice and carries the intellectual culture and the intellectually trained into positions of power that have no historical comparisons. Any tendency to avoid grappling with this interpenetration of intellectual technique with everyday practices therefore screens from view many of the meanings of those practices. A critique of the intellectual as elitist in no way touches the meanings of this material practice.

This is to say that we have to find ways of studying *our* own practices if we are to grasp the nature of the emergent social structure that we call postmodern, and this requires that we go well beyond the elitist aspect of intellectuality. Historically—certainly within modernity—we have always studied others, not the form and possibilities of our own practices. As members of the intellectual culture or the intellectually trained, Researchers are now placed more centrally in terms of power and development, and this must have implications for our methodology as well as how we need to think critically about practice or we fall into a quietism that protects our own newfound power.

The second notion of passivity poses some different ethical issues typically sidestepped by postmodern theory. To suggest that postmodernity should not merely happen to us and rather needs to be conceived with different possibilities—with intellectual responsibility for the working up of those possibilities—places a crucial emphasis on reconceiving the social whole and what overall shape it might take in supporting its internal diversity. That is, postmodern possibility will not be enhanced by a notion of postmodernity largely defined in terms of plurality, diversity, and difference.

Notions of postmodern difference are problematic in that they cannot give credence to the idea that postmodern choice is framed in a particular way. Postmodern choice is not "anything goes," as some theorists would have it. Rather, it is choice framed by the broad mediums that make those choices possible—in particular the social mediums associated with information and the media—and those framing mediums *shape* the nature of choice as well as generate new ones. In vitro fertilization, for example, as a choice draws us into new relations and necessarily remakes older ones. To be predominantly formed as an individual through technologized image means that any choice to be constituted with a greater emphasis upon social relations structured significantly around tangible others cannot be available to us. Choices that assume the dominance of high technology in our relations with others and with nature exclude other sorts of choices.

This is to suggest that the question of choice also requires a critical reflexivity on the part of the researcher. In fact, here one can pose the cultural politics of the situation fairly starkly, especially as it bears on education. If postmodernity is not to be conceived in terms of diverse surface flows but, rather, in terms of the underlying processes that structure those surface flows, certain things follow. Once the communication revolution occurs, postmodernity emerges. Once the communication revolution occurs, in an important sense there is no turning back. Yet what form postmodernity takes is another matter, one that depends on not only the uses of the communication revolution but also the degree to which that revolution is allowed to structure the shape of social relations generally.

The argument has been that one way to conceive the issues here is in terms of the degree to which the technologically mediated social relation is to characterize the social structure. In terms of social relations that value the tangible other, there is no reason in principle why these cannot be recreated as long as the instrumental orientation of high technology and the intellectually trained does not dominate. That is, another version of postmodernity would involve a reflexive reconstruction of relations that give significance to the presence of the other. A version of such an orientation, which values emancipation, would presumably find ways of avoiding the historical forms of asymmetry and exploitation with which we have come to associate such relations. But precisely how this is to be done, how a high-tech sector of production might relate to other forms of productive activity and social relations generally that are not so dominated in this way, remains to be worked out. These are cultural-political questions that need intellectual and practical effort to which education can make a worthwhile contribution.

But we must bear in mind that there are reasons, in spite of well-intentioned commitments to a "common humanity," why these questions will be brushed aside. In particular, the intellectual culture and the intellectually trained have certain interests here that support a resistance to the raising of such questions. As the information revolution skews the occupational structure in the direction of a job profile with heightened intellectual content, processes unfold that favor a certain kind of intellectual training. If one is to know how to work today, one must have a grasp of an abstract technique learned, not on the job, but in the educational institution. Or if it is to be learned on the job, as Carmichael recommends for the second tier of workers, there will have to be ways of engendering generic skills that are broader than any one workplace—carried in computer-based modules, for example.

The point is that at an objective level, in terms of intellectuals and the intellectually trained for themselves—no longer preoccupied with the rights of other social strata but with their own rights premised upon their emerging status as a constituency in their own right—there would seem to be an interest in a form of postmodern development that affirms the role of the intellectually trained. This would privilege the maximum development of the "clever country" and the internationalized economy, the information revolution unleashed in all its glory. So one could say, on the objective record, one might predict a disposition among intellectuals or the intellectually trained not to see very clearly their own interests in this version of postmodernity that as yet has no opposition; one where the employment of high technology supports intellectually trained strata who would be dominant in social arrangements. That is, other possible forms of development within a general postmodern frame might be ignored, a tendency that would be supported by a general lack of understanding among intellectuals of the nature of their own social practices and how they give expression to the communications revolution.

Curriculum and the Postmodern Subject

To this point this chapter has attempted to do two things: first, to identify through critique and theoretical development those processes, including their form or social logics, that underpin the emergence of postmodern social and educational settings; second, to allow the critical elaboration of more than one path within the general postmodern setting.

This approach has led into a criticism of certain versions of postmodernity and the postmodern self, especially those that seem overcommitted to the technologically mediated relation as though one can *live on that level alone* to the exclusion of relations of cooperation that value the tangible other, the presence of the other.

This last section of the chapter focuses on the problems of the postmodern self or selves and what this might mean for curriculum development in educational settings. Key themes from curriculum theory such as narrative, the universal, content, process, as well as the self *per se*, all gain a distinctive interpretation within postmodern theory. They have been implicitly drawn upon to restructure the curriculum and as such require careful evaluation. This is a very large task, one that can only be touched on in this chapter.

Interpreting postmodernity as a setting where diverse local narratives are its content can easily be seen as a recommendation for a particular form of curriculum, one that, for example, supports multicultural forms of the curriculum to the exclusion of any unified core. For any such core would typically be viewed as an example of modern universals that can only support the totalizing state and a form of cultural homogeneity that marginalizes difference. Yet to draw the conclusion that this version of postmodern curriculum is content oriented leads to confusion. For this is a very special form of the concrete akin to the way in which postmodern space takes a unique form. The transformations of content are more to the point here, and these gain intelligibility only if they are set within a contextual process. It is this combination that is able to engage postmodern sensibilities: Whether one speaks here of attraction to style related as it is to the mobility of the image or of themes promoted by Lyotard, such as the temporary contract.

In this respect a perspective that both sees a certain validity in the reality of postmodernity and wishes to preserve a critical perspective upon it must step back from the temptations of embracing the "concrete" and the "particular." These forms of the particular have a distinctive mobility, and it is this quality that suggests affinities with process. In this sense, the more conventional use of content carries connotations of stultification and modern "fixity."

This version of a postmodern orientation is therefore a distinctive ideological form. It presents itself as oriented toward the particular, the concrete, the local narrative, in opposition to grand narratives and universal forms, yet the nature of the postmodern particular cannot be grasped directly because of the broad setting that gives a special character to this particular. An alternative way of conceptualizing this postmodern reality would be to take up this background setting as a unifying setting that is an essential aspect of postmodern diversity. It so happens that this approach offers more hope of success against the encroachment of totalizing reason than the philosophical denial of totalities implicit in the orientation toward the local narrative. For the latter can only ground a practice in the misrecognition of the nature of the local narrative. *This* local narrative and a certain form of totality—that promoted by the information revolution— are bound together; they are two aspects of the same overall reality.

Similar arguments are also to be made about the postmodern self. A preoccupation with the personal combined with a strong wariness toward any concept of a unified self is typical of postmodern theory. In this respect there is something of an inversion of structuralist method that could give no decent place to the personal. Yet again it is a very distinctive form of the self one must speak of, for, Lyotard claims, there is nothing much to this postmodern self.

Why would he speak in this way? First of all, he has in mind the critique of the essentialist self of nineteenth-century philosophy, that untuited self ground to individualist liberal theory which has also been found to be a problem in Karl Marx. In contrast with this notion or intuition Lyotard is emphasizing the social constitutive processes that substitute for this notion of the self. This is a particular form of the social, notably that which is promoted by the linguistic sign; as such it is a form of the social that can give meaning only through its total set of interrelations and not through any particular signified. The second support to this reduced notion of the self is the sheer diversity and fragmentation of contemporary social relations that are generated by the information revolution and encourage him to refer to social relations in the image of the temporary contract. These two distinctive and mutually supportive approaches lead Lyotard and many other theorists to take up a variety of themes to characterize the modern self in contrast to the postmodern self.

Fixity and unfixity are one such example of how distinctions are made here. The modern self was so taken for granted as an (essential) self that one could say the self consisted of fixed qualities as well as being unified. There is no unified postmodern self; now the self is conceived in its contradictory phases, which allow a better description in terms of unfixity.

The problem is that where dichotomies such as these (unified-ununified and fixed-unfixed) are applied to postmodern education, they are likely to support distorted practices. They work at too superficial a level. If one were to investigate modernity and postmodernity with a synchronic mode of observation, one could easily agree that unified-fixed captures much of modernity and ununified-unfixed helps make "sense" of postmodernity. But this way of differentiating the two eras causes difficulties for education and social theory when we turn to *developmental* self process or, for that matter, to developmental social process. For it does not follow at all that the more fragmented, ununified, postmodern self has no interest in unity. From the standpoint of personal development, and appropriate curriculum for that development, this would have to be *the* educational question, one that is not really engaged by the way these dichotomies are typically employed.

The unified self of modernity was a construct of theory, or more to the point, not so much a construct as an intuitive assumption or starting point for philosophy. The self was also not a concern of social theory, whether one speaks of Marx or the sociological tradition. Arguably this was because the nature of the social form was such that the need to theorize the self was not as pressing as it became in the times of Sigmund Freud and George Herbert Mead and certainly not compared to current times. The relative fixity of modern social relations was such that, at least relative to later developments that bridge into postmodernity, the self was un-problematic.

This allows one to see how to affirm the sense in which the postmodern self can be described as ununified. It does not matter much whether one refers here to the sorts of contradictory elements that constitute the self from a Freudian or Lacanian perspective or the sorts of processes emphasized by Mead: One can certainly acknowledge that there can be no simple unity for the self. But it can still be argued that in terms of process, the individual strains toward unity. This is to take up what Mead calls the universalizing tendency in individual and social process. Thus any stress on lack of unity makes sense only if we can also recognize and act on the undeniable reality that young people, as well as adults, still attempt to make sense of, and make meaning in, their lives. This is to say that however ununified they feel, unity of some kind is terribly important.

This is not to speak of universals in a static mode. It is not to refer to the universals of modern philosophy, the other side of the modern essentialist self. What Mead identifies is a straining toward unity between self and other, a straining toward mutuality that lies at the heart of the social and the cooperative *process*.

For any person this process is always frustrated in this way or that. Certainly one can freely acknowledge the dangers associated with those who seek a simple resolution by reaching for an undifferentiated unity. Nevertheless, this strain toward unity is a fact: It is observable in all historically constituted settings and is also crucial for any educative relation.

Contrary to the popular postmodern view, there is no reason why postmodernity should be seen to contradict *this* process of universalization. Rather, to see postmodernity as profoundly tied to the universal in two possible ways generates more insight. The first way, that version of the postmodern that I believe must be struggled against, a version dominated by intellectual technique, the information revolution, and the commodity, offers a mode of life that in principle and increasingly in practice foregoes the process of mutual interchange suggested by writers such as Mead. This is the meaning of the consumption lifestyle that offers a mode of universalization whereby the other need not take any tangible form and is increasingly displaced by image, style, and the commodity. In this mode there is no need for a unifying perspective for individual identities because all control passes to the market and the intellectually trained. In this notion of the postmodern, it is in relations of *this* type where unity lies. This is the hidden unity of the diverse ununified postmodern self.

The second form of unity one could envisage here in relation to postmodernity entails a much stronger sense of contestation of appropriate social settings and the indispensability of some conception of the social whole for such an oppositional practice. To cling here to modern forms of grand narratives or subjects certainly will not do. But there is a need for the students who emerge from this shift in formative institutions toward the more abstract social medium to have some way of synthesizing their experience. And this would entail a defense of "grand" narratives *after* the essentialized self.

Such narratives would need to be more tentative than their modern versions—have more of a sense of process and reflexive reevaluation as well as an appreciation of cultural difference—and also engage the self and its developmental problems. Education can help in such efforts to universalize experience, to experience unity in difference; and it can help students to see through some of the more seductive pathways of the commodity-based postmodern form.

What might be involved here can be seen in small part through a reflection on the content-process question in education. We have seen how, despite an attraction to the particular and the local, familiar forms of postmodern theory come down in favor of process or form. This can be seen in the (universalizing) generic skill of the new education. It can also be seen in the constant transformation of contents set within the flow of image that typifies the postmodern cultural lifestyle. The postmodern, to recap, is where we enter a form that has a level of association that is repulsed by the stable content and, more crucially, cannot work through it.

Within curriculum theory, content questions, which gain support from diverse interests, are often raised in order to insist that the curriculum should not be trivial, that it should have substance. However, that claim, which in a general way I would argue needs support, gets intertwined with more basic issues of social and cultural development in settings like our own, where the social form is hostile to stable content.

Accordingly, at first glance modern curriculum can, relative to the postmodern, be associated with substance simply because of the relative stability of its setting. But this version of the content-process argument, where there is a rejection of the postmodern essentially because of the nature of the emergent relations in its social form, is a blind alley for education. Although the postmodern setting cannot work through stable contents, it does not follow that stable contents challenge that setting. On the contrary they are easily sidestepped via ridicule because they cannot engage the emergent sensibility. The question is how to go beyond an emphasis on conventional notions of content without simply opting out of the issue of substance.

The Victorian Certificate of Education (VCE) in Australia, for example, like many of the educational reforms that preceded it, is broadly committed to process, with free choice as to content. This is surely influenced by the new methods associated with poststructuralism, themselves giving expression to the emergent social setting. Assuming that there is no grand antedeluvian return to some modern kind of stability, is there any way to strengthen the process of curriculum development? Can any selective principle be used to choose some contents over others that does not turn its back on postmodern sensibilities?

Here the question is not what to do on Monday. It is, rather, what to use as the framing orientation of the curriculum process. The basic point is that stable content can give some insight into the modern social setting but *not* into the postmodern. For the latter a different strategy is called for because any particular content is misleading. Here, varying content is not the problem: rather, it is the lack of a discernible pattern to the variation as well as an inability to regard certain patterns as preferable to others that is the difficulty. For example, selection of content can follow the principle of attempting to give insight into the way the new commodity-based version of postmodernity works, that is, as a social setting that *consumes* content and style.

If one were to study work, for example, one could contrast historical forms of work with contemporary forms: where the technologies and social relations of production were relatively stable, where the forms of cooperation were relatively direct, contrasted with productive modes in the postmodern era of intellectual training where flexible skills and the lifelong need to retrain are combined with work methods where any cooperation is mediated by massive technological forms and the opportunity to work is denied to growing proportions of the population. The development of a skill in the modern context could be seen as stable content, but in postmodernity the skill can be described only more and more abstractly: Any one content or skill is quickly dissolved back to a more general skill—the generic skill. The contrast can help to illuminate the nature of our social setting. If work were related to ways of life, the interconnections might become clearer. The degree to which there are other possibilities for development would be yet another step. A critical postmodern curriculum would, then, not choose between content and process; it would, rather, emphasize in its selection those contents that help illuminate the underlying process. The illumination of the form and its contradictions would thus be the selective principle for content, whose range would be both limited and open to regular change.

Such an approach would mark education off from that knowledge found in the media that clearly has other principles of selection, ones that can give no place to a critical consciousness seeking to reflexively build relations that still value emancipatory relations of presence. It would be the beginning of a process of reclaiming an interpretive place for education.

CONCLUSION: EVALUATING LYOTARD

There seem to be good reasons to differentiate what postmodern theorists say from any conception of our contemporary social settings that describes them as postmodern. At bottom the need for this caveat derives from the limits of the methods typically taken up by poststructuralists. This is certainly a criticism that applies to the work of Jean-François Lyotard.

The strength of his arguments lies in his determination to spell out the profound nature of the changes to our social and educational settings in the circumstances of the information revolution. These run well beyond those matters discussed directly in this chapter such as economic rationality and the end of the educated self. They include the possibilities of technoscience shaping a profoundly new future, one structured around the norm of transsexuality on the one hand and the colonization of space on the other.[23] In taking up the question of the reconstitution of society and attempting to work it through in a great variety of ways, one could certainly sympathize with the difficulty of the task he has set himself. Yet a critical evaluation cannot allow itself to be influenced in this way too strongly.

There is no doubt that Lyotard sets himself the task of developing a critique of technoscience and information, and he is quite right to avoid a critique that can only suggest a rejection of that revolution. Any critique needs to work within a broad recognition that this is one of those epochal revolutions that will be with us forever. But the question is *how* will it be with us?

When Lyotard turns to this question, the kind of answer he can give is, as one must expect, partly dictated by his method. Here it is the way in which theories of the sign have retranslated the nature of the social that requires our attention.

The linguistic turn that has so overwhelmed social interpetation has generated many new insights but does so at a cost. By redescribing the social as linguistic communication, where the basic elements of communication are self-referential or arbitrary, one consequence has been an increasing difficulty to give any meaning to reference.

From a practical standpoint a theory unable to give significance to reference has insurmountable problems. For this would mean that place and the particular other will have no significance in self and social formation. In other words, such a method would have little resistance toward social settings restructured around unconstrained expressions of the mobile image and information. It is this closeness of fit between the linguistic methods and an information revolution, which globalizes place and makes over the particular other into a fleeting other, that demands of us that we go forward, rather than rest satisfied, after digesting the insights of poststructuralist method.

These limits come into the foreground when the time comes for Lyotard to spell out what his critique of technoscience means. He faces a definition of the social that gives him very little space to move. He reflects on the crisis of meaning when our bodies are dematerialized, but his method suggests that our bodies are inconsequential. This in turn allows him to be excited by that era which promises dematerialization, whether through in vitro or via the exchange of body parts. He acknowledges that no society can function with most of its potential workforce unemployed, but the information revolution remains the only social and productive reality within his frame of reference. Consequently, such arguments can only appear to be nostalgic. He acknowledges the significance of place and the other but is resigned to the implications of the "temporary contract" making over all relations. Ultimately he can only offer a critical limit to the information revolution by the contrast of local and grand narratives. Even here he can see that the local is shaped by the information revolution in ways that generate a crisis of meaning, and so by implication his limit comes down to one recommendation: If you fear the consequences of the information revolution upon local narratives, make sure that that revolution does not become attached to a grand narrative! With his frame of reference, this is as far as he can go.

There is good reason to think that it is far too late for such a recommendation. The commodity-oriented social form promoted so actively by significant sections of the intellectually trained is well advanced and is supported by narratives of progress and the good life that have taken hold and possess large sections of "advanced" societies. Another mode of critique and practical orientation is essential, and in this article it has been suggested that one way of pursuing such a goal is by means of a more differentiated concept of the social that is able to give insight into the nature of postmodernity. If there are some very useful points of initial reference in Lyotard, they are certainly not sufficient for us to rethink education in the circumstances of postmodernity.

NOTES

1. This chapter is an edited version of a keynote paper presented to the Australian Association for Research in Education, Deakin University, November 22–25, 1992.

2. In other words, although this chapter is preoccupied with postmodernity as a perspective and practice of special relevance to education, I am not satisfied with a concept that can have only a diffuse politics. Rather, postmodernity is taken up with a critical standpoint, which will have to be argued, and which tries to establish a basis for differentiating between opposing postmodern social formations. The crucial issue is not this or that name but how to conceptualize a profound process of change.

3. Both these master themes are given an insightful account in Fredric Jameson's well-known article "Postmodernism, or the Cultural Logic of Late Capitalism," *New Left Review* 146 (1984): 53–92.

4. See Ernesto Laclau and Chantal Mouffe, *Hegemony and Socialist Strategy* (London: Verso, 1985); Michel Foucault, "Introduction" to G. Deleuze and F. Guattari, *Anti-Oedipus: Capitalism and Schizophrenia* (Minneapolis: University of Minnesota Press, 1977).

5. See Laclau and Mouffe, *Hegemony and Socialist Strategy*, for one attempt to work out this notion.

6. This is not a naive affirmation of the media as if they were in some way desirable relative to other mediums of association. It is merely a recognition of a new reality whose effects remain to be evaluated.

7. To say this is not necessarily to slip into an apolitical functionalist theory. Any general medium can be given political interpretations, but the point here is that it is a shift in general mediums that needs to be initially grasped in terms of broad consequences for self formation and how we approach the other, and for social settings as well. It so happens that *this* general shift has major implications for class divisions as well.

8. These transformations in educational orientation in the light of the media's emergence are discussed more thoroughly in my *Postmodernity: State and Education* (Deakin: Deakin University Press, 1992).

9. The social order is no longer so tied to a certain conjunction of state and educational institutions. The media, which actually transform the "market" [see my "Misreading the Deeper Current: The Limits of Economic Rationality," *Arena* 98 (1992)], also transform the way in which the state is placed within a general setting of social order.

10. Jean-François Lyotard, *The Postmodern Condition: A Report on Knowledge* (Minneapolis: University of Minnesota Press, 1984). Henceforth referred to as *PMC*.

11. See ibid.

12. Which is to say that his critique of performative science, which is meant to lay the basis for postmodern science, is unconvincing. A postmodern science, identified by its discontinuities, is more at the heart of contemporary forms of performativity than he is willing to acknowledge. See my "Post-Lyotard: A Critique of the Information Society," *Arena* 80 (1987).

13. Fundamentally, this is a problem of method that is caused by an attachment to certain forms of social relation—the liberatory social relations facilitated by local narratives set within high-tech means. This is much too complex a topic for this article, but see my "Post-Lyotard" and *Postmodernity: State and Education.*

14. In other words, it is possible to get some clues from his work on how to avoid a technological determinist argument, although to follow this through means going beyond Foucault.

15. Michel Foucault, "Truth and Power," in *Foucault Reader*, ed. Paul Rabinow (New York: Pantheon, 1984).

16. Ibid., p. 68.

17. Ibid., pp. 69–70.

18. To be respected, I submit, but only up to a certain point. The question is, then, how to have an interpretation of these intuitions.

19. There is an ambiguity here that needs some clarification. The well-known critique of universality is where one speaks for the whole human race as though all cultures were constituted in the same historical settings as "us"—for example, the "West" is implicitly imposed on all other cultures—or where dominant cultures are undifferentiated from marginalized cultures, which are then oppressed. Such a use of an ahistorical notion of universality is certainly a clear example of cultural hegemony. Foucault is drawing on this type of critique, but he allows it to bridge into other processes that are actually a different form of universality. Here one can speak of historically formed social relations that are simultaneously universal in the sense that they have a relatively strong tendency to be able to reach across time and place. Thus one can speak of the historically grounded universalizing culture of science or the communications revolution, which is "free" from the constraints of place and has displaced another historically formed universalizing culture with an attenuated relation to place, that of Christianity. That both have the potential to draw on their cultural powers to take apart *other* cultures illustrates their peculiar historically formed power, which derives from their universalizing techniques.

The tendency for these universalizing cultures to present themselves as outside of history certainly generates confusion, but it is a confusion best interpreted as an ideological strategy. That "the nuclear threat affected the whole human race" does *not* derive from an ahistorical universality but, rather, as will be argued below, from techniques generated by the historically formed universalizing practice of science itself. Of course, this requires a further level of clarification about the special or distinctive qualities of such relations that allow them to achieve their quite powerful effect. There is no doubt that these questions are closely related to Foucault's rethinking of the theory of power, or of Friedrich Nietzsche describing the priest as inscribing a form of power outside of class power, but a failure to separate these different forms of universality makes it impossible to conceptualize the peculiar power of the sciences and the specific intellectual in postmodernity. For a discussion of these matters that informs the argument of this chapter, see Geoff Sharp, "Constitutive Abstraction and Social Practice," *Arena* 70 (1985): 48–82, and further arguments below.

20. See ibid., 221–37.

21. This is not, however, a search for what Jacques Derrida would call "full presence." That indeed is a dangerous holy grail that denies the profound ways in which we are socially constituted. However, some social mediums—technologically extended ones—give no significance to the presence of the other, whereas others largely demand it. This is a perspective that can actually be turned against Derrida's notion of "writing."

22. Indeed, there is a need to make a place for the intellectual who is distanced in some respects from the broad society, although simultaneously morally and practically engaged with that society and its contradictions.

23. See footnotes 29, 30, and 31 in my "Post-Lyotard," p. 144.

8 Is Education at the End of a Sovereign Story or at the Beginning of Another? Cultural-Political Possibilities and Lyotard

Barry Kanpol

> We must infuse our definition of politics with a common sense of ethics and spirituality which challenges the structures of oppression, power and privilege within the dominant social order . . . as a critical project which transforms the larger society.[1]

It has been argued by the academic left that in order to help alleviate forms of subordination, alienation, and oppression, a new conception of democracy must be attained.[2] Within a modernistic enlightenment discourse informed by the principles of freedom, equality, and social justice, we live in an age where political subjects on the left reject the authoritarianism of any master narrative. Under this rubric, interpretation and meaning-making within the construction of a democratic environment is prioritized, particularly as the world finds itself increasingly within a crisis of difference. The Palestinian Uprising involving the Palestinians' particular quest for autonomy, the ongoing Middle-East peace process, the fall of the Berlin Wall, indigenous movements in Ecuador, Colombia, and Mexico, and the fall of Stalinist communist parties in Eastern Europe, for example, all suggest that the negotiation of democracy is indispensable to the sanctity and meaning-construction of *any* nation. It is certainly the case in the United States, with the recent Los Angeles uprising, the tax protest movement, and citizens' action movement, coupled with the feminist, race, and gay movements. Critical educationalists have connected the moral imperatives of a novel democratic vision to schools and the public sphere.[3] It is no small argument to make, as these theorists generally do, that schools represent an institution of hope and possibility, a terrain of constant and ongoing contestation against totalizing hegemonic and metanarrative forces. Against the backdrop of national and global capitalism, critical theorists are unified in their commitment to a democratic citizenry. They have advanced our understanding of the relationship among schooling, cultural formations, and the production of subjectivity within a declining social and moral order. The past two decades have produced much research on the demoralizing conditions of schools,[4] documenting the savage inequalities of our urban school centers.[5] Yet the struggle for democratic hopes persist for the educational left, despite the seeming and persistent undercutting of progressive democratic dreams, hopes, and aspirations.

As a form of collective struggle, critical educationalists have "taken on" the postmodern sensibility as one avenue to theorize over democratic contingencies. But critical educationalists are perplexed as to what counts as legitimate democratic inferences. The confusion runs deep into the modern-postmodern debate, at both the theoretical and pragmatic levels.[6] Although this is not the time nor place to make such grand theoretical distinctions, a task attempted by many others,[7] it is important to mention Jean-François Lyotard's position. Postmodernism for Lyotard is "undoubtedly part of the modern."[8] Postmodernism has more to do with the particular in emancipation rather than the universal. It represents an end to master narratives rather than a totalizing acceptance of master narratives.[9] Clearly, for Lyotard postmodernism is deeply concerned with multiple and fluid subjects who construct particular identities and subjectivities in an ongoing meaning-making context, uninhabited by totalizing master narratives.

Lyotard's theoretical constructions allow many new possibilities for thought. We can view the modern within the postmodern and vice versa. Particularity runs within generality or the universal, generality within particularity, master narratives within the personal, and the personal within master narratives. Ernesto Laclau is instructive here:

And, in actual fact, the spectacle of the social and political struggles in the 1990s confronts us with a proliferation of particularisms, while the point of view of universality is increasingly put aside as an old fashioned totalitarian dream. I want to argue, however, that an appeal to pure particularism is no solution to the problems we are facing in contemporary societies. The assertion of pure particularism, independent of any content and of any appeal to a universality, is a self-defeating enterprise.[10]

David Purpel refers to master narratives or universals as dominant modalities of American culture.[11] Indeed, for Purpel schools become contradictory sites of cultural struggle where human beings should be the central cultural, humane, and morally upstanding agents of democracy. Schools, Purpel argues, represent the master, universal narratives of positivism, capitalism, and patriarchy, yet contradictorily they present the particular and different micronarratives of nurture, care, sensitivity, and compassion. It is partly because of these contradictions that I find some modicum of hope for emancipatory outlets within the education field. As Chantal Mouffe claims, democracy is possible because the universal (or in this case the master narrative) does not possess one particular body or any necessary content. Instead, as Mouffe goes on, "different groups compete to give their particular aims a temporary function of universal representation."[12]

In my own teaching, as a philosopher and critical educationalist, I like to think that I am not simply getting students to perform or conform for and to a stagnant social system; nor am I *only* presenting higher learning "to supply the social system with the skills to fulfill society's own needs of internal cohesion" or master narrative.[13] I attempt to use my privileged and professional role to present students with the critical tool for thinking within possible universal social cohesion and social democratic hopes, dreams, and possibilities. I want to argue, against Lyotard,[14] that the death of the Professor is *not* at hand, despite technological advances that may seem to undercut the role of the professor. Put differently, how can the critical educationalist, albeit high school teacher or university professor, who is struggling for community and democracy, use the best of modernism's emancipatory commitment to freedom, rationality, and choice while incorporating postmodernism's basic tenets of difference, multiple-subject positionality, and identity confusion? The "moral and political content of one's identity," especially as it is related to the "maldistribution of human resources," as Cornel West claims, becomes the stuff of democracy.[15] How democracy is embodied within the particular struggle that initiates a universal sensibility is of major concern to me, particularly when linked to the educational context. For example, the Outcome-Based Education reform movement in my home state of Pennsylvania asks teachers to adhere to fifty-three different basic outcomes for assessing and measuring the abilities of all students before they graduate from high school. It would be foolish of me to argue that all students who have been assessed against these outcomes have performed similarly. A critically important feature of this reform movement is that it *allows* teachers *time* to accomplish the outcomes and define what an outcome could mean, given the context of its occurance.[16] So although the outcome concerned with *citizenship* requires that "all students understand the history and nature of prejudice and relate their knowledge to current issues facing communities, the United States and other nations," particular teachers and students are left to struggle over its interpretation. These struggles over meaning can have *potentially pragmatic* "critical" applications to various educational contexts.

With the above in mind, I want to argue that education has come to the "moral" end of one sovereign metanarrative story. That is, schools can no longer afford to continue their belief in the grand narrative of emancipation. The results have been devastating.[17] Race, class, and gender disparities are simply overwhelming. The institutionalism of ghettoism borders on a plague. AIDS, high school dropout, and teenage suicide rates are drastically increasing.[18] Indeed, another sovereign story, or another narrative, must be negotiated in lieu of the old demoralizing and decapitating one. I want to argue that this new sovereign story is theoretically loaded with both modern and postmodern tendencies, and particular and universal generalities. More importantly, however, the idea of another sovereign narrative is a moral and spiritual struggle that transcends mere theoretical deconstruction and, instead, enters into the guts of democratic hopes, possibilities, and dreams. Thus, to begin to address the moral content of identity within democracy forces us to raise interesting questions of the radical democratic project as related to education: the death of master narratives and the possible construction of others.

I will discuss Lyotard's view of the sovereign. I view the sovereign within the context of a critical democratic theoretical and practical struggle in schools. I conclude my argument with an evaluation of a new sovereignty, despite postmodern difference—a narrative that is both moral and spiritual, in agreement and in disagreement with Lyotard. It is one that involves the particular within the universal, and one that presents us with cultural political possibilities indebted, in large part, to the legacy of Lyotard's thinking.

LYOTARD AND THE SOVEREIGN

It is interesting to note, as Lyotard argues, that "the project of modernity (the realization of universality) has not been forsaken or forgotten but destroyed, liquidated."[19] Lyotard forcefully argues that although there may be some credible local narratives, the idea that any grand narrative may exist has no credibility. Despite all this, Lyotard is vehement that his argument is not to obliterate others' stories or small narratives "from continuing to weave the fabric of everyday life."[20]

Lyotard, like Foucault, argues that regimes of truth imply many small narratives of the everyday, what other postmodernists generally conceive of as "differences." In related fashion, Peter McLaren has tied social struggle to the notion of "voice,"[21] and Henry Giroux has coined democratic struggles as "borders" of understanding and interpretations of micronarrative theoretical and practical accounts.[22] Feminists in education have argued for gender space to contest grand hegemonic narratives,[23] and multiculturalists in and out of education have called for constructing border identities to challenge social and cultural imposition, such as patriarchy and white middle-class domination.[24]

Within the above theoretical formulations, critical educationalists argue, following Lyotard, that indeed there cannot be a grand narrative that governs academic institutions. These critics cite how the conservative and even liberal views of education have only exacerbated the power structure of the dominant order, either by masking what really is (a more conservative discourse) or by making pseudo-liberal progressive changes to instructional sites (such as site-based management, educational reform movements, or empowering teachers and students). Within the modern, Lyotard states, history has not ended with a grand narrative or sovereign story; indeed, "the finality of human history is another means of destroying the project of modernity while giving the impression of completing it."[25] Lyotard attests that there can be no grand narrative or sovereign story if there is always a process of delegitimation, where educators face a world both seduced and sanctioned by the live power of dead signs. Delegitimation occurs in schools when the projects of teacher effectiveness, teacher and student empowerment, school choice, site-based management, and outcome-based education, for instance, obfuscate the urgency of addressing demoralizing school conditions. Legitimation functions, argues Lyotard, to tell stories of others, to create "different regimes of phrases and different genres of discourse."[26] Legitimation also functions through "parology," the ability to "identify and undermine the metaprescriptions of established language games by constant innovation and experimentation in order to generate new ideas."[27] Not only language games but other cultural artifacts, symbols, and gestures become the stuff of "affective investment" into a realm of postmodern, emancipatory democratic struggle and possibility.[28]

It is no small claim to make, as Lyotard does, that "postmodernity is at the end of the people as sovereign of their stories,"[29] that "we can resort neither to the dialectic of Spirit nor even to the emancipation of humanity as a validation for postmodern scientific discourse."[30] Disturbing to me are two issues. First, if there are regimes of truth and phrases and/or discourses as legitimation processes within *particular* subjective experiences, it follows that particular kinds of sovereignty and spirits of emancipation can exist. Where, then, does the postmodern condition turn to for legitimation if there is no sovereignty? Pure ludic deconstruction by bourgeois theorists who impose postmodern suavities simply exalt theory as a type of travelogue, a form "of fatal attentiveness to difference and infinite heterogeneity."[31] Second, if there is no general, master, or grand narrative made up of smaller emancipatory narratives, where does this leave critical educational postmodernists regarding a committed political and common agenda of social transformation within our schools? If we are to take Lyotard's argument to the extreme—that postmodernism is the end of people as sovereign stories, despite the "particular," sovereign emancipatory story—then we must ask ourselves: Is there any room for a radical politics of solidarity that can make a coordinated social transformation stance or "narrative" a plausible process?

Lyotard has thus provided the impetus for me to argue, at least theoretically, for a development of a social project that can further explain and perhaps prove more capable of transforming the education context. Optimistically I move ahead, despite my constant reminder of George Counts's old revolutionary question: Dare the school build a new social order?[32] Within this question lie the same inevitable challenges to postmodernists in education that the progressive views of Counts faced over sixty years ago! Although I believe that critical pedagogy needs to play a greater part in reformulating the role of historical and educational agency in this postmodern era, we must take pains to avoid this democratic possibility's becoming another master narrative, sovereign truth, or essentialist reconstruction. However, to ask the question that the democratic postmodern critics in education still ask—Dare the school build a new social order?—presupposes that particular narrative accounts (voices, borders, fragmented identities, multiple subjectivities) be placed within a sovereign possibility, hope, or ideal, indeed, a sovereign utopia, or what I will later argue for as moral and spiritual possibilities. It is this imperative as a transitionary or provisional state that may lead to democratic hopes, one that Lyotard abandons in his deconstruction of the postmodern condition.

THE ABANDONMENT OF UNITY IN LYOTARD AND DEMOCRATIC POSSIBILITIES

It is no small claim for Lyotard and other postmodernists to make, that the unity of experience, particularly sociocultural unity as an organic whole, *cannot* be conceived within the postmodern condition. I have argued elsewhere, however, that while unity of experience is not real in that subjects can never experience the same totality of "experience," there still can be sets of experiences that bind social agents together despite their particular differences (race, class, gender, identity, etc.).[33]

Lost within the critical emancipatory discourse of difference and disharmony committed to promoting a more democratic (communal, dialogical) public sphere is the notion of identity within solidarity, unity, and commonality. The deconstruction of difference in education has not been tolerated or amplified as the totality of unified exploration of *similar* struggles that will oppose oppressive, alienating, and subordinative conditions and may lead to affirmations of community, dialogue, identity, and intersubjective relatedness. Lost within education postmodernity is the enlightenment hope that Jürgen Habermas brought to our attention within his unified communicative subject position.[34] Lost in postmodern education theorizing is any hope that democracy can rear its head. And absent within postmodern theorizing in education is development of the particularity of experience within a unified subject or common goal or good. The above comments are *not* an argument to abandon metanarrative experiences or particularity of difference. It is an argument, however, to seriously consider Lyotard's interesting assumption: "A work can become modern only if it is first postmodern. Postmodernism thus understood is not modernism at its end but in the nascent state, and this state is constant."[35] I query if modernism exists for Lyotard at all, yet the above quote suggests that somewhere within the postmodern "nascent" state there exists modernistic assumptions and norms.

Some postmodernist theorists in education have argued for the incorporation of the best of modernity, its most emancipatory and democratic impulses as a necessary condition for understanding postmodern sensibilities, particularly in relation to borders of understanding between race, class, and gender configurations.[36] For the moment, anyway, I would like to consider Lyotard's notion of work, quoted above, as more than art or text production; something related to education as site-specific, with its own artistic design, text, and museum, one that has its own postmodern transitional "nascent" state. It is no new argument to make that schools in the United States are filled with difference, disparity, oppression, alienation, and subordination. One of the grandest mistakes made by education policy makers over the years is the creation of the conservative view that schools are places where everyone has an equal opportunity to commodify their schooling. One visit to an inner-city school will quickly dispel this notion. In its best and most emancipatory senses, schools talk a good "modern" lingo: empowering teachers and students, site-based management, creating student critical thinkers, and so on. Lyotard's position here would cite schools as markers of multiple difference. Schools are first postmodern. I remind readers of Lyotard's position: A work can become modern only if it is first postmodern; "postmodernism thus understood, is not modernism at its end but in the nascent state, and this state is constant." If one takes this argument further, schools represent moving and transitional states of the postmodern, within multiple sensibilities, realities, differences, and narratives, but moving toward what I have described in my earlier works as a democratic possibility, or as Ernesto Laclau and Mouffe have argued for earlier,[37] as a "democratic imaginary"—those common acts of subjects that lead to struggle against alienation, subordination, and domination.

As an aside to schools for the moment, the postmodern political project has not viewed common and different elements of cultural conflict as connected to emancipatory and democratic intents.[38] Social movements described earlier can be labeled as extending a common democratic denominator, in which resistances to the oppressive conditions of advanced capitalism, with its resulting alienation and subordination of workers, the poor and the underpaid, give rise to a new set of social relations. Opposing the class-reductionistic view of the subject, I believe that these democratically inspired conflicts are at least a starting point for understanding how acts of meaning and interpretation, politicizing identity and ending subordination, can share similar features. In a larger sense, the new social movements create forms of participatory democracy. Recognizing the similarities and differences of movements of oppressed peoples partially ameliorates the one-sidedness of these social movements. Bound within the multiple constructions of different and competing discourses, aspirations, and hopes is the *commonality* of struggle that binds social agents in their existential and intersubjective experiences. Laclau and Mouffe argue that these cultural frictions serve as the inevitable challenge of the postmodern and are intimately tied to a counterhegemonic strategy or "democratic imaginary."

Related to schools, if we are to take Lyotard's view that the postmodern exists prior to the modern or any commonality of emancipatory ex-

perience, we must seriously ask, as Lyotard does, if the totality of experience is even possible given these postmodern sensibilities? Or is a
common view of democracy, given multifarious differences of school sites
and race, class, and gender disparities at schools, an alternative to the
already stultifying system in place? The answer would seem to be simple:
Within the postmodern condition of difference—the moving subject and
identity confusion—lies the hope that schools *can* progressively move in
a common way to the modernistic quest for human emancipation. Put more
practically, there may be gender conflicts in one school and racial tensions
in another, or there may be racial and gender contestation in different parts
of the same school. What guides the democratic imaginary and emancipatory hopes is the reliance of postmodern difference as a marker to help
make schools qualitatively better places for students, teachers, and connected employees. Perhaps the multicultural movement the world over,
but particularly in the United States, is an example of postmodern difference infiltrating the curriculum of public schools and higher learning
institutions. I am not arguing that all institutes adopt into their curriculum
what critical educationalists generally call critical multiculturalism. Nor
am I arguing that on-site management, for example, be viewed as a border
for teachers and principals only to cash out differences. Nor can teacher
empowerment be viewed as the end to teacher alienation. Enough literature
has shown how these areas of educational interests act to hegemonize
social relations.[39] What I am arguing is that multifarious difference has
been raised in the consciousness of educational institutions as well as of
businesses in training their minority personnel.

Teacher empowerment and on-site management hold postmodern possibilities and sensibilities, particularly as meaning-making can be negotiated. The movement to the modern notion of community, characterized by
freedom, democracy, and the struggle for space among the disadvantaged
and minority, especially on the institutional level, though admittedly in its
infancy is, nevertheless, a movement based on the emancipatory modernistic hope of equalizing social relations. At best the struggles and hopes
within the postmodern world, supported by democratic imaginary pos-
sibiliites at schools, share a sense of community, dialogue, and intersubjectivity that bind people together despite their sundry differences. Lyotard
states the postmodern to be "that which denies itself the solace of good
forms, the consensus of a taste which would make it possible to share
collectively the nostalgia for the unattainable; that which searches for new
presentations not in order to enjoy them but in order to impart a stronger
sense of the 'unpresentable.' "[40] Lost within the un*re*presentable is the
proliferation of particular social and political struggles in the 1990s that

point to the *particular* within universal hopes, dreams, and aspirations.[41] It seems to me that if critical educators are to affect public schools or higher-learning institutions, the particular must be represented within a broader context of democratic struggle, meaning-making, and challenges to dominant and oppressive social forms. Such was the case with the studies of teachers that I conducted in a number of different social sites (albeit different schools), where gender, race, and class struggles expressed a manifest difference, struggle over identity, and multiple subjectivity. These features did not mean, however, that within difference there was not a struggled-for common good sought by teachers to conquer unequal social relations.[42] The common good can function as a "social imaginary," one function of which it is to consider "a condition of possibility of any representation within the space that it delimits."[43]

As critical educators we need to understand that the kinds of struggles engaged in by teachers and professors who adopt a critical approach borders on what McLaren has described as an "epochal transition," in which there are multiple Marxisms, feminisms, and so on, that while promising liberation also splinter the left social movement. What both McLaren and I, among other critical educationalists, are calling for is not the abandonment of the unrepresentable but some form of totalizing vision, an "arch of social dreaming" that "gives shape, coherence, and protection to the unity of our collective struggles . . . against domination and for freedom while preserving the specificity of difference."[44]

SOVEREIGN OF POSSIBILITY

Critical educators need to understand that within multiple theoretical formulations of liberalisms, Marxisms, feminisms, and so on, a sovereign of possibility must be sought as a common good if we are to make any social and political inroads into the dominant culture. I am not suggesting that we abandon multiple theoretical formulations as the knowledge construction of regimes of truth. Nor am I suggesting that all desires, hopes, and dreams (or oppressions) are totally similar. Equally so, I am not suggesting that all school sites are similar, with the same empowerment, on-site management, and multicultural agendas. I *am*, however, calling for a form of a totalizing vision. McLaren's view of an "arch of social dreaming" is pertinent to my argument: "This arch of social dreaming is meant to give shape, coherence, and protection to the unity of our collective struggles. It means the conquest of a vision of what the total transformation of society might mean."[45] This vision necessarily starts within the postmodern rupture of difference as a reference point for a renewal of the modernistic democratic possibility. Of course, this possibility presupposes that a "common struggle against domination and for freedom while preserving the specificity of difference" *itself* becomes a totalizing and sovereign force and discourse.[46]

This sovereign of possibility, in my mind, borders on a spiritual struggle that connects and intertwines theoretical and practical difference. It centers on what David Purpel and other liberation theologists describe as a search for a vision of possibility that has its roots in connectedness with a higher belief in Spirit, or even God.[47] For Cornel West, this struggle for meaning, and ultimately for democracy, "is an ethical implication of the Christian conception of what it means to be human, how we understand democracy, what is its content, its substance."[48] For bell hooks and West, struggle is rooted in one's faith and commitment to a higher moral vision. Democracy for West and hooks is necessarily a belief in God that "is understood in relation to a particular context, to particular circumstances."[49] They see it as a commitment to enduring one's faith despite the suffering that might occur because of one's belief or the particular circumstances one may experience.[50] Within the specific context of struggle and belief, Lyotard's notion of difference allows the educator the space to hold at bay the desire for closure, coherence, and totality. And within absence, uncertainty, partiality, and relativity, it provides a reason for the search within the conflict of meanings for a common dream of moral certitude, a certitude that begs criteria and yet suggests a moral imperative and a fabric of the highest "faithful" order. It is a commonplace to claim, as Purpel and other liberation theologists argue, that we live in times of moral and spiritual decay. Within the declining moral order critical educators are faced with postmodern uncertainties. There is a desperate need for critically searching for common, democratic imperatives that attempt to replace the present state of uncertainty and moral ineptness. Clearly, this is a daunting task that cannot be viewed from one theoretical or practical context. In the face of the moral and spiritual debacles of our culture and schools, I begin to wonder whether postmodernism has to offer any pragmatic emancipatory hope and I am driven to interrogate the moral fabric of the nihilistic postmodernist theorists, Lyotard included, who lack a unified vision for the common good, a vision of faith or order, to repair or represent the common hopes and dreams of ordinary people—that is, a new vision of sovereignty. As bell hooks comments: "I am waiting for them to stop talking about the 'other,' to stop even describing how important it is to be able to speak about difference . . . often this speech about the other is also a mask, and annihilates, erases."[51] Hooks does not mean to abandon the other, or even to deny difference; rather, he elaborates a sense of calling upon the tradition to "break bread together," to sit in commonality, as Jews do the world over during Passover, or Christ did when he broke bread with his Jewish disciples before his self-sacrifice. In Judeo-Christian tradition the image of searching for and finding freedom and salvation through sacrifice, of giving of oneself to others, is an ongoing process that involves the metaphor of breaking bread, "sharing in domestic, secular and sacred life where we come together to give of ourselves to one another fully."[52] This necessarily implies coming together, or as Nicholas Burbules and S. Rice comment in terms of the liberal tradition, simply "talking together" across differences.[53] It is within this "coming together" that critical educators are faced with the intellectual and moral task of first combining theoretical understandings (despite postmodern ruptures) and then attempting to create a new moral and democratic imperative that does not impose authoritatively but speaks for and with others in a unified vision of the social, moral, and spiritual.

CONCLUSION

In calling for the end to all metanarratives, Lyotard is arguing for the abandonment of all forms of totality. Yet as A. T. Nuyen comments, according to Lyotard:

There is no longer any point in talking about God, Spirit, Form, humanity, ego cogito, other than an attempt to achieve some local effects, with values confined to a localized context (such as God in the context of worship, Spirit in the context of dialectics, and so on). Instead of a grand narrative that can legitimate other discourses, we are faced with a series of petits récits, of local "perspectives," of diverse language games, each with its own set of rules. Such is the postmodern condition as far as Lyotard is concerned.[54]

Despite the presence of "differends," critical educational theorists argue that for democracy to flourish within education, teachers and professors must teach students to make informed judgment and commitment in a social world where "solidarity with the human condition or sensitivity to the human environment" are both necessary and desirable.[55]

I conclude this chapter on two levels. First, at the theoretical level are two important questions raised by Mustafa Kiziltan, William Bain, and Anita Canizares concerning the relation between enlightenment and education, given the postmodern condition. They ask:

Can the concept of enlightenment be reconsidered in such a way that it provides meaning and purpose to a disenchanted discourse of public education? If the answer is positive, or at least promising, then, can we envision a theory of public education, one which breaks from the metanarratives of modernity and which is not bound to the technicist logic of performativity and yet can be supported by the new idea of enlightenment?[56]

Embedded within these questions is an understanding that a new theory of democracy in education must begin by abandoning the "banking" concept of education, which is an instrument of oppression for both students and teachers.[57] Although this idea is not new, it is a first step toward revitalizing a democratic education. More specifically, and as a result of reading Lyotard's work, within this revitalization—what Kiziltan and his colleagues call the new idea of enlightenment—can there also be a renewed vigor of social and cultural commitment, a solidarity of sorts, or simply "a common voice"?[58] That is, can there be a new or provisional sovereignty that has at its roots human compassion and care, nurture and justice, equity and faith? I have argued that in order to overcome oppression, alienation, and subordination a revitalized democratic ideal—different and yet holding similar emancipatory qualities—must be struggled over for any significant change to occur. This must take place on the pragmatic level.

Of course, this means that the postmodern social milieu must be understood within specific sites as both partial and transitional. I have also argued that within a discourse of possibility and "arch of social dreaming," enlightenment ideals will have to be met by adhering to the very norms of modernity: the quest for free thinking, rational behavior, and normative criteria for simply living one's life everyday. This necessarily has to do with a *prophetic* democratic ideal where "democracy becomes an ethical implication about content and substance."[59] It is a vision that, as West asserts, "has to do with the coming of the kingdom, with the empowerment that flows from the breaking and invading of a kingdom that on the one hand is beyond our power and on the other hand is inseparable from what we do. We are kingdom-bound. We are never kingdom-creating, but we stay in contact with its power."[60] Within the kingdom that West describes lie both postmodern and modern ideals. Postmodernism is *beyond our power* as well as *inseparable from* what we do. To begin to deconstruct the postmodern kingdom from a critical perspective is to create and stay in contact with what a new kingdom or new sovereignty may look and feel like. This represents the best of modernist ideals where democracy can be renegotiated and reconstructed. Education, then, rests within the striving to attain the highest moral norms and standards to build what could be considered a just and fair "kingdom" for others.

On the more pragmatic level, what could this mean? First, within difference, every school site has its own kingdom or "internal cohesion," its own possible democratic site—its own particular "subsystem of the social system."[61] It was argued earlier that all school sites display different kinds of struggles, be they based on race, class, or gender. And because of this, and because children's experiences differ culturally and socially, special concessions will have to be made by teachers to "hear" or "listen to" diversity. Lyotard makes an apposite remark in this regard:

As child or immigrant, one enters a culture through an apprenticeship in proper names. One must learn the names that designate near relations, heroes (in a general sense), places, dates, and also, I would add, units of measure, space, time and exchange value. . . . Names are not learned by themselves—they are lodged in little stories. Again, narrative's strength lies in its capacity to hold together a multiplicity of heterogeneous families of discourse . . . narrative arranges these families into a sequence of events.[62]

Clearly, the individual voice and the "particular" story or narrative play a part in Lyotard's "politics of difference." Within the everyday world occupied by teachers, the particular must be understood within the universal in order to grasp the nature of a unified vision of democracy. This means a tremendous amount of work by critical educationalists—a daunting task given the current bureaucratic and positivistic gestalt of education, which functions as a field of knowledge and also involves the social and cultural reproduction of teachers not only as pawns of the state but also as race-, class-, and gender-inflicted subjects.

Within schools, subject areas such as social studies, geography, English literature, art, ethnic literature, or dance appreciation must critically center each child's particular narrative—each child's similar and different cultural experiences—within a common, albeit shifting, democratic imaginary. Democratic participation of students in learning about multiple meanings could open up these subject areas to both more individual and more collective dialogue, their multiple interpretations, and the way meanings are negotiated. A new and revitalized sovereignty in schools, one that is passionate and committed to a communal vision of democracy, will be further supported by teachers' collective questioning of oppressive school policies and practices such as "tracking," all forms of gate-keeping, exams, sexual and racial discrimination, state mandates about curriculum, and union activities. This vision also implies that teachers take on cooperative learning as an emancipatory norm, where difference is negotiated and expressed, and possessive individualism and rampant forms of competition are challenged as part of a democratic process of learning. Under such a regime each individual voice and narrative is heard as different but nevertheless remains a part of this "arch of social dreaming" called democracy. Thus, each school must develop its own internal narrative, despite its social-class location. Each school has the potential to break down old structures and create its own "regimes of truth," its own provisional and particular democracy within the general, universal whole.

As an educator I feel that it is imperative not to lose sight of the democratic imperative enshrined in our constitution. Within this constitution lies the possibility of building a community of faith that transcends similarities and differences and, eventually, even human suffering and travails. As educators we must seriously scrutinize Lyotard's view of the abandonment of the sovereign and the grand narrative, even if we agree with him. Those of us who remain somewhat idealistic and utopian, wedded to democratic hope and, therefore, in opposition to Lyotard's total abandonment of any metanarrative, must remain committed to a compelling vision that begins to build bridges of faith, borders of similarities and differences, and instill ethics into discussion and bring politics into all phases of our theoretical discourses. Only when we seriously and studiously accept this challenge as a *common framework* of reference will critical postmodernism become a theoretical referent to challenge mainstream consciousness, epistemological certainty, ideological tentativeness, and any metanarrative tradition. Only then can we in solidarity confront the possibility of a new sovereignty for education, a revitalized and provisional metanarrative that is always open to scrutiny, always negotiable, but that has as its core basic human dignity, respect, and care. Maxine Greene perhaps best sums up the moral imperative we face as a united body of critical educators:

There has to be some reference to, some taking into account of, certain notions of good and bad, right and wrong. In this time of numbness and multiplicity, we are not only interested in feelings of "oughtness" or obligatoriness. We are interested in certain shared beliefs about what is to be considered desirable and undesirable, good and bad, right and wrong. At once, we are concerned with how conscience is or can be developed in diverse human beings and how persons can be moved to define their moral purposes as they tell the stories of their lives.[63]

NOTES

1. Manning Marable, *The Crisis of Color and Democracy* (Maine: Common Courage Press, 1992), p. 258.

2. See, for instance, Ernesto Laclau and Chantal Mouffe, *Hegemony and the Socialist Strategy: Towards a Radical Democratic Politics* (London: Verso, 1985); Chantal Mouffe, "Hegemony and New Political Subjects: Towards a New Concept of Democracy," in *Marxism and the Interpretation of Culture*, ed. Cary Nelson and Lawrence Grossberg (Chicago: University of Illinois Press, 1988); Chantal Mouffe, "Citizenship and Political Identity," *October* 61 (1992): 33–45; Ernesto Laclau, "Metaphor and Social Antagonisms," in *Marxism and the Interpretation of Culture*, ed. Cary Nelson and Lawrence Grossberg; Ernesto Laclau, "Universalism, Particularism, and the Question of Identity," *October* 61 (1992): 83–90; Cornel West, *Prophetic Reflections* (Maine: Common Courage Press, 1993); Lawrence Grossberg, *We Gotta Get out of This Place: Popular, Conservative and Postmodern Culture* (New York: Routledge, 1992); Linda Hutcheon, *The Politics of Postmodernism* (London: Routledge, 1989); Marable, *The Crisis of Color and Democracy.*

3. See, for instance, Svi Shapiro, *Between Capitalism and Democracy* (New York: Bergin and Garvey, 1990); Barry Kanpol and Peter McLaren, eds., *Critical Multiculturalism: Uncommon Voices in a Common Struggle* (New York: Bergin and Garvey, 1994); Barry Kanpol, *Towards a Theory and Practice of Teacher Cultural Politics: Continuing the Postmodern Debate* (New Jersey: Ablex, 1992); Michael Peters, "Radical Democracy, the Politics of Difference and Education," in *Critical Multiculturalism: Uncommon Voices in a Common Struggle*, ed. Kanpol and McLaren; Kathleen Weiler, *Women Teaching for Change* (New York: Bergin and Garvey, 1987); Michelle Fine, *Framing Dropouts: Notes on the Politics of an Urban High School* (Albany, N.Y.: SUNY Press, 1991); Frank Pignatelli, "Towards a Postprogressive Theory of Education," *Educational Foundations* 7, 3 (1993): 7–26; Henry Giroux, *Living Dangerously* (New York: Peter Lang, 1993).

4. For example, the deskilling literature; see Michael Apple, *Teachers and Texts* (London: Routledge, 1988); P. S. Hbelewitsh, "The Teacher Technician: Causes and Consequences," *Journal of Educational Thought* 24, 3A (1990): 147–60.

5. Jonathan Kozol, *Savage Inequalities* (New York: Crown, 1991); Fred Yeo, "The Conflicts of Differences in an Inner City School: Experiencing Border Crossings in the Ghetto," in *Critical Multiculturalism: Uncommon Voices in a Common Struggle*, ed. Kanpol and McLaren; Michelle Fine, "Sexuality Schooling and Adolescent Females: The Missing Discourse of Desire," *Harvard Educational Review* 58, 1 (1988): 29–53.

6. On the pragmatic aspects of the debate see Kanpol, *Theory and Practice.*

7. See Douglas Kellner, *Critical Theory, Marxism and Modernity* (Cambridge and Baltimore: Polity Press and Johns Hopkins University Press, 1989); Kanpol, *Theory and Practice*; Lisa Appignanesi, ed., *Postmodernism: ICA Documents* (London: Free Association Books, 1989); Scott Lash, *Sociology of Postmodernism* (Boston: Routledge, 1990); Henry Giroux, *Border Crossings* (Boston: Routledge, 1992).

8. Jean-François Lyotard, *The Postmodern Explained to Children: Correspondence 1982–1985*, trans. and ed. Julian Pefanis and Morgan Thomas (Minneapolis: University of Minnesota Press, 1992), p. 12.

9. Ibid., p. 27 and p. 31.

10. Laclau, "Universalism, Particularism, and the Question of Identity," p. 87.

11. David Purpel, *The Moral and Spiritual Crisis in Public Education* (New York: Bergin and Garvey, 1989).

12. Mouffe, "Citizenship and Political Identity," p. 90.

13. Jean-François Lyotard, *The Postmodern Condition: A Report on Knowledge*, trans. Geoff Bennington and Brian Massumi (Minneapolis: University of Minnesota Press, 1984), p. 48.

14. Ibid.

15. Cornel West, "A Matter of Life and Death," *October* 61 (1992): 21.

16. Unlike the older system where teachers had specific time slots to complete academic units, teachers can now choose to complete or extend an outcome based upon their particular perspective and/or preference. This opens the door for the more socially conscious teacher to introduce more socially oriented material without state control.

17. See Kozol, *Savage Inequalities*.

18. See Donna Gaines, *Teenage Wasteland* (New York: Harper-Collins, 1992).

19. Lyotard, *The Postmodern Explained*, p. 18.

20. Ibid., p. 19.

21. Peter McLaren, *Life in Schools*, 2nd. ed. (Boston: Longman, 1994).

22. Giroux, *Border Crossings*.

23. See Madeline Grumet, *Bitter Milk* (Boston: Routledge, 1988); Elizabeth Ellsworth, "Why Doesn't This Feel Empowering? Working through the Repressive Myths of Critical Pedagogy," *Harvard Educational Review* 58, 3 (1989): 280–98; Patti Lather, *Getting Smart* (Boston: Routledge, 1991); Jennifer Gore, "What Can We Do for You! What Can 'We' Do for 'You'? Struggling over Empowerment in Critical and Feminist Pedagogy," *Educational Foundations* 4, 3 (1990): 5–26.

24. See, for example, Carl Grant and Judith Sachs, "Multicultural Education and Postmodernism: Movement Toward Dialogue," in *Critical Multiculturalism: Uncommon Voices in a Common Struggle*, ed. Kanpol and McLaren; West, "A Matter of Life and Death"; bell hooks, *Talking Back* (Boston: South End Press, 1989); Beverly Gordon, "Fringe Dwellers: African American Women Scholars in the Postmodern Condition," in *Critical Multiculturalism: Uncommon Voices in a Common Struggle*, ed. Kanpol and McLaren.

25. Lyotard, *The Postmodern Explained*, p. 18.

26. Ibid., p. 20.

27. Carol Nicholson, "Postmodernism, Feminism, and Education: The Need for Solidarity," *Educational Theory* 39, 3 (1989): 199.

28. For the use of this term see Grossberg, *We Gotta Get out of This Place*.

29. Lyotard, *The Postmodern Explained*, p. 20.

30. Ibid., p. 60.

31. Barry Kanpol and Peter McLaren, "Introduction," in *Critical Multiculturalism: Uncommon Voices in a Common Struggle*, ed. Kanpol and McLaren, p. 3.

32. George Counts, *Dare the School Build a New Social Order?* (New York: John Day Co., 1932).

33. Kanpol, *Theory and Practice*.

34. Jürgen Habermas, "Modernity versus Postmodernity," *New German Critique* 22 (1981): 3–22.

35. Lyotard, *The Postmodern Condition*, p. 79.

36. See Giroux, *Border Crossings*; Nicholson, "Postmodernism, Feminism and Education"; Nicholas Burbules and S. Rice, "Dialogue across Differences: Continuing the Conversation," *Harvard Educational Review* 61, 4 (1991): 393–416.

37. Laclau and Mouffe, *Hegemony and the Socialist Strategy*.

38. Kellner, *Critical Theory, Marxism and Modernity*.

39. See, for example, Michael Apple, "The Text and Cultural Politics," *Journal of Educational Thought* 24, 3A (1990): 17–33; Kevin Harris, *Teachers and Social Classes* (Boston: Routledge, 1982); Phillip Corrigan, "Untying the Knots: The Texts of the State," *Journal of Educational Thought* 24, 3A (1990): 46–67.

40. Lyotard, *The Postmodern Condition*, p. 81.

41. Laclau, "Universalism, Particularism, and the Question of Identity."

42. See Kanpol, *Theory and Practice*.

43. Mouffe, "Citizenship and Political Identity," p. 30.

44. Peter McLaren, "Schooling and the Postmodern Body: Critical Pedagogy and the Politics of Enfleshment," in *Postmodernism, Feminism and Cultural Politics*, ed. Henry Giroux (New York: Bergin and Garvey, 1991), p. 170.

45. Ibid.

46. Ibid.

47. Purpel, *The Moral and Spiritual Crisis in Education*.

48. Cornel West, *Beyond Eurocentrism and Multiculturalism*, vol. 1, *Prophetic Thought in Postmodern Times* (Maine: Common Courage Press, 1993), p. 225.

49. bell hooks and Cornel West, *Breaking Bread* (Boston: South End Press, 1991), p. 9.

50. We could refer to the suffering of Paul in the New Testament as well as the sufferings of others. Paul's commitment to the teaching of Jesus, particularly while in jail, can be viewed as a reference point to understand struggle of the highest moral and spiritual order. Nothing could stop Paul in his commitment of faith. No less can be said of Martin Luther King's struggle or those of other black leaders (including black feminists), or for that matter the Israelites' struggle out of slavery in Egypt and Moses' commitment to his vision of faith. They, as Paul, also "rejoiced in our sufferings, because we know that suffering produces perseverance; perseverance, character; and character hope, and hope does not disappoint us" (Romans 5:3–5). Their hopes, I believe, extended a humane vision of democratic community justice in the world of the everyday, despite the particular circumstances people find themselves in. West (*Beyond Eurocentrism*, vol. 2, *Prophetic Reflections: Notes on Race and Power in America*, p. 16) argues, quite forcefully, that despite slavery, it was a commitment to a "faith" vision of prophetic Christianity—"that every individual regardless of class, country, caste, race, or sex should have the opportunity to fulfill his or her potentialities"—that drove black Christians to an understanding of and commitment to this world liberation *and* other world liberation, *despite the circumstances*. The this world liberation was a political and social quest, a social freedom. The other world liberation was an existential freedom to do with one's enduring faith commitment.

51. bell hooks, "Marginality as Site of Resistance," in Russell Ferguson, Martha Gever, Trinh T. Minh-ha, and Cornel West, *Out There: Marginalization and Contemporary Cultures* (Cambridge, Mass.: MIT Press, 1992), p. 342.

52. hooks and West, *Breaking Bread*, p. 6.

53. Burbules and Rice, "Dialogue across Differences."

54. A. T. Nuyen, "Lyotard on the Death of the Professor," *Educational Theory* 42, 1 (1992): 30. See Chapter 3 this volume for a revised version of this article.

55. Nicholson, "Postmodernism, Feminism and Education," p. 200.

56. Mustafa U. Kiziltan, William J. Bain, and Anita Canizares M., "Postmodern Conditions: Rethinking Public Education," *Educational Theory* 40, 3 (Summer 1990): 361.

57. Paulo Friere, *Education for Critical Consciousness* (New York: Seabury Press, 1973).

58. Eamonn Callan, "Finding a Common Voice," *Educational Theory* 42, 4 (1992): 429–41.

59. West, *Prophetic Thought in Postmodern Times*, p. 225.

60. Ibid.

61. Lyotard, *The Postmodern Condition*, p. 48.

62. Lyotard, *The Postmodern Explained*, p. 31.

63. Maxine Greene, "Values Education in the Contemporary Moment," *Clearing House*, May/June 1991: 302.

9 Pedagogy and Apedagogy: Lyotard and Foucault at Vincennes

James Marshall

We must be the salt of truth in the wound of alienation.
Jean-François Lyotard, "Preamble to a Charter"

The events of May-June 1968 in France were described by Edgar Morin as "the student maelstrom,"[1] and by André Gorz as "the first major revolutionary crisis to have shaken capitalist Europe in the last thirty years."[2] Alain Touraine said, "The May Movement was a thunderbolt announcing the social struggles of the future."[3] In response to the student uprisings, President Charles de Gaulle said on May 19, 1968, "Les reforms, oui, la chienlit, non."[4] Later he was to say that the students' activities were "misadventures" and that "there had been a crisis of civilization," as opposed to a "drama of students."[5] There were clearly major disagreements about these events and what they represented. In education there were those who saw the proposed educational reforms as even further manifestations of the technocratic-capitalist state, and they had good reason, as the technocratic wing of the Gaullist party certainly wished for major technocratic reforms of the universities, if not to destroy the liberal university.[6] There were those—reformists—who saw the universities and the schools as being hopelessly outmoded, though not all who saw the universities as being in need of reform were technocratic-capitalist reformers (Michel Foucault was one such person). Within those two broad factions were considerable minor factions, locked in disagreements and internal battles.

Jean-François Lyotard was at Nanterre where events erupted educationally on May 3rd, and he was involved in the movement of March 22nd.[7] He was therefore at the center of the action. Michel Foucault was not even in France but in Tunisia (though he did visit very briefly in May); and for some people, that "he hadn't done anything" was cause for reproach.[8] But in late 1968 Foucault was to become head of the philosophy department at the new "experimental" campus of the University of Paris, at Vincennes. Lyotard was to join the department later. Broadly, Lyotard and Foucault were both on the left, and intellectually there are certain similarities between their positions on a number of issues. For example they both discounted metanarratives, grand theory, and foundational approaches to reason, believing in multiplicities of reason, and of power; both believed that the notion of the intellectual, as portrayed, for example, by Jean-Paul Sartre, was dead; both attacked Sartre;[9] both questioned the liberating claims of the Enlightenment message; and both believed in the importance of "art" in providing a counter to the logocentric rationalistic claims of Western thought. But there were differences.[10]

In particular at Vincennes they held different positions toward pedagogy, and therefore toward the form that participation and education at Vincennes should and could take. A part of the political response to May-June, Vincennes was to be the model of the "new" universities; it was to be interdisciplinary, on the cutting edge of research, and it was to be democratically structured. Here the Gaullist catchword was *participation*. But participation had meant one thing for ministers of education Christian Fouchet and Edgar Faure, and another for the students. The position adopted by Foucault and Lyotard rested clearly on the side of the students, but they took different paths on the form that pedagogy should take to enhance the left's version of participation. Foucault remained almost as a classical academic, whereas Lyotard sought a different form of pedagogy, coining the term *apedagogy*.[11] Their different positions on pedagogy will be developed below.

This chapter is divided into three main sections. The first section looks at the reforms promoted by the de Gaulle government between 1966 and 1970, and in particular at those reforms of the universities promoted by Christian Fouchet in 1966, and at Edgar Faure's 1968 proposals for the *loi d'orientation*, which was accompanied by the setting up of Vincennes. Foucault's and Lyotard's respective responses to participation and pedagogy are discussed in the last two sections.

FRENCH EDUCATIONAL REFORMS IN THE 1960s

This section concerns itself with the educational reforms introduced in the Fifth Republic mainly by Christian Fouchet in 1967, but also with the reforms introduced in 1968 by Edgar Faure in response to the events of May-June of that year. This information sets the scene for Foucault's and Lyotard's reactions to the educational issues at Vincennes post–November 1968.

In a speech to the National Assembly of France on May 19, 1965, Premier Georges Pompidou said of French education:

It still lives for the most part on postulates bequeathed to it by the Jesuits of the 17th. century and which were only slightly modified at the end of the last century. Of course we have become aware of the increased importance assumed by the sciences and also of the accretion of new knowledge. But we have contented ourselves with adding to the syllabus . . . [that which is] . . . often increasingly abstract. . . . Children arrive at the end of their secondary studies with a level of knowledge which is becoming more and more worthless.[12]

The Fifth Republic had marked four major areas for reform on assuming office. Education was one of them, and changes were initiated as early as 1959. Within education the aim initially was at "modernizing teaching methods, improving methods of selection at the ages of eleven and thirteen, changing the conditions of the baccaleauréat examination and eventually of raising the school leaving age to sixteen."[13] Later there were to be emphases on modernizing the universities and taking higher education down the technocratic path the Fifth Republic deemed necessary for a strong France.

There can be little doubt that at the outset of the Fifth Republic, de Gaulle had a strong commitment to education. Indeed, it was said that in the area of educational reforms in the first ten years of the Fifth Republic, France had been "more innovative and dynamic than most other Western European countries."[14] However, de Gaulle's commitment, like that of Napoleon, had been based upon the notion of stability and the grounding of teaching upon "sound principles."[15] By the end of his period in office he was generally disillusioned with education; first, with teachers and, second, with the students. Although he desired a form of education that would develop powers of reasoning and reflection as well as a critical attitude, perhaps exemplified by his own earlier reflective and critical behavior in the army, he was in turn, and as already noted, highly critical of the students' political activities.

Georges Pompidou, who became premier in 1962 and president in 1969, was himself an ex–school teacher with a literary and classics background. Yet he never questioned the importance of the need for industrial expansion and growth or for a scientific and technocratic education that would meet such needs. Fouchet became minister of education in 1962 and held office for four years and four months, which was the longest tenure by a minister of education for a century. He was not a specialist in education but he was certainly a technocrat determined to rationalize educational provision and administration at all levels. However, it is with the "reforms" of upper-secondary and university education that his name will be associated.

Considerable rapid changes were made in higher education during this decade, but the secondary changes impinged heavily upon higher education also, not only in the demands for places by successful baccaleauréat candidates, but also in the shifts in the curriculum away from an essentially classical, humanistic form of study toward a practical technocratic education through which progress, and the demands of industry, were to be met. This shift reflects Pompidou's notion of worth expressed in his 1965 comments on education to the National Assembly (quoted earlier).

A major "reform" that impinged directly upon the universities was the changes to the baccaleauréat examination. At the start of the decade success in the baccaleauréat examination gave unlimited access to all of the faculties in the universities. It had been possible for a student whose interests had been in the classics at the lycée to be admitted to a science faculty. Fouchet's reforms were to restructure the course and the examination into a number of sections—five in all—so that access to a university faculty came to be predetermined by the section of the course. The main innovations were the introduction of economics with statistics, to be studied along with Latin or a foreign language (even with his leanings toward technology and progress Pompidou could not foresee abandoning Latin); the inclusion of languages in modern studies, a section previously denoting science; and the institution of student-counseling services provided by the staff council and orientation programs. Clearly the role of the classics had been diminished, and a major shift from the literary humanistic education that preceded the decade had been initiated, if not put in place and made operational.

In effect, selection to the universities had been introduced. The left, which was almost fanatically attached to a principle of nonselection, held that possession of the baccalauréat was not merely a universally acceptable admission qualification but also an admission qualification to whatever faculty the student might choose.[16] This right of access was regarded as an expression of an irrevocable bottom-line principle of equality. Principles of selection, for the left, smacked of pre-Revolutionary class privilege. Ironically, in the vast expansion of French higher education, many teachers and administrators, concerned about falling standards, had advocated some form of limitation.[17] Sam White, writing in the *Evening Standard* of May 17, 1968, noted that Raymond Aron was insisting upon this "solution" to the student unrest.[18] Spokesperson for *Le Figaro*, Aron, "saw himself as the lone voice of sanity amidst a general madness."[19]

Within higher education were two powerful forces, those of democratization and those of modernization. The former, usually expressed as equality of opportunity, in the main represented the increased demand from the lower middle classes (and not the working classes) for access to higher education. As late as 1971 the Organization for Economic Cooperation and Development (OECD) reported that the push for access had " not yet started from the urban working class or from the small farmers and agricultural workers."[20] (It was really middle-class students—Daddy's little darlings—that revolted in May-June.) It was also believed that these demands would be better met by a form of "classless style" and a reduction in the level of correlation between the level of social class and the level of education. To a certain extent these factors required greater access to higher education and greater access to a variety of forms of education. Those pressing for democratization wanted access then, and open access to all forms of education, whereas those pressing for modernization wished to control the growth, to control the size of the forms of development, and to control the forms of institution in which such education would be given. These were competing pressures in France and called in question many of the assumptions upon which traditional higher education had been based.

For example the universities saw their traditional role widening dangerously and were concerned about a loss of standards in rapid expansions of higher education. For many in the university, modernization involved a distortion, if not an abdication, of the traditional function of the university—its humanizing, cultural transmission function. Others, and before the upheavals of 1968, began to look at ways of resolving these conflicts by looking at curricula, pedagogy, and better ways of involving students in the university.

The main tensions identified by OECD up to 1968 were the following:

1. *The Pressure of Numbers.* The numbers gaining the baccalauréat and thereby an entry certificate to the faculties had risen immensely. There were enormous classes and considerable anonymity. However, the faculties that could not select tried to gain breathing space by failing large numbers at the end of the first year—up to 45 percent.[21] This was bound to cause problems.

2. *Faculties and les Grandes Écoles. Les grandes écoles* were highly selective and access was highly competitive. In Foucault's case this involved two years' preparation at Lycée Henri IV, and on the first occasion he failed. Whereas the faculties were not overly concerned with their teaching, *les grandes écoles* were very attentive to their teaching. Given their function to prepare the future political and intelligentsia elites, this is hardly surprising. But they conducted little research. Whereas their failure rate and dropout rates were low, those of the faculties were high. According to OECD, whilst the faculties supported one another, they also supported one another's weaknesses.

3. *Modernization and the Institutions of Higher Education.* Between these sectors was a yawning gap with little variety. There was little attempt to meet between faculties and the world of industry and commerce. Industry sought the traditionally liberally educated person from the faculties but were finding that their education was old fashioned and scholarly.

The *OECD Report* was written in 1971. Additional universities had been established throughout the 1960s, and Fouchet addressed these general difficulties in May 1965 with the proposals for implementing the "reform" of the universities from the Implementation Commission.[22] The reforms of the earlier commission—"*les dix-huit*"—proposed to do away with the introductory year (*la année propédeutique*), tested by the eliminatory exam, and replace the existing structures with three stages of university study. The first stage was to be a two-year cycle leading to a diploma in literature or science. In literature, for those preparing to teach there were six main sections: classics, modern studies, languages, history, geography, and philosophy. Within the sciences were divisions, but the important feature for science was that students were required to fulfill prerequisites in science or mathematics. In addition to the literature and science sections were three other sections: psychology, sociology, and history of art and archaeology. The second stage was either a further year leading to a license, which was required for secondary teaching, or two years leading to a *maîtrise* or master's degree. Finally there was the competitively won *agrégation* and a doctorate.

Another innovation was the creation of university institutes of technology for the training of highly specialized technicians with more general education than technicians had possessed in the past. W. R. Fraser comments, "For the universities this did represent the acceptance of a new function: the training of skilled personnel in civil engineering, mechanical construction, dynamics, electronics and automation, chemistry, labour management, applied biology, administration, local government, documentation and statistics."[23]

These changes proposed by Fouchet had major implications for teachers and researchers. First, they represented a split between research and teaching and a separation of lycée teaching from university work. Previously *professeurs* could move reasonably freely between *lycée* and university—as in the cases of Georges Canguilhelm, who had taught Foucault at Lycée Henri IV and taught later at the universities of Strasbourg and the Sorbonne, and Lyotard, who had taught for several years in lycées and subsequently at Nanterre and Vincennes. But the main problem was that expansion had been so rapid, and the changes so major, that sufficient attention had not been given to the implementation and integration of these major innovations into what had been a very traditional system concerned with the preservation and transmission of culture. Generalist and innovative teachers were required, yet the centralized curriculum and structures militated against such autonomy and innovation.

Within a year of Fouchet's higher-education reforms students and workers began a series of revolts and disturbances. The reforms had not been a settlement of student grievances and left- and right-wing political beliefs and attitudes toward education. The intellectual differences underlying these differences are well summarized by Ray Macrides:

While Pompidou and his associates never questioned what had become known as the "industrial imperative," that is, the need of industrial expansion and growth, many among the intellectuals, some of the left wing parties and some of the trade unions began to subordinate it to social and qualitative requirements: security, leisure, improved conditions of everyday life, education, culture, and above all the elimination of sharp income inequalities. Many people demanded the freedom to control and decide for themselves—in the factory, in the universities, in towns and villages—instead of allowing an impersonal and highly centralized state to make decisions for them. The French men and women began to reject the tutelage of the centralised administrative state and to yearn for what we call "community control."[24]

Fouchet had made a serious mistake in underestimating the students' desire for real participation in the functioning of education.[25] It was the students themselves who cracked the university system in 1968. This led to the *loi d'orientation* in which was granted considerable autonomy to institutions and participation to students. This November 1968 bill was a response to the revolutionary student challenge of May-June 1968. Fouchet's changes had done little to meet the left's demands for democratization, and the students' demands for participation in 1968 necessitated more serious modification to the system. Given that some people were committed to the system, for it "was an object of national pride,"[26] then it was hardly surprising that opposition to the 1968 bill came from both left and right.

If it is accepted that the main student grievances in May-June were educational and not political (contra *Time*, May-June 1968), then indeed the students had cracked the system. Daniel Cohn-Bendit's account makes the grievances point well, namely, that the students were in the main driven not by political but by educational motives (assuming that these can be separated for this discussion).[27]

The students' main grievances centered on the problems caused by the rapid expansion of the 1960s; these included a shortage of teachers, the inadequacies of the buildings, the irrelevance of many courses, a remoteness of staff, and petty administrative restrictions, particularly in residence halls. Students were concerned about selection and their rights to engage in political activities on university premises, such activities having been restricted to those occasions arising as part of the normal curriculum. They wanted self-management for the universities, a change of teaching methods, and changes to curricula and examinations.

The 1968 bill did not address selection even though the previous government had announced that selection would be introduced in 1969. The issue was too difficult politically. In theory political discussions could be held only if they arose as part of an established course, though the posting of notices and the holding of meetings were generally tolerated. The bill proposed to allow debates on political issues providing that the life of the university was not disrupted. On the question of the reorganization and restructuring of the universities, the bill "steered a cautious course between concessions and precautions, with the aim of preventing any irrevocable weakening of the State's fundamental responsibility for education."[28] The number of universities was to be increased, and universities were defined as possessing financial autonomy, but they were no longer to be composed of the traditional faculties. Instead, they were to be composed of smaller units or departments. Universities were to be administratively autonomous, and university councils were to be "expressions of the principle of participation, comprising teachers, researchers, students and administration" (ibid.). Although examinations were to be supplemented by a form of continuous assessment, examinations that conferred the national diplomas remained firmly under the control of the Ministry of Education (as evidenced at Vincennes—see below). Although the universities were to have financial and accounting autonomy, they still depended upon government grants, and their accounts and administration remained firmly under the control of the central administration through auditing and inspection. The students' June 1968 demands for the universities' total autonomy from the state had not been met. Yet in the parliamentary debates that preceded passage of the bill on November 11, 1968, fears were expressed that "M. Faure had gone too far to meet the students."[29]

Nevertheless, Faure's successor, Oliver Guichard, continued decentralization of academic decision making, the establishment of interdisciplinary curricula, and the founding of new university centers in the Paris region. The emphasis on a technological business-oriented curriculum continued, with further reforms of this type introduced by Minister of Education René Haby in 1974. For many professors this meant an end of the notion of a cultured person and the co-option of the university for business purposes.[30]

Vincennes was part of this response. It was to be experimental but interdisciplinary, on the cutting edge of research, and democratic. It was to be a magnet to draw the dissidents from the Latin-Quarter, to isolate and confine them. If the faculty attracted to Vincennes contained idealists, liberals, and intolerant ultra-leftists in a potentially interesting intellectual mix, the students were the cream of the militant crop from the street-fighting days.[31] Somewhat ironically the site on which this new campus erupted, both physically and politically, was leased from the army, which had owned the land for more than one hundred years.

Vincennes was to be a model of the reforms, of the *loi d'orientation*; it was to be participatory (democratic) and interdisciplinary in the sense of the new structures contained within the reforms. Faure had stressed the need for more participation in a speech to the Assemblée Nationale earlier in July 1968 in a major response to the events of May-June. New relations between teachers and staff, and new structures for the universities, were said to be of paramount concern. Participation was then the dominant theme of Faure's declaration.[32] But how was participation to be understood?

Participation had been a concern of de Gaulle in his immediate postwar government, and it almost became a slogan in the later years of the Fifth Republic. As with many Gaullist ideas, it was vague and rhetorical, alluding to notions of shared management and profit-sharing schemes. At Vincennes participation was to be interpreted by students and a number of faculty in a particular way, not at all as envisaged by the Fifth Republic, and this was perhaps the downfall of the philosophy department.

But then the teaching of philosophy had not been addressed adequately by the Fouchet reforms. Under the control of edicts from the 1920s, philosophy syllabii and teaching methodology compounded the severe overcrowding at the universities.[33] For the Fouchet reforms addressed structures but not pedagogy.

FOUCAULT'S PEDAGOGICAL RESPONSE TO VINCENNES

Foucault, at Canguilhelm's request, was appointed early to the faculty at Vincennes.[34] Prior to that he had been at Clermont-Ferand and the University of Tunis. Despite his Gaullist acquaintances and his lack of sympathy for left political parties and theories, Foucault was essentially on the left. He was not in France during many of the important formative years of French left politics leading up to 1968. Nor was he involved in party politics, though in the 1950s he had briefly been a member of le Parti Communiste Française (PCF). What was clear was that after his experiences in Warsaw, he was strongly anticommunist (manifested, for example, in a violent series of attacks upon Roger Garaudy, former secretary of the PCF, when he was appointed to Clermont-Ferrand contrary to the department's wish for Gilles Deleuze[35]). Though he was fiercely interested in politics, he remained at a distance from any militant political involvement. Many of his friends from Clermont-Ferrand times were surprised at his later swing to the far left and the radical positions that he was to adopt. His assistant (Foucault's "sister") from 1962 to 1966, Francine Pariente, said of his attitudes and positions in the 1970s: "I never managed to believe it really."[36] Others had seen him as a Gaullist, but this was denied by Jules Vuillemin, who had appointed him to Clermont-Ferrand. Foucault had several contacts with Gaullist power in the 1960s, often through his friend from Warsaw days, Etienne Burin des Roziers. He said of Foucault that "when he visited me sometime during 1962 the future of our higher education was his dearest project."[37] He was even considered for an administrative post as assistant director of higher education in the Ministry of Education, but that was to be blocked by those who objected to his homosexuality. A homosexual as a director of higher education was not acceptable to certain people. What is important here, as Didier Eribon points out, is that Foucault did not find the idea of such a post repugnant. Eribon notes, "This anecdote reveals the sort of man Foucault was in those days—an academic in the most classic sense of the word."[38]

In 1965 Foucault took part in elaborating the reforms in education that Christian Fouchet had begun. As we have seen, these reforms were an important part of the Gaullist program, with both de Gaulle and Pompidou committed and involved. In a 1966 statement Foucault seems to be very much in accord with the *spirit* of university reform: "If an honest man, today, has the impression of a barbarous culture this impression is due to a single fact: our system of education dates from the nineteenth century and there still reigns there the most insipid psychology, the most antiquated humanism. . . . This is the fault of the organisation of education."[39]

Traces of Foucault's remarks are to be found in the report of the Implementation Commission, but Foucault had also prepared other reports and made verbal reports to the commission (e.g., the meeting of February 15, 1965, when he spoke to a report already circulated). Also, other inputs by Foucault into the discussions are formally noted in the minutes.[40]

Foucault's contributions can, then, be summarized as contributions to technical problems involved in implementing the reforms and as contributions on the teaching of philosophy and the doctoral thesis.[41] He also raised a number of objections and questions concerning the technological thrust of the implemented reforms. These contributions, which included two written reports, indicate a person committed to both university education and the traditional approach to knowledge through a firm foundation in the disciplines, especially for students going down the technical paths in the proposed university institutes of technology.

If Foucault did not at any time dissent from the broad general thrust of the proposed reforms,[42] he did, it is clear from the minutes, perceive problems and express concerns. The nature of many of these concerns is important. First is the concern about the teaching of philosophy and the training of future teachers of philosophy. And these are concerns about the *discipline* of philosophy. Philosophy mattered to Foucault. Second is a concern expressed about the doctoral thesis. Foucault believed that preparation for dissertations took too long and that many theses were abstracted from the practical professional life of the candidates. The status of the thesis appears to fall under his attacks upon grand abstract and universalizing theories. If theory can only be local and specific, then it must arise from particular contingencies. Hence Foucault was arguing for the importance of the intellectual and professional life of the candidate. The doctoral thesis must arise from, and be part of, the candidate's lived experience.

His major concern, though, seems to be with the disciplines and the necessity of a sound grounding in knowledge and methodology. Although it is clear from the concerns already noted that Foucault was committed to philosophy, it is not so clear in the minutes that he was at those points in time committed more widely. His questioning of Fouchet on these matters makes that wider commitment clear. But how wide? To all disciplines and to all forms of knowledge? That cannot be discerned from the minutes. If we add to the picture his general antagonism toward the human sciences, as well as the 1966 statement quoted above, then it is clear that he is talking about the more traditional disciplines within the faculties of science, arts, and law, and not about the humanistic social sciences.

Faure's approval of Foucault's appointment to Vincennes cannot then have been accidental. Foucault had proven himself to be committed to the traditional disciplines, he had made major proposals on the subject of philosophy to the Implementation Commission, and he was at the cutting edge of his subject as *Les Mots et Les Choses* had shown.

Foucault's position on these matters did not seem to have changed while he was at Vincennes, for in his inaugural lecture at the College de France on December 2, 1970, on his departure from Vincennes, he was very careful to insert himself and his work into both historical and contemporary scholarship. In doing so he paid tributes to many, but especially to Georges Dumézil, Georges Canguilhelm, and Jean Hyppolite.[43]

If this is a picture of a classical academic, compare it with the Foucault who returned to Paris from Tunisia in late 1968. He had been hardened by unrest and violent encounters with the police there, and he was to take part physically and with considerable courage, along with students and faculty members, in several demonstrations at Vincennes. Foucault had hoped that the events of May-June 1968 would signal new forms of life and social organization. But if he was more overtly politicized by his experiences in Tunisia, he was also to be attacked for not being in Paris in May-June. This caused difficulties for him at Vincennes, for he was seen by some to have been compromised by his absence in Tunisia. However, his earlier work on madness was taken up by the antipsychiatry movement and by the left in general, so that he began to enjoy a growing reputation as a leftist.[44]

The arguments and fights over participation and the continual disruption of teaching, fired by the right-wing press, did not make life easy for Foucault. Yet he aligned himself with the students:

It seems to me that what students are trying to do . . . and what I myself am trying to accomplish in the dust of my books is basically the same thing. . . . We must free ourselves from cultural conservatism as well as from political conservatism. We must see our rituals for what they are: completely arbitrary things . . . it is good . . . to transcend them . . . show up, transform, and reverse the systems which quietly order us about. . . . This is what I try to do in my work.[45]

The phrase "dust on my books" cannot be ignored, as it represents a certain displacement, a certain lack of praxis or involvement.

Certainly Foucault made a number of very interesting appointments to Vincennes. Deleuze declined because of his health, but acceptances included Alain Badiou, Etienne Balibar, François Chatelet, Janette Colombel, Judith Miller (Jacques Lacan's daughter), Jacques Ranciere, René Schérer, Michel Serres, and Henri Weber. These appointments represented an intriguing variety of political positions from moderate leftism to the PCF, to an extreme version of Maoism, and to Trotskyism. Eribon suggests that Foucault sought to moderate the extremisms of some of the appointees. Other possible explanations are that he created a space in which it would be possible for marginalized philosphers to work and that he sought specialists in power and specialists in knowledge.[46]

Perhaps Foucault did not fully recognize or acknowledge that the first victim of the May-June maelstrom was the teacher, the person professing to knowledge, and the person whose authority was based upon competencies in a field or fields of knowledge.[47] Foucault was challenging both political authority and authority in the areas of the human sciences, but in his actions and teaching behavior he did not seem to see that this also called in question his own status as a teacher. His emerging interest in power and knowledge was not employed in a self-reflective and reflexive manner at Vincennes to critique his own teaching.

Foucault taught courses on Friedrich Nietzsche and on sexuality and individuality. But the remainder of the program was much more openly political. (Details of the courses taught are provided by Eribon.) The content attracted the ire of the Minister of Education, who in January 1970 announced that because of the specialized content of the courses any degrees awarded would not be recognized nationally. On February 9 Foucault defended his choice to experiment with freedom at Vincennes in *Le Nouvel Observateur*:

We have defined two broad areas of teaching: one that is basically devoted to the political analysis of society and one that is devoted to the analysis of the scientific fact and to the analysis of a certain number of scientific domains. These two regions, politics and science, seemed to all of us, students and teachers alike, to be the most active and the most fruitful.[48]

Although Foucault had selected the right staff and developed the right curriculum, his approach to pedagogy did not appear to recognize the critical importance this occupied for any genuine reforms of the universities. Participation was interpreted by many of the student factions and faculty as requiring more than agreement on the form of the curriculum. Foucault could not cope with the constant interruptions to lectures, the pickets and demonstrations that became commonplace at Vincennes, and the rambling forums and debates that often replaced formal teaching.

Foucault expressed solidarity with the students and attempted to modify some of his pedagogic practices, yet according to James Miller, "he continued to lecture *ex cathedra*, making no effort (as many radical professors did in those years) to conceal or soften the power and authority of his own intellect." Here Miller quotes Foucault:

When I lecture dogmatically I tell myself: I am paid to bring to my students a certain form and content of knowledge; I must fashion my lecture or my course a little as one might make a shoe, no more and no less. I design an object. I try to make it as well as possible. I make a lot of trouble for myself (not always, perhaps, but often). I bring the object to the desk. I show it and then I leave it up to the audience to do with it what they want.

And Miller concludes: "If his students had a question Foucault would try to answer it; if they needed help, he would try to provide it. Otherwise he preferred simply to let them go their own way, offering himself as an example, rather than trying to impose doctrinal conformity."[49]

Foucault saw students as apprentices and himself as the master crafts-man, even in those difficult times. He never saw himself as a guru with disciples but offered himself only as an example. His teaching, then, was compatible with his view of his works, of theory, and of the general role of intellectuals in society.

In his inaugural lecture at the Collége de France he addressed projects on the traditional and centuries-old subjects of truth, rationality, and normality, though emphasizing his explicit interest in the subject of power and noting that he was crossing the boundaries of these traditional subjects. Yet he emphasized, particularly in the debts he paid to Hyppolite, that he wished to be "among other things, a scholar among scholars."[50] The lecture contained then elements of both scholarship and radical "things to come."

In the ensuing years, and within these parameters, Foucault performed his scholarly duties assiduously.

LYOTARD AND APEDAGOGY

When the events of May-June 1968 erupted, Lyotard was at the center of the maelstrom, at Nanterre. Prior to that he taught for ten years in lycées and at the Sorbonne and had received his agrégation in 1950, the year in which Foucault was failed. But he was not an idle spectator at Nanterre, for he took part and was a member of the movement of May 22, talking about "our movement," our critique, and "our violence."[51] Daniel Cohn-Bendit, a leader of the students in 1968, was very familiar with the ideas of the group *Socialism ou Barbarie*,[52] of which Lyotard had been a leader in the 1950s and early 1960s, though he had left and broken with Marxism in 1963. Furthermore, he had specific theoretical views on the nature of the pedagogy required at Vincennes. These had been articulated at Nanterre in direct response to May-June, and they clearly addressed the problem of the teacher's knowledge and authority. If Lyotard saw this as a major problem in any proper reforms of the universities, it is not clear that Foucault did.

Lyotard saw the starting point of the struggle at Nanterre as the rejection of the thrust of the Fouchet reforms and the even more overt politicizing of the universities in the cause of capitalism.[53] Democratization as promised by Fouchet and Faure was seen as a sham, as a means by which the Gaullist reformers could more effectively insert the themes and practices of modernization into social and working life. But for Lyotard these reforms were not merely to be resisted in any conservative manner so as to preserve the universities' traditional role of transmission of a humanistic culture. Instead, the whole function of the university and its ossified and rarefied culture had themselves to be transformed. So for Lyotard the so-called crisis of May-June "ushers us into a new period of history" where the will is not "for political renewal, but the desire for something different, the desire for another society, for different relations between people,"and for a fundamental decentering of education from centralized academic and institutional authority.[54]

Some events at Nanterre were indicative of student and faculty views on participation. A campaign was launched at Nanterre on May 1 in which teaching methods, course content, and university organization were critiqued, and on May 2 when Cohn-Bendit appeared in court, Pierre Grappin, the dean, closed the Nanterre faculty. The May 22 movement condemned the closure claiming that dialogue had been refused by Grappin, and the police entered the campus the following day. Strikes and demonstrations spread gradually to other educational institutions throughout France. The Nanterre faculty reopened on May 10 but was immediately disrupted. On May 13 fifty-eight professors at Nanterre stated that the university system was dead and that they no longer recognized the educational system. On May 14 the Nanterre faculty declared itself an autonomous university and general assemblies of students and staff were held in Paris to discuss reorganization of the universities. But by May 20 Nanterre was experiencing difficulty in setting up its management committees. Cohn-Bendit, a student of Henri Lefebrve, was supported by staff (Lefebrve, Alain Touraine, and Guy Michaud) at a hearing in the Sorbonne on May 3. We can note here shared staff and student demands and mutual support for different forms of pedagogy, different course content, and university reorganization, which included greater autonomy for individual institutions.[55]

Mark Poster's interpretation of the events of May-June is in terms of existential Marxism, claiming that "to the extent that a new theory is needed for this unprecedented process, existential Marxism seems appropriate."[56] Whether or not that interpretation is correct, and it would certainly accord a prime place to Lefebrve through his praxis at Nanterre, by 1968 Lyotard held a particular theoretical position that accords well with the events at Nanterre and Vincennes and with how these were elaborated into his points on apedagogy.[57]

From his understanding of Nietzsche, Lyotard argued thus:[58] The revolutionary militant believes that his struggle and contestation are based upon truth. The militant appeals to a revolutionary theory that condemns the whole mode of production and its entire superstructure and consigns people to catastrophe unless changes are made to the mode of production and its superstructure. However, the militant realizes that he or she is not appealing to *truth* but to a moral *ideal*. Further, socialism becomes far less revolutionary than capitalism, which is both cynical and devoid of moral concerns, leading to the destruction of beliefs.

The conclusion the militant must draw is that the revolutionary theory was after all only an ideal and not truth. This "permits" Lyotard to launch a polemic against truth and to promote a form of Nietzschean philosophy as the means of demystifying the search for eternal truth. Insofar as traditional philosophy was constructed as a measure against tales, myths, and other forms of narrative, then the logos itself must be shown to be a myth. The outcome of this is that all discourse is to be considered as narrative. The properties of the narrative are that narrative has already begun and its referent is not an event or fact but other narratives. It is therefore never finished, as narrator confronts narratee, who may in turn become the narrator of a fresh narration. The story cannot end, as the narrator holds no privileged position in relation to the narratee. It is clear, then, that Lyotard did not simply wish to replace the teacher by the student.

What should be further noted is that Lyotard did not write about these matters a priori. Instead, his work is situated in day-to-day matters. Here there is an underlying emphasis upon the pragmatics of language use. His comments on pedagogy also are closely intertwined with comments on the forms and structures of educational institutions. The forms that teaching takes reflect the forms of authority and power that structure and constitute the institution. What follows from the narrator-narratee notion is that in writing the writer is also required to listen. Just as the listener is addressed, so too is the reader addressed and the writer must "listen" to the ongoing narrative.

In both cases of narrator and listener Lyotard is presenting an argument against the notion of autonomy because for him autonomy is but the "autonomy" to occupy a preconstituted position in the technocratic mode of education and production. Autonomy, with a right to speak with the "authority" of the educated person, provides an independence that in technocratic mode occludes the voices of the Other (in the classroom, for example, culture, thought, desire, tradition, the immemorial, the sublime) and "frees" one from relations of obligation to others.[59]

Thus for Lyotard in 1968 *theoretically* neither the reformists, nor the conservative faculty members, nor any one of the militant factions held the truth in May-June. They had stories that had to be told and weighed against the other stories, so that a new story could emerge. Hence the need for endless meetings and for forms of dialogue and practice in which power relations were eliminated so that a "new" narrative and a praxis could emerge. Didactic forms of teaching and the teacher as authority, which presumed truth, or the interpretation of facts and events were theoretically precluded.

What did Lyotard say in particular in relation to teaching, curriculum content, and the organization of the universities? In relation to the university he said that the movement of May 22

addressed the exteriority of knowledge to life, its connivance with power, along with its persistence of hierarchical relations. . . . Our critique is not only verbal; it is critical practical. It involves the offensive blockage of the university and its diversion to revolutionary ends, it involves physical combat against the so-called order, transgressions. . . . The movement affirms the freedom to speak equally, the mockery of the hierarchy, the courage to submit all questions to open debate.[60]

Lyotard stressed that this needed cooperation between workers and students as well as resistance to slander and propaganda. This raised concerns and fears in 1968 about the politicizing of teaching and the failure to return to serious work. Lyotard's response was that the movement also feared the politicizing of teaching and the university, but by Fouchet.[61]

According to Lyotard, the faculty was not independent and "dedicated to the elaboration and transmission of knowledge in itself." Rather, the faculty prevents genuine understanding and expression through the operations of defusing and recuperation.

The defusing of the means of understanding and expression is carried out by the faculty of dead letters: their recuperation is the task of the faculty of human relations. The former diverts intelligence and inventiveness away from praxis towards the fetishization of finished works, of the past, of that which is established; the latter employs the same intelligence and inventiveness in the conditioning of the workforce and the raising of its output. The work of defusing produces the scholar; the work of recuperation produces the expert. The imagination of the working class cannot come up with anything more innovative than to make the faculty make experts rather than scholars. That was the Fouchet plan.[62]

As a consequence, he claims, the means of understanding and expression remain the province of a few. This limitation leads to a closed-off culture within the universities, with the remainder alienated from true understanding and expression of reality. There is no point in democratization into such alienated institutions, Lyotard claims, because it would be participation in manipulative and alienating processes. Instead, he continues, we must "impose institutions and modes of teaching and research that allow the critical comprehension of reality in all of its forms and the liberation of power of expression." Nor can this be left to moderates, for in their very form of liberal moderation they are but allies of the powers that be. Unable to carry out the reforms required, they would allow the universities to drift back into the older forms because

the distinction would not always get made between the critique of a university judged to be inadequate because it is *not adapted* to the requirements of modern capitalism and the critique of a university judged inadequate precisely because it would *remain adapted* to these requirements, and contestation would continue to be confused with reformism.[63]

What Lyotard saw clearly was that the teacher and pedagogy were critical to any genuine or meaningful reform of the universities. The role of the teacher and the nature of pedagogy had to be rethought because if they were not, the alienation of knowledge and students would certainly continue if the Gaullist reformists won on the direction the reforms should take, and would be reinforced if the conservative reactionaries won. The students and those who contested the universities, their structures and pedagogy, would be interpreted by the reformists as conservatives, and by the conservatives as reformists, *unless* the role of the teacher and the form that pedagogy was to take in the reformed universities were addressed as a critical issue. Lyotard attempted to address these issues.

In the older form of the university the function of the teacher, according to Lyotard was "to consume cultural contents in order to produce cultural content that can be consumed by the students; to produce saleable students (consumable labour force)."[64] In order to achieve genuine understanding and expression pedagogy must be kept *open*, he argued. By this he meant "offered to critical consciousness." In particular,

the teacher/pupil ought to be permanently protected against both a falling back into the old hierarchical magisterial relation and the demagogy that proposes between the teacher and the pupil, as well as against the training of the pupil as a mere expert/counsellor. . . . The splitting apart of knowledge . . . must also be disrupted, and the purposes of knowledge must be the object of a permanent indictment: in this society knowledge is constantly compromised with power. . . . We have no catechism to be recited, no dogma to insinuate, no conviction to suggest. We want the questions that are asked of humanity to be asked and to continue to be asked in all the seminars, workshops, and commissions of the faculty.[65]

In later writing Lyotard argued that a university policy on the transmission of knowledge had to be formulated around a series of questions: Who transmits learning and to whom? What is transmitted and in what form? What is the medium of transmission?[66] Lyotard's concern was that performativity of the overall social system would be taken as the framework of relevance for answering these questions so that the "desired goal becomes the optimal contribution of higher education to the best performativity of the social system." As performativity increases its control over questions of relevance and quality in higher education, knowledge ceases to become an end in itself and its transmission is no longer the exclusive responsibility of teachers and students. Emancipation becomes the catchcry of a bygone age and the grand narratives of legitimation, and the "autonomy" granted the universities in the *loi d'orientation* "has very little meaning." Finally, the partial replacement of teachers by machines could only be intolerable against the background of those grand old narratives. As these have been pushed aside by the demands of performativity," the process of delegitimation and the predominance of the performance criterion are sounding the knell of the death of the Professor."[67]

In response to the questions on university policy, cited above, Lyotard provided these answers between 1968 and 1970. What was required, he determined, was a certain form of transmission by teachers of a certain kind to students of a certain kind. This he referred to as apedagogy, a here-and-now attitude that attacked powers but did not merely attempt to reverse the powers of the oppressed by *seizing* power. Apedagogy was not a pedagogy of the oppressed for him, as he claimed that *all* pedagogy participates in forms of oppression. Instead apedagogy required reciprocal relations of a nonmanipulative kind.

Thus Lyotard should not be interpreted here as advocating a Freirean form of pedagogy, as in *Pedagogy of the Oppressed.*[68] Freire's point is that through consciousness raising and proper literacy it is possible for the oppressed to name the world, thereby obtaining the power necessary to free them from their oppression. This is merely an oppositional form of pedagogy that reverses forms of power and is mired in the grand metanarrative of emancipation. Also, Freire was writing from a Marxist position rejected by Lyotard, whose break with Marxism is exemplified in his 1963 *Socialism ou Barbarie.*

Lyotard appeared to be advocating a form of pedagogy in which power relations were absent and in which, instead, there existed reciprocal relations of mutuality. But Foucault's point was that in disciplinary blocks such as the universities, power relations were closely intermingled with all forms of communication.[69] What was required, according to Foucault, was a form of pedagogy that was nonmanipulative. Foucault, however, did not provide criteria for "good" power relations. Both Foucault and Lyotard believed in the close connection between power and knowledge, but by the early 1970s only Lyotard seemed to have provided a way through the power-knowledge nexus.

Both men were interested in art and literature, but it is Lyotard who in the early 1970s laid "the groundwork for a radical critical aesthetics by using art to reveal the limitations of theory."[70] Although Foucault also realized the disruptive potential of art and literature—and in spite of using art, such as Velázquez's *Las Meninas* in *The Order of Things*, and writing on Raymond Roussel[71]—he did not seem to fully integrate the aesthetic into his analyses. In relation to literature he said in 1975 that he accorded it no role in the process of analysis and that, in particular, it had been deliberately excluded from *Discipline and Punish.*[72] The aesthetic, then, provided Lyotard with a critical theoretical tool that had the potential to attack the power-knowledge nexus. No such critical tool seems to have been available to Foucault at the time he was at Vincennes.

Lyotard did not go to Vincennes until Foucault had departed. Clearly the events at Vincennes that had so disturbed and frustrated Foucault had parallels at Nanterre in 1969–70. Indeed, Lyotard records some of these events.[73] There are disruptions, police, confrontations with police and administration, demands for freedom against armed gangs, splits in the student movement among communists, Trotskyites, and Maoists, the destruction of amenities, and a general harassment from the right-wing media. Lyotard referred to some of the students as maniacs.

In a sense Vincennes was designed to fail, where "fail" is understood in terms of failure to resist the types of reform presaged by Fouchet and Faure and implemented by Guichard, and to achieve the cultural, political, and educational aims of the May 22 movement. Vincennes also did not address the main problems of the universities and the student grievances prior to May-June. A brief summary of these issues is needed.

First was the problem of overcrowding. This was an immediate problem at Vincennes on opening day in January 1969 with more than 5,000 students cramped into a makeshift campus. This may have been exacerbated by a policy of free entry (without having the baccalauréat), which, though one solution to the problem of selection and the use of the baccalauréat to determine life options, may not have been the right option for Vincennes at that time. Second was the inadequacy of amenities. Vincennes was at the end of a metro line, but a bus was still needed to the campus, and there was no equivalent of the Latin-Quarter to which students could disperse for coffee and conversation. These two student grievances were not addressed at Vincennes.

Third was the alleged irrelevance of courses. There is little doubt that the offerings of the philosophy department at Vincennes did address the aims of the movement of May 22. If Foucault got the curriculum right, the minister of education did not agree. Even though students and teachers thought it to be about right and even though there had obviously been some participation, Guichard declared that any degrees awarded would not be nationally recognized because the curriculum was too specialized. So much for devolution. Writing some eight years later, and with the philosophy syllabus still not recognized, Lyotard wondered about his students at Vincennes: "Why do they come? One day you asked this question solemnly during class. They told you it was their business, not yours."[74]

Examinations were also changed in the philosophy department under the reforms of 1968. But, according to Judith Miller, examining and awarding of credits in the philosophy department became almost farcical.[75] Committed to the destruction of the university, Miller was eventually fired by the minister over misconduct in examining.

This issue contributed to the bad public perception of Vincennes and to the belief that a Vincennes degree was of little value. Of course the minister "had" to act on Judith Miller, but this issue and the actions of the minister on other matters as well can be seen as part of the exclusion, confinement, and carcerel treatment that had been "designed" for Vincennes. Like Foucault's prisons, Vincennes was almost designed to fail.

Lyotard was to say of his time at Vincennes in the 1970s:

We used to fight a bit. Only once did it lead to anything worthwhile. It was on a day of active strike. What could we do? At the time we were working on the operators in persuasive discourse, making use of Plato's dialogues and Aristotle's Rhetoric and Sophistic refutation. We subjected the statements relative to the strike to the same analysis. . . . Enter the commando unit armed with clubs, shouting that we were breaking the strike. A fight starts, quickly followed by palavers between the two groups, the besiegers and the besieged. The latter argue as follows: on the one hand our "normal" activity is to study persuasive discourse. . . . On the other hand, to participate in an active strike is to occupy the workplace and to think together about the discourses that persuade or dissuade us from striking. The difference between these two activities is not distinguishable. . . . Most of the assailants backed off, admitting that we were as much "out of it" as they were.[76]

Gradually the student movement disappeared. Lyotard knew that it would, and he knew why. Writing of May-June, and in 1968, he said, "Whatever we may be able to do here can and will be recuperated by the powers that be, until society as a whole is reconstructed differently."[77]

CONCLUSION

Who got it right at Vincennes, Foucault or Lyotard? This is probably not the right way to formulate a question that can be asked. Given some commitment to a leftist position, some commitment to resisting the oppressive modernist tendencies of the reforms, and some positive commitment to new social and cultural structures after the events of May-June, the question might be framed in terms of who proposed or practiced a more appropriate pedagogy to attain educational aims consistent with those commitments. In my view Lyotard is the answer to the reformulated question. Foucault realized later that the left's problem was that they had not been able to formulate an appropriate theory of *governance*, which would have had to include a proper form of pedagogy.[78] Work on this had been planned with Pierre Bourdieu, but it was never done.

NOTES

1. Edgar Morin, "The Student Commune," in *Reflections on the Revolution in France: 1968*, ed. Charles Posner (Harmondsworth, England: Pelican, 1968), p. 111. Morin, a sociologist, was expelled from the Parti Communiste Français in 1951 and was a director of the journal *Arguments*. In 1968 he was at the Centre National de la Recherche Scientifique.

2. André Gorz, "What Are the Lessons of the May Events?" in *Reflections on the Revolution*, ed. Posner, p. 251. Gorz was a disciple of Jean-Paul Sartre and political editor of *Les Temps Moderne* in the 1960s.

3. Alan Touraine, *The Movement of May*, trans. Leonard Mayhew (New York: 1971), p. 347. Touraine, a sociologist, was at Nanterre in May-June, along with Henri Lefebrve and Jean-François Lyotard. He was one of the first members of staff to express solidarity with the students, even though he was attacked by them as part of a general attack on the social sciences and sociology in particular as having become "the regime's handmaiden." Edgar Morin, "The Student Commune," p. 112.

4. Quoted by Posner, *Reflections on the Revolution*, p. 87. De Gaulle is talking about his much-desired reforms in education and the workplace. These were to be concerned with major technocratic thrusts and "participation." Vincennes was. an outcome of the educational "reforms."

5. Charles de Gaulle, quoted in André Malraux, *Felled Oaks: Conversations with de Gaulle* (New York: Holt, Rhinehart & Winston, 1972).

6. Posner, *Reflections on the Revolution*, pp. 69–74.

7. Named after the date when students began to mobilize at Nanterre after the arrest of leaders of the National Committee for Vietnam. The amphitheater and then an administrative block were occupied by 142 students and a committee formed after discussions on how to change society. Initially called the Committee of 142.

8. Didier Eribon, *Michel Foucault* (Cambridge, Mass.: Harvard University Press, 1991), p. 202. See also James Miller, *The Passion of Michel Foucault* (New York: Simon & Schuster, 1993), Chapter 6; and David Macey, *The Lives of Michel Foucault* (London: Hutchinson, 1993), Chapter 9.

9. For example, Foucault's attacks on Sartre as the man of the Enlightenment and Lyotard on Sartre's notion of aesthetics.

10. See, for example, David Carroll, *Paraesthetics: Foucault, Lyotard, Derrida* (London: Methuen, 1989).

11. See for example, "Nanterre, Here, Now," trans. Bill Readings, in Jean-François Lyotard, *Political Writings*, trans. Bill Readings and Kevin Paul Geiman (Minneapolis: University of Minnesota Press, 1991), pp. 46–59.

12. Compare the 1971 Organization for Economic Cooperation and Development Report *Review of National Policies for Education: France* (Paris: OECD, 1971), pp. 20–22. Hereafter cited as OECD.

13. Dorothy M. Pickles, *The Government and Politics of France*, Vol. 2 (London: Methuen, 1973).

14. W. Safran, *The French Polity* (New York: MacKay, 1977).

15. W. D. Halls, *Education, Culture and Politics in Modern France* (Oxford: Pergammon Press, 1976).

16. Pickles, *Government and Politics of France*, p. 152.

17. Halls, *Education, Culture and Politics in Modern France*, p. 183.

18. Sam White, *Sam White's Paris* (Dundon Green Sevenoaks Kent, England: New English Library, 1984).

19. Mark Poster, *Existential Marxism in Post-War France* (Princeton, N.J.: Princeton University Press, 1975), p. 356.

20. OECD, p. 68.

21. Ibid., p. 70.

22. The principles for educational reform were identified by 1964 by the Commission d'Étude de l'Enseignment Supérieure (known as *les dix-huits* because of the number of members). The Commission des Enseignments Scientifiques at Littéraire des Faculties was then formed for the implementation of policies identified by the earlier commission. It met in early 1965.

23. W. R. Fraser, *Reforms and Restraints in Modern French Education* (London: Routledge & Kegan Paul, 1974), p. 77.

24. Roy Constantine Macrides, *French Politics in Transition* (Cambridge, Mass.: Winthrop, 1975), p. 55.

25. Fraser, *Reforms and Restraints in Modern French Education*, p. 140.

26. Pickles, *Government and Politics of France*, p. 153.

27. Daniel Cohn-Bendit, *Obsolete Communism* (Harmondsworth, England: Penguin, 1969).

28. Pickles, *Government and Politics of France*, p. 156.

29. Ibid.

30. Safran, *The French Polity*.

31. Miller, *The Passion of Foucault*, p. 175.

32. Edgar Faure, *Déclarations de M. Edgar Faure, Ministre de l'Education, Nationale, Devant le Parliament* (Assemblée Nationale, le 8 October et Senat, le 28 Octobre, 1968), e.g., p. 7.

33. See, for example, Ministère de l'Education Nationale, *Horaires, Programmes, Instructions—Philosophie* (Paris: M.E.N., 1967).

34. Eribon, *Michel Foucault*, p. 202.

35. See ibid.; see also Macey, *The Lives of Michel Foucault*.

36. Eribon, *Michel Foucault*, p. 132.

37. Quoted in ibid.

38. Ibid., pp. 132–33. Miller, *The Passion of Foucault*, p. 172, says that "during those years, Foucault also seems to have played the academic game with genuine relish and cunning."

39. Michel Foucault, "Entretien" (avec Madeleine Chapsal), *La Quinzaine Littéraire*, May 16, 1966: 14–15.

40. See the minutes of the Commission des Enseignments Scientifiques et Littéraire, *Minutes of Meetings*, unpublished (Mission des Archives, Ministère de l'Education Nationale, Paris, 1964–65).

41. A similar proposal was made by Minister of Education Edgar Faure in his address to the Senate in October 1968. See note 30.

42. Eribon, *Michel Foucault*, p. 135.

43. Michel Foucault, "The Discourse on Language," in *The Archaeology of Knowledge* (London: Tavistock, 1972).

44. Macey, *The Lives of Michel Foucault*, Chapter 9.

45. "A Conversation with Michel Foucault," *Partisan Review* 38, 2 (1971): 208. This was excluded from its reprint as "Rituals of Exclusion" in *Foucault Live* (Columbia: Semiotexte, 1989). Quoted by Miller, *The Passion of Foucault*, p. 180.

46. Macey, *The Lives of Michel Foucault*, p. 225.

47. See Vincent Descombes, *Modern French Philosophy* (Cambridge: Cambridge University Press, 1973), Chapter 6.

48. "Le Piege de Vincennes," quoted by Macey, *The Lives of Foucault*, pp. 230–31.

49. Miller, *The Passion of Foucault*, p. 181.

50. Ibid., p. 184.

51. Jean-Françoise Lyotard, "Preamble to a Charter," 1968, reprinted in *Political Writings*, trans. Bill Readings (Minneapolis: University of Minnesota Press, 1993), pp. 41–45.

52. Cohn-Bendit, *Obsolete Communism.*

53. Ibid.

54. Ibid., p. 41.

55. These are extracted from Posner's diary of events. See Posner, *Reflections on the Revolution*, Chapter 2.

56. Poster, *Existential Marxism in Post-War France*, p. 396. This is discussed fully in Chapter 9.

57. I take this interpretation of Lyotard's position from Vincent Descombes, *Modern French Philosophy* (Cambridge: Cambridge University Press, 1973), pp. 180–86.

58. Jean-François Lyotard, *Dérive a Partir de Marx et Freud* (Paris: Union Générale d'Editions, 1973).

59. I am grateful to Bill Readings for the discussion of this point (Chapter 10, this volume).

60. Lyotard, "Preamble to a Charter," in *Political Writings*, p. 42.

61. Ibid., p. 45.

62. Ibid., p. 44.

63. Ibid.

64. Lyotard, "Nanterre, Here, Now," in *Political Writings*, p. 57.

65. Lyotard, "Preamble to a Charter," p. 45.

66. Jean-François Lyotard, *The Postmodern Condition: A Report on Knowledge*, trans. Geoff Bennington and Brian Massumi, Foreword by Fredric Jameson (Minneapolis: University of Minnesota Press, 1984), p. 57.

67. Ibid., p. 53.

68. Paulo Freire, *Pedagogy of the Oppressed* (Harmondsworth, England: Penguin, 1972).

69. Michel Foucault, "Afterword" in *Michel Foucault: Beyond Structuralism and Hermeneutics*, ed. Hubert Dreyfuss and Paul Rabinow (Brighton, England: Harvester Press, 1982), pp. 208–26.

70. Carroll, *Paraesthetics*, p. 24.

71. Michel Foucault, *Death and the Labyrinth: The World of Raymond Roussel* (London: Athlone Press, 1987); originally published in 1963.

72. Michel Foucault, "The Functions of Literature," reprinted in *Michel Foucault: Politics, Philosophy, Culture*, ed. Lawrence D. Kritzman (London and New York: Routledge, Chapman and Hall, 1988), pp. 307–13.

73. See Lyotard, "Nanterre, Here, Now," in *Political Writings*, pp. 46–59.

74. Lyotard, "Endurance and the Profession," in *Political Writings*, p. 70.

75. Ibid., p. 229.

76. Ibid., p. 72.

77. Lyotard, "Preamble to a Charter," p. 44.

78. See Michel Foucault, "Governmentality," *Ideology and Consciousness* 6 (1979): 1–26.

10 From Emancipation to Obligation: Sketch for a Heteronomous Politics of Education

Bill Readings

Audiences are surprising.

Jean-François Lyotard

When people address the question of education, they tend to do so from one of several points of view. The administrator is concerned to understand education as a process in which the production and distribution of knowledge will repay the costs in time and capital expended. The professor wants to justify a life spent in the pursuit of objectives that, analyzed in terms of cost and benefit, seem to produce little personal payoff, so he or she will tend to make large claims for his or her power to train a certain kind of student subject: critical, well rounded, or empowered. The student usually complains about an institution or a practice to which he or she feels forced to submit without first understanding why, about a hierarchy that seems not to acknowledge the student to which it appeals, as product, in order to justify itself (in a consumer society, these complaints become harder to ignore). Each of these descriptions of education performs an initial gesture of centering: Each writer takes him or herself to stand at the *center* of the educational process. What seems to me most worthwhile about Jean-François Lyotard's long history of writings on education is a persistent move to *decenter* the educational process, to insist that it is not best understood from the point of view of a sovereign subject that takes itself to be the sole guarantor of the meaning of that process. In this chapter I argue that this decentering is grounded in an attention to the pragmatic scene of teaching, an attention that refuses the possibility of any privileged point of view so as to make teaching something other than self-reproduction of an autonomous subject: neither the administrator taking the system in hand, nor the professor taking the student in hand, nor the student taking him or herself in hand.

First of all, it should be noted that Lyotard does not write *on* education in the obvious sense. That is to say, he does not take a body of theoretical work, a system of concepts, and apply it instrumentally to the realm of education. Lyotard does not speak to education from outside the scene of teaching; his meditations tend to insist upon their setting within the scene of pedagogy, be it in the seminar room, as in "Endurance and the Profession," or on the battlefield, as in "Nanterre, Here, Now."[1] Reflective or urgent, this is a form of writing that resists the temptation of transcendence, of speaking from a position in which the intellectual subject takes itself to incarnate the voice of the universal. Taking into account these various pedagogical scenes, Lyotard's thinking is resolutely pedagogical. Consistently, his writing is marked by an attention to the pragmatics of language use in the pedagogical scene, a pragmatics most overtly theorized in *The Differend*.[2]

The extent of this concern has not necessarily been acknowledged: The renown gained by *The Postmodern Condition* has tended to obscure its status as a report written for the Conseil des Universités of the government of Québec.[3] As Lyotard remarks in his introduction, the book is an "occasional" text, a report on the contemporary nature of knowledge in Western societies that is addressed to university administrators, a text that "situates" the analysis of the epistemological legitimation.[4] One significant gesture is the initial refusal of the role of expert in favor of the uncertainty of the philosopher, who is not sure what it is that he does and does not know.[5] This is not just a matter of epistemological modesty; it is also a refusal to situate the writer of *The Postmodern Condition* in a position of transcendence, outside the institution he analyzes. Neither outside the institution nor completely at home in it, Lyotard foregrounds the institutional question, unable to take the institution as either merely an object of knowledge or a way of life. One of the ironies of Fredric Jameson's widely accepted critique of *The Postmodern Condition* is the way in which his implications of insufficient political seriousness ignore this highly "practical" discursive location.[6] One has to be very careful what one says to governments, after all.

Not that this insistence upon the situatedness of writing is anything new for Lyotard: As early as 1962, in "Dead Letter," his reflection on culture is inseparable from the institutional questions of the university faculties within which culture is supposedly preserved, produced, and inculcated.[7] And his involvement in the events of spring 1968, as both a militant in and an apologist for the movement of March 23, accompanies an extended reflection upon the specific site and function of the university within contemporary capitalism. These are crucial points to which I shall return later in a more detailed discussion of this question so as to frame my analysis of the pedagogic scene.

In what follows, I trace the nature of Lyotard's double attention to the question of education, focused as it is upon both the pragmatic scene of pedagogy and the institutional question of the university. In so doing, for the benefit of English-speaking readers I focus on the selection of texts recently published in the collection of *Political Writings*, a collection that overtly acknowledges the position of the intellectual and the question of the students as preeminent sites of political reflection for Lyotard. At the expense of a certain analytic crudity, let me begin by isolating two general propositions that structure Lyotard's varying analyses of education:

1. An insistence on the pedagogic scene as structured by a dissymmetrical pragmatics, and a concomitant insistence that this relation must be addressed in terms of ethical awareness—that it belongs to the sphere of justice rather than of truth.
2. A reflection on the institutional context of education, which refuses both the isolation of education in relation to wider social practices and the subjugation of education to predetermined or externally derived social imperatives.

The first of these propositions is important in that it refuses to make the pedagogical relation into an object of knowledge: Understanding teaching is not a matter of drawing flowcharts that track and police the movements of knowledge, power, or desire. Such charts, even when drawn up with the best of intentions, always tend to install a single and authoritative point of view, reducing teaching to an object of knowledge for a sovereign subject who will play the role of policeman. Reminding us that teaching is always a practice, Lyotard insists that the concern of our reflections upon such a practice must be for justice rather than for truth: We must seek to do justice to teaching rather than to know what it is (and, in fact, a belief that we know what teaching is or should be is a major impediment to just teaching). I devote the body of this chapter to attempting to trace how such an understanding of teaching as an ethical practice works in Lyotard's writings. My second proposition is more easily recognizable, although it equally imposes upon us a responsibility of the utmost watchfulness: namely, never to take for granted the nature and function of the institutional forms within and against which teaching takes place. In fact, one could say that this means never separating the two propositions, never imagining that attention to pedagogic pragmatics can be divorced from an attention to institutional forms, a warning that Samuel Weber has theorized in exemplary fashion in his *Institution and Interpretation*.[8] First, then, I will sketch the terms of Lyotard's decentering of the pedagogic situation, of his refusal of the ideology of autonomy in matters of teaching.

The most obvious symptom of this decentering is an attention to the addressee, to the listener, in the pedagogic situation. Even a cursory glance at the extended body of Lyotard's writing reveals a persistent concern with forms of address, be it the dialogue of *Just Gaming*, the fictional dialogue of *Instructions Païennes*, the diatribe of *Economie Libidinale*, or the epistolary form of *The Postmodern Explained*.[9] More significantly, this is not merely a matter of preciosity or formal experiment—which is to say that Lyotard's dialogues are not divided monologues. By this I mean that the dialogue form is not designed to display his capacity to occupy both sides of a question; rather, it is *dialogic* in M. M. Bakhtin's sense. The dialogue form is not organized dialectically, to arrive at a single conclusion that will either be the vindication and reinforcement of one position (Socrates' opponent is forced to agree with Socrates) or a synthesis of the two (as in Hans-Georg Gadamer's account of the fusion of horizons or James Joyce's "jewgreek is greekjew").[10] The dialogue does not thaw and resolve into a monologue. To put this another way, the dialogic form is not controlled solely by the sender; it is not a formal instrument in the grasp of the writing subject, like Stephane Mallarmé's use of *mise en page*. I call Lyotard's writing dialogic because it evokes the dialogue form in order to refuse the modernist privileging of the sender over the addressee, to refuse the figure of the lone artist who synthesizes reality either through a rational understanding or a romantic effort of will.

Lyotard's writing does not merely speak monologically; it seeks to listen, to do justice to the pole of the addressee.[11] To pay attention in this way to the addressee is not simply to attempt to determine the conditions of reception of a discourse, is not simply to reinforce a monologue. On the contrary, it is to inscribe within discourse a radical aporia, to write in a way that respects what might be called the abyssal space of reading by the other, the fact that we never know to whom our writings may speak, that "audiences are surprising."[12]

This is why Lyotard has paid such attention to the writings of Emmanuel Lévinas in formulating his account of the ethical. Lévinas serves to remind us that no individual can *be* just, since to do justice is to recognize that the question of justice exceeds individual consciousness, cannot be answered by an individual moral stance. This is because justice involves respect for an absolute other, a respect that must precede knowledge: "This is what makes the thought of a Lévinas so important: it shows that the relation with the other, what he calls 'the Other' of 'the absolutely Other' is such that the request that is made of me by the other, by the simple fact that he speaks to me, is a request that can never be justified" (*JG*, 22).

To be hailed as an addressee is to be commanded to listen, and the ethical nature of this relation cannot be justified: We have to listen, without knowing why, before we know what it is that we are to listen to. To be spoken to is to be placed under an obligation, to be situated within a narrative pragmatics. Even a preliminary discussion of the framework within which discussions are to be undertaken requires this initial respect, a respect that is senseless in that it has no constative content. Nor is this "respect" a matter of deference; it is the simple fact of alertness to otherness, something that the German word *Achtung* conveys, linking as it does respect and warning: *Achtung! Ein andere* is perhaps the rule of this ethics.

When I call Lyotard's writing pedagogical, it is because it is structured by the pedagogic scene of address, with all its ethical weight: The condition of pedagogical practice is, in Maurice Blanchot's words, "an infinite attention to the other."[13] Of course, the nature of this attention is up for grabs: It can be the attention of the Lacanian analytic scene, which, to paraphrase Mikkel Borch-Jacobsen, can be characterized as "absolute mastery."[14] This is not an empirical argument about the practices of the École Freudienne, though Lyotard has had something to say about them.[15]

The difference between Lyotard's pedagogy and Jacques Lacan's analysis is that the "other" to whom Lacan pays attention is not the analysand but the Unconscious. The pragmatics of Lacanian analytic discourse thus remain modernist in that the pole of the addressee is suppressed, becoming the empty relay that marks the place of castration, of absence, the black hole around which the privileged encounter of the analytic master and the unconscious instance of the signifier occurs. Of course, the action of this signifier is purely referential; pointing to its own slippage along the signifying chain, it has no signification other than the absence of the signified. Hence analytic mastery is not a matter of simple interpretation, of decoding; rather, as the case of Dupin reminds us, it is a privileged capacity for following the defiles of the signifier without being entrapped into the illusion of hermeneutic mastery, the lure of the search for a contentual meaning by which the Prefect of Police is transfixed.[16] Yet this abnegation of one kind of mastery is compensated by another: the privileged knowledge that there is no such meaning, armed with which the analyst can fix the analysand in the place of blindness or castration, pretext for and inert support of an encounter with the unconscious signifier. While I applaud the exemplary antihumanism of this gesture, I find it somewhat unjust to the analysand, who, as the rich tradition of feminist readings of Jacques Lacan has pointed out, may hesitate before the absolute identification of castration with lack and absence. In this respect, Jane Gallop's the *Daughter's Seduction* seems to me an exemplary reassertion of the analysand/addressee within the framework of the Lacanian refusal of depth psychology, which is perhaps what makes it such a successful text for classroom use.[17] However, the limitation of Gallop's Lacanian analysis is that the emergence of the addressee is contained within the dialectic of transference and countertransference, which tends to produce an account of pedagogic affect that fits too easily into an instrumental rhetoric of manipulative seduction. Desire remains a transaction between subjects, and as such can be too easily complicit with power, its flow channeled within the hierarchical distribution of places.

In the classroom, the Other should not serve to erase the addressee; the pragmatic instance that she or he occupies is not simply the pretext for a communication between the philosopher-master and the tradition of Western Thought (or the Unconscious). That is the lesson of Lyotard's pedagogy. There is some Other, in the classroom, and it has many names: culture, thought, desire, energy, tradition, the event, the immemorial, the sublime. The educational institution seeks to process it, to dampen the shock it gives the system. *Qua* institution, education seeks to channel and circulate this otherness so that some form of profit can be made from it. Yet this shock arises, since it is *the minimal condition of pedagogy*. It opens a series of incalculable differences, the exploration of which is the business of pedagogy. Education, as *educere*, a drawing out, is not for Lyotard a maieutic revelation of the student to him or herself, a process of clearly remembering what the student in fact already knew. Rather, education is this drawing out of the otherness of thought that undoes the pretension of self-presence, that always demands further study. And it works over both the students and the teachers, though in a dissymmetrical fashion.

Lyotard's demand that the pole of the addressee should be respected is not a demagoguery: If he refuses to make the students into the locus of a simple reproduction, either of the professor or of the faithful servants that the system requires, this is not in order to suggest that the students occupy a position of autonomy or authenticity, that in order to be educated they need only to affirm who they already are. Here, Lyotard avoids subjugating education to a Marxist grand narrative. The students are not a proletariat by analogy; they do not incarnate the repressed meaning of the educational process. Lyotard's attack on the professor's authority, on the professor as the transcendent subject of the educational process, does not simply seek to replace the professor with the student. This would, of course, be the demagogic version of 1968: the inversion of hierarchy, so that the students embody the real university. But as Lyotard reminds us in his "Preamble to a Charter,"

we must keep the pedagogical relation as a whole open, offered to critical consciousness. The teacher/pupil relation ought to be permanently protected against both a falling back into the old hierarchic magisterial relation and the demagogy that proposes a symmetry between the teacher and the pupil, as well as against the training of the pupil as a mere expert/counsellor. Knowledge must also be ceaselessly kept from reverting back into a known thing. (*PW*, 45)

Three pitfalls attend the pedagogic relation. First is the hierarchy that makes the professor an absolute authority and the students so many receptacles for the transmission of a preconstituted and unquestionable knowledge. Second is the claim that teaching raises no difference between teachers and students, the demagoguery that suggests that there is nothing to learn. And third is the reduction of education to the development and training of technocrats without questioning the purposes and functions to which that training is dedicated. Each seeks to put an end to questioning, most obviously in the first and third cases, but more insidiously in the second, where thought is sacrificed rather than questioned—sacrificed precisely because it might question the presumption of an indifferent egalitarianism.

What each of these threats to the pedagogic relation has in common is an orientation toward autonomy, an assertion that knowledge involves the abandonment of a network of ethical obligations: to have knowledge is to gain a self-sufficient, monologic voice. The voice of the *magister*, whose authority rests upon his (usually *his*) privileged relation to the meaning of knowledge, a relation that is secured against any irruption of the pole of the addressee—authoritative discourse means that it makes no difference to whom he (usually *he*) is talking. The pole of the addressee is empty, an empty vessel. And the end of the process will be a replication of that autonomy, as the student becomes another professor, in turn. Thus, student autonomy is the end-product of the pedagogical process, which replicates the autonomy of the master.

On the other hand, in the demagogic mode the students' autonomy becomes an a priori given, is asserted from the beginning as the unrecognized condition of possibility of education. Students have the autonomy to decide what it is they know, what it is they should or should not learn; they have no particular relation to the professor. This might look like a claim for the recognition of the student addressee, but in fact it is merely the redescription of that addressee as always already the sender of any message, able to listen to a message only insofar as he or she has in fact (or *in potentia*) already sent it to him or herself. In the technocratic mode of training, autonomy is accorded to the referent, to a technical knowledge that is indifferent to the specificity of its inculcation: the pedagogic relation is reduced to a mere replication once more, this time the replication of the bureaucratic state as it fits subjects to tasks. Here, the educational subject is in fact the system, and the autonomy that the student gains through education is the freedom to occupy a preconstituted place in the system, which we usually describe in terms of the illusion of "working for oneself."

The narrative that underlies these three accounts of the function of education is thus parallel in that it argues that the goal of education is the achievement of a certain mimetic identity by the student, either as replication of the professor, as self-replication, or as the replication of a place in the system. With this identity comes autonomy, or to put it more clearly, *independence*: the end of dependence, of obligated relation to others. The student has acquired a certain freedom, a position of self-sufficient identity. He or she has been granted it by the professor, by the consensus of his or her peers, by the employer. The student will not have to listen any more—indeed, should not listen any more, since listening would be tantamount to questioning.

This is part of the long narrative of education that the Enlightenment, above all in France, inculcated: that knowledge would make humankind free, that education is a process of transforming children into adults. Transforming children, who are by definition dependent upon adults (who have to be held by the hand, as Lyotard puts it in "The Grip"), into independent beings, the free citizens that the modern state requires. They will judge for themselves, they will vote individually, in private, in little boxes that cut them off from all relation to others. Hence, as Lyotard points out in *The Postmodern Condition*, the French educational system has always privileged primary education rather than the university, since the state's interest in education is primarily in the production of citizen-subjects.[18] The subject's "freedom" is the freedom to be subjected to a state, which subjection is held to be no constraint by virtue of the fiction that the existence and nature of that state holds only insofar as it is the object of the free choice of subjects—a fiction whose limits appear the moment one remarks, "But I didn't vote for that."[19] If we are perhaps ready to recognize that this freedom is bought at the price of subjection to the abstract entity that is the modern state, we have yet to think through its implications for our understanding of pedagogy.

In the place of the lure of autonomy, of independence from all obligation, then, Lyotard insists upon the fact that pedagogy is a relation, a network of obligation. In this sense, we might want to talk of the teacher as *rhetor* rather than *magister*, one who speaks in a rhetorical context rather than one whose discourse is self-authorizing. The advantage here would be to recognize that the legitimation of the teacher's discourse is not immanent to that discourse but is always dependent, at least in part, on the rhetorical context of its reception. The rhetor is a speaker who takes account of the audience, whereas the magister is indifferent to the specificity of his or her addressees. Lyotard's description of himself, in *Instructions Païennes*, as a *métèque*,[20] a peripatetic foreign rhetorician, does seem to head in this direction: His lessons claim for themselves the "open duplicity" of the sophist.[21]

Yet there is room for a certain reservation with regard to the embrace of sophistic rhetoric as a *model* for the pedagogic scene in that the appeal to persuasion risks turning the pedagogic relation back into a site of subjective calculation. To be blunt, this is the epistemology of a Stanley Fish, in which the act of rhetorical persuasion is an agonistic contest of subjective wills who continue to use language instrumentally, as the instrument of persuasion that will create an effect of conviction and cause the addressee to become, for him or herself, what she or he is for the speaker. Here, rhetoric does not display a prudent respect for the pole of the addressee but seeks to erase it, to render it identical to the pole of the speaker, to make the listener adopt the same "position." Lyotard's critique, in *Rudiments Païens*, of the effect of conviction, shows that he is aware of this danger:

Normally, a theory is accompanied by a specific affect: conviction. There are witnesses, attestations, supported by observations, and they allow the constitution of a kind of discourse (a narrative, for example) which evokes belief, not only in the hearer but also in the speaker. This does not imply that the discourse is universally valid, but that at least it belongs to the domain in which the question of its validity can and must be asked. Conviction is the affect that corresponds to the closure of an inquiry, to the providing of conclusions.[22]

Reading Freud's *Beyond the Pleasure Principle*, Lyotard notes an *effect of uncertainty* that accompanies Freud's hypothesis about the economy of the pleasure drive. This is not a weak conviction but an irrepressible uncertainty that arises from the exposure of theory to the question of affect:

"All of a sudden theory ceases to deal with the true and the false, what matters above all to theory is the question of whether or not there is pathos. . . . It is a *theory-fiction*, whose specific affect is *impassivity*, not conviction. By impassivity I mean the impossibility of feeling the 'yes' and the 'no' of conviction" (*RP*, 24–25). On the basis of this account of Sigmund Freud, Lyotard argues for a rejection of the closure that accompanies conviction, a refusal of the theoretical terror that seeks to put an end to discussions: "The important thing for us now is to destroy theory, and we will not do this by taking a vow of silence. On the contrary, silence walks hand in hand with theoretical terror, it is its accomplice and guarantor. We are always told: if you are not speaking so as to speak the truth, shut up" (*RP*, 29).

If the rhetorical pragmatics of the pedagogue is not directed at conviction, how then are we to characterize the ethical obligation that teaching aims to evoke? The second problem that an instrumentalized account of the pragmatics of teaching can cause is a focus solely directed at an intersubjective relation. Lyotard's account of pedagogy does insist upon its intersubjectivity, upon the pole of the addressee, but it does not do so exclusively. That is to say, teaching is not exhausted in the achievement of intersubjective communication. The student-teacher relationship is not one of magisterial domination—nor is it one of dyadic fusion, in which mutual understanding would serve as an end in itself, the mutual unveiling of teachers and students of which Johann Fichte speaks in his writings on the university.[23] Neither convincing students nor fusing with them, teaching, like psychoanalysis, is an interminable process.

What prevents such a fusion and thus makes teaching interminable is the fact that the network of obligation extends to all four poles of the pragmatic linguistic situation, as described by Lyotard in *The Differend*: the sender, the addressee, the referent, and the signification. The referent of teaching, that to which it points, is the name of Thought. Let me stress the point that this is not a religious dedication. I say "name" and I capitalize "thought" not to indicate a mystical transcendence but to avoid the confusion of the referent with any particular signification. The name of Thought precisely is a name in that it *has no intrinsic meaning*. As a horizon, it cannot be given a content that will allow the closure of debate. Debate may occur as to its signification, but this will always be an agonistic contest of prescriptives about what thought should be: Nothing in the nature of thought, as a bare name, will legitimate any one or other of these accounts. To put this another way, any attempt to say what thought should be must take responsibility for itself as such an attempt: the name of Thought, since it has no content, cannot be invoked as an *alibi* that might excuse us from the necessity of thinking about what we are saying and when, and from where. The name of Thought is one of many names that operate in the pedagogic scene, and the attribution of any signification to it is an act that must understand itself as such, as having a certain rhetorical and ethical weight. Such an act must take responsibility for itself, must not invoke thought as an alibi. As Lyotard puts it:

To admit that competence in scientific and technical matters is not illusory and that scientists, engineers and technicians really are learned, although at times there is evidence to the contrary, does not prove that the same thing goes for all questions. One can, for example, provide a rigorous demonstration that the just is not an object of knowledge and there is no science of justice.

One can show the same thing for what is beautiful, or what is agreeable. Hence there is no true and certain competence in these domains, domains that, however, have a great significance in everyday life. In these domains there are only opinions. And all these opinions have to be discussed.[24]

Hence, for instance, I admit that these reflections are written from the point of view of someone who is, professionally, a teacher, though he does not in any absolute sense know the signification of the name of teacher.

In the classroom, Thought intervenes as a third term that undoes the presumption to autonomy of professors, of students, of a body of knowledge. Thought names a differend; it is a name over which arguments take place, arguments that occur in heterogeneous idioms. Most importantly, this third term does not resolve these arguments; it does not provide a metalanguage that can translate all other idioms into its own so that their dispute can be settled, their claims arranged and evaluated on a homogeneous scale. What is drawn out in education is not the hidden meaning of Thought, nor is it the true identity of students, nor is it the true identity of the professor (replicated in the students). Rather, what is drawn out is the aporetic nature of this differend, the necessity and impossibility that it should be discussed, despite the absence of a univocal or common language for that discussion to occur. Thought is, in this sense, an empty transcendence, not one that can be worshipped, believed in, but one that throws those who participate in pedagogy back into a reflection upon the ungroundedness of their situation: their obligation to each other and to a name that hails them as addressees, before they can think about it.

Thus, to attribute a signification to thought, the act of saying what it means to think, is inevitably a political question, in the minimal sense of an agonistic moment of conflict where a difference is opened as to the nature of discourse. To put this another way, "what is called thinking?" is never, for Lyotard, simply a theoretical question, one that a fully grounded epistemology might answer. Whence proceeds the second aspect of Lyotard's writing on education that retains our attention: the persistent refusal to engage in abstract reflection on pedagogy in isolation from a reflection on the institutions within and against which that teaching takes place.

Lyotard's militant position in the events of 1968 in Paris is now perhaps more widely acknowledged, however much it may surprise those accustomed, like Peter Dews, to associate his writings with the undermining of the possibility of political action.[25] The essays that come out of the events of 1968 insist upon the concrete fact of militant action, as in "Nanterre, Here, Now," which interweaves student accounts of battles with police with the text of an analysis of the situation that Lyotard had prepared for a meeting of teachers' union groups. Lyotard begins by noting that he failed to deliver this address owing to the intervention of security marshals—underlining the point that one of the primary effects of the student revolt was to provide the proof that no institutional space of enunciation or of reflection is completely independent of the violence and disruption of political conflict, that "in this society, knowledge is constantly compromised with power."[26]

Hence Lyotard's analysis of 1968 refuses the choice proposed by the Fouchet plan, which offered to bring the French university system "up to date." This offered a choice between a quasi-feudal institution that produces erudite scholarly knowledge and a modernized, practical institution that will produce the technical know-how required in advanced capitalist society. As he argues in "Preamble to a Charter," the traditional and modern images of the university are in fact more complicit than they might seem: The humanities stress the separation of the university from society, and thus defuse critical energies in producing scholars, whereas the social sciences technologize social reality to produce experts. As we have seen, Lyotard's description of the role of the philosopher in the introduction to *The Postmodern Condition* is precisely a refusal to be either an expert or a scholar. The production of scholars in the humanities and the production of experts in the social sciences combine to prevent social critique, be it by defusing critical energies or by recuperating them so as to refine the functioning of the existing social order.[27]

The question of the university cannot be answered by reforming it so as to produce knowledge more efficiently, or so as to produce more efficient knowledge. Rather, the analogy of production itself must be brought into question: the analogy that makes the university into a bureaucratic apparatus for the production, distribution, and consumption of knowledge. For what is at stake here is the extent to which the university *as an institution* participates in the capitalist-bureaucratic system.[28] That is to say, the university as an institution can deal with all kinds of knowledges, even oppositional ones, so as to make them circulate to the benefit of the system as a whole (this is something we know very well—radicalism sells well, in the university milieu). Hence the futility of the radicalism that calls for a university that will produce more radical kinds of knowledge, more radical students, more of anything. Such appeals, because they do not take into account the institutional status of the university as a capitalist bureaucracy, are doomed to confirm the very system they oppose. The ideological content of the knowledges produced in the university is increasingly indifferent to its functioning as a bureaucratic enterprise; the only proviso is that such radical knowledges fit into the cycle of production, exchange, and consumption. Produce what knowledge you like, only produce more of it so that the system can speculate on knowledge differentials and profit from the accumulation of intellectual capital.[29]

This, it seems to me, is the situation in which we find ourselves now. Lyotard's insistence on institutional critique requires of us that we find a way to make our pedagogical activities, as students and teachers, difficult for the system to swallow, hard to insert within the generalized economy of capitalist exchange. The exponential growth in the commodification of information itself, thanks to new technologies, renders this situation even more acute. If pedagogy is to pose a challenge to the ever-increasing bureaucratization of the university as a whole, this will require a decentering of our vision of the educational process. Only in this way can we hope to open up pedagogy, to lend it a temporality that resists commodification, by arguing that listening to Thought is not the spending of time in the production of an autonomous subject or in an autonomous body of knowledge. Rather, to listen to thought, to think beside each other and beside ourselves, is to explore an open network of obligations that keeps the question of meaning open, a locus of debate—doing justice to thought, listening to our interlocutors, means trying to hear what cannot be said, but which tries to make itself heard, a process incompatible with the production of (even relatively) stable and exchangeable knowledge.

This may prove surprising.

NOTES

1. These essays are reprinted in Jean-François Lyotard, *Political Writings*, trans. Bill Readings and Kevin Paul Geiman (Minneapolis: University of Minnesota Press, 1993). Henceforth referred to as *PW*).

2. Jean-François Lyotard, *The Differend: Phrases in Dispute*, trans. Georges Van Den Abbeele (Minneapolis: University of Minnesota Press, 1988).

3. J.-F. Lyotard, *The Postmodern Condition*, trans. Geoffrey Bennington and Brian Massumi (Minneapolis: University of Minnesota Press, 1979). Henceforth referred to as *PMC*.

4. Ibid., p. xxv.

5. Ibid.

6. Fredric Jameson, in his "Foreword" to *The Postmodern Condition*, notes an apparent neutrality of tone but then goes on to imply that Lyotard's argument is not "genuinely political" because its appeal is to symbolic or protopolitical forms of action (*PMC*, pp. xx).

7. J.-F. Lyotard, "Dead Letter," in *PW*.

8. Samuel Weber, *Institution and Interpretation* (Minneapolis: University of Minnesota Press, 1987).

9. J.-F. Lyotard, *Instructions Païennes* (Paris: Galilée, 1977); *The Postmodern Explained*, trans. Julian Pefanis et al. (Minneapolis: University of Minnesota Press, 1993); *Économie Libidinale* (Paris: Minuit, 1984); J.-F. Lyotard and Jean-Loup Thébaud, *Just Gaming*, trans. Wlad Godzich (Minneapolis: University of Minnesota Press, 1985) (henceforth referred to as *JG*).

10. Here I am thinking in particular of the dialogue form in the penultimate section of *Ulysses*, in which a question-and-answer session leads to a synthesis of Bloom and Stephen Dedalus, Hebraic and Hellenic traditions.

11. "Culture is lending an ear to what strives to be said," Lyotard, "Dead Letter," *PW*, p. 33. The recourse to culture here is perhaps no longer relevant, since it is linked to a somewhat romantic vision of the force of "poetry" as "the activity that lets what demands to be said be spoken," p. 39. Such an expressivist account is considerably revised in *The Differend*, which deals with the fact that clash of heterogeneous idioms undermines any such simple opposition between silence and voice, an opposition that leaves unproblematized the liberatory narrative of passage from one to the other.

12. J.-F. Lyotard, "Endurance and the Profession," *PW*, p. 73.

13. Maurice Blanchot, *The Unavowable Community*, trans. Pierre Joris (Barrytown, N.Y.: Station Hill Press, 1988).

14. See Mikkel Borch-Jacobsen, *Lacan: The Absolute Master*, trans. Douglas Brick (Stanford, Calif.: Stanford University Press, 1991).

15. See Gilles Deleuze and J.-F. Lyotard, "Concerning the Vincennes Psychoanalytic Department," in *PW*, in which they detail the autocratic attempt by the Lacanian school to "purge" the department of psychoanalysis and install only orthodox Lacanians.

16. See "Séminaire sur *La Lettre volée*," in Lacan, *Écrits* (Paris: Seuil, 1966).

17. Jane Gallop, *The Daughter's Seduction* (Ithaca, N.Y.: Cornell University Press, 1982).

18. "The subject of the first of these versions [of the narrative of legitimation] is humanity as the hero of liberty. All peoples have a right to science. If the social subject is not already the subject of scientific knowledge, it is because that has been forbidden

by priests and tyrants. The right to science must be reconquered. It is understandable that this narrative would be directed more towards a politics of primary education, rather than of universities and high schools. The educational policy of the French Third Republic powerfully illustrates these presuppositions." *PMC*, p. 31.

19. As Wlad Godzich puts it, "Those who hold state power first co-opt individuals, thereby making them other with respect to the rest of society, and then let the state as an apparatus of power determine the configuration of the social. Thus neither the production of the other nor that of the social is collective." From "Afterword: Religion, the State, and Post(al) Modernism" in Weber, *Institution and Interpretation*, p. 161.

20. See the partial translation, "Lessons in Paganism," in *The Lyotard Reader*, ed. Andrew Benjamin (Oxford: Basil Blackwell, 1989), p. 133.

21. Ibid., p. 136.

22. J.-F. Lyotard, *Rudiments Païens* (Paris: Union générale d'éditions, 1977), pp. 17–18 (my translation). Henceforth referred to as *RP*.

23. Johann Gottlieb Fichte, "Plan déductif d'un établissement d'enseignement supérieur à fonder à Berlin," in *Philosophies de l'Université: l'idéalisme allemande et la question de l'Université*, ed. L. Ferry, J. P. Pesron, and A. Renaut, trans. G. Coffin, J.-F. Courtine, L. Ferry, A. Laks, O. Masson, A. Renaut, and J. Rivelaygue, pp. 180–81: "A common spiritual existence, . . . where they have learnt early on to know each other deeply, and to respect each other, where all their reflections begin from a base which is known to all identically and which gives no grounds for dispute" (my translation from the French).

24. "A Podium without a Podium," in *PW*, p. 94.

25. Peter Dews, *Logic of Disintegration: Post-Structuralist Thought and the Claims of Critical Theory* (London: Verso, 1987). I shall not examine the problems of Dews's argument here. Instead, I would urge readers to consult Richard Beardsworth's excellent essay "Lyotard's Agitated Judgement" in *Judging Lyotard*, ed. Andrew Benjamin (London: Routledge, 1992), which persuasively rebuts Dews's accusations.

26. "Preamble to a Charter," in *PW*, p. 45.

27. Ibid., p. 44.

28. "The university belongs to the system insofar as the system is capitalist and bureaucratic," "Nanterre, Here, Now," in *PW*, p. 56.

29. It is perhaps worthwhile distinguishing this analysis from Pierre Bourdieu's concept of "cultural capital," which animates John Guillory's analysis of the university in *Cultural Capital* (Chicago: University of Chicago Press, 1993). For Guillory, as for Bourdieu, cultural capital retains a primarily ideological function despite the fact that the term seems relatively indifferent to the ideological content of cultural production. This is because cultural capital is conceived as circulating within a cultural system that is closed off by national boundaries. In order for symbolic status to be quantifiable, to be analyzed analogously to financial value, the system within which it is distributed must be closed, and hence Bourdieu and his epigones tend to limit the field of their studies, often appealing to a need for contextual specificity. From this perspective, the university necessarily appears as an ideological apparatus of the nation-state rather than a potentially transnational bureaucratic-capitalist enterprise.

Selected Bibliography

Appignanesi, Lisa. ed. *Postmodernism: ICA Documents*. London: Free Association Books, 1989.

Apple, Michael. *Teachers and Texts*. London: Routledge, 1988.

Apple, Michael. "The Text and Cultural Politics." *Journal of Educational Thought* 24, 3A (1990): 17–33.

Arendt, Hannah. "The Crisis in Education." In *Between Past and Future*. New York: Viking Press, 1961.

Arnold, Matthew. *Culture and Anarchy*. Ed. Ian Gregor. Indianapolis: Bobbs-Merrill, 1971.

Aronowitz, Stanley, and Henry A. Giroux. *Postmodern Education: Politics, Culture, and Social Criticism*. Minneapolis: University of Minnesota Press, 1991.

Bakhtin, M. M. *Speech Genres and Other Late Essays*. Trans. Vern W. McGee. Ed. Caryl Emerson and Michael Holquist. Austin: University of Texas Press, 1986.

Beardsworth, Richard. "Lyotard's Agitated Judgement." In *Judging Lyotard*, ed. Andrew Benjamin, 43–80. London: Routledge, 1992.

Bell, Daniel. *The Coming of Post-Industrial Society*. London: Wildwood House, 1974.

Benamou, Michel, and Charles Caramello, eds. *Performance in Postmodern Culture*. Wisconsin: Center for Twentieth Century Studies and Coda Press, 1977.

Bernauer, James W. *Michel Foucault's Force of Flight: Toward an Ethics for Thought*. New Jersey: Humanities Press International, 1990.

Bernstein, Richard J. *The New Constellation: The Ethical-Political Horizons of Modernity/Postmodernity*. Cambridge, Mass.: MIT Press, 1992.

Blanchot, Maurice. *The Unavowable Community*. Trans. Pierre Joris. Barrytown, N.Y.: Station Hill Press, 1988.

Bloom, Alan. *The Closing of the American Mind*. New York: Simon & Schuster, 1987.

Bogue, Ronald. "Gilles Deleuze: Postmodern Philosopher?" *Criticism* 32, 4 (Fall 1990): 401–18.

Borch-Jacobsen, Mikkel. *Lacan: The Absolute Master*. Trans. Douglas Brick. Stanford, Calif.: Stanford University Press, 1991.

Burbules, Nicholas, and S. Rice. "Dialogue across Differences: Continuing the Conversation." *Harvard Educational Review* 61, 4 (1991): 393–416.

Bürger, Peter. "The Decline of the Modern Age." *Telos* 62 (Winter 1985): 117–30.

Calinescu, Matei. *Faces of Modernity: Avant-Garde, Decadence, Kitsch*. Bloomington: Indiana University Press, 1977.

Carroll, David. "Narrative, Heterogeneity, and the Question of the Political: Bakhtin and Lyotard." In *The Aims of Representation: Subject/Text/History*, ed. Murray Krieger, 69–106. New York: Columbia University Press, 1987.

Carroll, David. *Paraesthetics: Foucault, Lyotard, Derrida*. London: Methuen, 1989.

Cohn-Bendit, Daniel. *Obsolete Communism*. Harmondsworth, England: Penguin, 1969.

Cook, Deborah. "Remapping Modernity." *British Journal of Aesthetics* 30, 1 (January 1990): 35–45.

Corrigan, Phillip. "Untying the Knots: The Texts of the State." *Journal of Educational Thought* 24, 3A (1990): 46–67.

D'Souza, Dinesh. *Illiberal Education: The Politics of Race and Sex on Campus*. New York: Macmillan, 1991.

Deleuze, Gilles. *Nietzsche and Philosophy*. Trans. Hugh Tomlinson. New York: Columbia University Press, 1983.

Descombes, Vincent. *Modern French Philosophy*. Cambridge: Cambridge University Press, 1973.

Dews, Peter. *Logic of Disintegration: Post-Structuralist Thought and the Claims of Critical Theory*. London: Verso, 1987.

Di Stefano, Christine. "Dilemmas of Difference: Feminism, Modernity, and Postmodernism." In *Feminism/Postmodernism*, ed. Linda J. Nicholson. New York: Routledge, 1990.

Dreyfuss, Hubert L., and Paul Rabinow. *Michel Foucault: Beyond Structuralism and Hermeneutics*. Chicago: University of Chicago Press, 1983.

Dreyfuss, Hubert L., and Paul Rabinow. "What Is Maturity? Habermas and Foucault on 'What Is Enlightenment?' " In *Foucault: A Critical Reader*, ed. David Couzens Hoy. New York: Basil Blackwell, 1986.

Ellsworth, Elizabeth. "Why Doesn't This Feel Empowering? Working through the Repressive Myths of Critical Pedagogy." *Harvard Educational Review* 58, 3 (1989): 280–98.

Eribon, Didier. *Michel Foucault*. Cambridge, Mass.: Harvard University Press, 1991.

Fine, Michelle. "Sexuality Schooling and Adolescent Females: The Missing Discourse of Desire." *Harvard Educational Review* 58, 1 (1988): 29–53.

Fine, Michelle. *Framing Dropouts: Notes on the Politics of an Urban High School*. Albany, N.Y.: State University of New York Press, 1991.

Flax, Jane. "Postmodernism and Gender Relations in Feminist Theory." In *Feminism/Postmodernism*, ed. Linda J. Nicholson. New York: Routledge, 1990.

Flax, Jane. "The End of Innocence." In *Feminists Theorize the Political*, ed. Judith Butler and Joan W. Scott. New York: Routledge, 1992.

Foster, Hal, ed. *Postmodern Culture*. London: Pluto Press, 1983.

Foucault, Michel. *The Archaeology of Knowledge and the Discourse on Language*. Trans. A. M. Sheridan Smith. New York: Pantheon Books, 1972.

Foucault, Michel. *The Order of Things: An Archaeology of the Human Sciences*. New York: Vintage Books, 1973.

Foucault, Michel. "Introduction" to G. Deleuze and F. Guattari, *Anti-Oedipus: Capitalism and Schizophrenia*. Minneapolis: University of Minnesota Press, 1977.

Foucault, Michel. *Language, Counter-Memory, Practice*. Ed. Donald F. Bouchard. Ithaca, N.Y.: Cornell University Press, 1977.

Foucault, Michel. *Discipline and Punish: The Birth of the Prison*. Trans. Alan Sheridan. New York: Vintage Books, 1979.

Foucault, Michel. "Governmentality." *Ideology and Consciousness* 6 (1979): 1–26.

Foucault, Michel. *Power/Knowledge*. Ed. Colin Gordon. New York: Pantheon Books, 1980.

Foucault, Michel. *Foucault Reader*. Ed. Paul Rabinow. New York: Pantheon Books, 1984.

Foucault, Michel. *Death and the Labyrinth: The World of Raymond Roussel*. London: Athlone Press, 1987.

Foucault, Michel. *Michel Foucault: Politics, Philosophy, Culture*. Ed. Lawrence D. Kritzman. London and New York: Routledge, Chapman and Hall, 1988.

Frankel, Boris. *The Post-Industrial Utopians*. Cambridge: Polity Press/Basil Blackwell, 1987.

Fraser, Nancy. "Foucault on Modern Power: Empirical Insights and Normative Confusions." *Praxis International* 1 (1981): 272–87.

Fraser, Nancy. "Foucault's Body-Language: A Post-Humanist Political Rhetoric?" *Salmagundi* 61 (1983): 55–70.

Fraser, Nancy. "Michel Foucault: A 'Young Conservative'?" *Ethics* 96 (1985): 165–84.

Fraser, Nancy, and Linda J. Nicholson. "Social Criticism without Philosophy: An Encounter between Feminism and Postmodernism." In *Feminism/Postmodernism*, ed. Linda J. Nicholson. New York: Routledge, 1990.

Freire, Paulo. *Pedagogy of the Oppressed*. Harmondsworth, England: Penguin Books, 1972.

Friere, Paulo. *Education for Critical Consciousness*. New York: Seabury Press, 1973.

Fritzman, J. M. "Lyotard's Paralogy and Rorty's Pluralism: Their Differences and Pedagogical Implications." *Educational Theory* 40 (1990): 371–80.

Galanter, E. *Automatic Teaching: The State of the Art*. New York: John Wiley and Sons, 1959.

Gallop, Jane. *The Daughter's Seduction*. Ithaca, N.Y.: Cornell University Press, 1982.

Giroux, Henry. *Living Dangerously*. New York: Peter Lang, 1993.

Gless, Darryl J., and Barbara Herrnstein Smith, eds. *The Politics of Liberal Education*. Durham, N.C.: Duke University Press, 1992.

Gordon, Colin. "Question, Ethos, Event: Foucault on Kant and Enlightenment." *Economy and Society* 15, 1 (February 1986).

Gore, Jennifer. "What Can We Do for You! What Can 'We' Do for 'You'? Struggling over Empowerment in Critical and Feminist Pedagogy." *Educational Foundations* 4, 3 (1990): 5–26.

Greene, Maxine. "Values Education in the Contemporary Moment." *Clearing House*, May/June 1991.

Grossberg, Lawrence. *We Gotta Get out of This Place: Popular, Conservative and Postmodern Culture*. New York: Routledge, 1992.

Habermas, Jürgen. "Modernity versus Postmodernity." *New German Critique* 22 (1981): 3–22.

Habermas, Jürgen. "The Entwinement of Myth and Enlightenment: Rereading *Dialectic of Enlightenment*." *New German Critique* 26 (Spring–Summer 1982): 13–31.

Habermas, Jürgen. *The Philosophical Discourse of Modernity*. Trans. F. Lawrence. Cambridge, Mass.: MIT Press, 1987.

Halls, W. D. *Education, Culture and Politics in Modern France*. Oxford: Pergammon Press, 1976.

Harris, Kevin. *Teachers and Social Classes*. Boston: Routledge, 1982.

Hartsock, Nancy. "Rethinking Modernism: Minority and Majority Theories." *Cultural Critique* 7 (Fall 1987).

Hassan, Ihab. *The Dismemberment of Orpheus: Towards a Post Modern Literature*. New York: Oxford University Press, 1971.

Hinkson, John. *Postmodernity: State and Education*. Deakin: Deakin University Press, 1992.

Hirsch, E. D. *Cultural Literacy*. Boston: Houghton Mifflin, 1987.

Hollis, Martin. *The Cunning of Reason*. Cambridge: Cambridge University Press, 1987.

hooks, bell. "Marginality as Site of Resistance." In *Out There: Marginalization and Contemporary Cultures*, ed. Russell Ferguson, Martha Gever, Trinh T. Minh-ha, and Cornel West. Cambridge, Mass.: MIT Press, 1992.

hooks, bell. *Talking Back*. Boston: South End Press, 1989.

Howe, Irving. "Mass Society and Postmodern Fiction." *Partisan Review* 26 (1959): 430–36.

Hutcheon, Linda. *The Politics of Postmodernism*. London: Routledge, 1989.

Huyssen, Andreas. "The Search for Tradition: Avant-Garde and Postmodernism in the 1970s." *New German Critique* 22 (Winter 1981): 23–40.

Nicholson, Linda J., ed. *Feminism/Postmodernism*. New York: Routledge, 1990.

Jameson, Fredric. "Postmodernism, or the Cultural Logic of Late Capitalism." *New Left Review* 146 (1984): 53–92.

Kanpol, Barry. *Towards a Theory and Practice of Teacher Cultural Politics: Continuing the Postmodern Debate*. New Jersey: Ablex, 1992.

Kanpol, Barry, and Peter McLaren, eds. *Critical Multiculturalism: Uncommon Voices in a Common Struggle*. New York: Bergin and Garvey, 1994.

Kaplan, Ann E., ed. *Postmodernism and Its Discontents*. New York: Verso, 1988.

Kearney, Richard. *The Wake of Imagination*. Minneapolis: University of Minnesota Press, 1988.

Kellner, Douglas. *Critical Theory, Marxism and Modernity*. Cambridge and Baltimore: Polity Press and Johns Hopkins University Press, 1989.

Kiziltan, Mustafa U., William J. Bain, and Anita Canizares M. "Postmodern Conditions: Rethinking Public Education." *Educational Theory* 40, 3 (Summer 1990): 351–69.

Koelb, Clayton. "Introduction: So What's the Story?" In *Nietzsche as Postmodernist: Essays Pro and Contra*, ed. Clayton Koelb. New York: SUNY Press, 1990.

Köhler, M. "Postmodernismus: ein Begriffgeschichtlicher Überblick." *Amerikastudien* 22, 1 (1977).

Kozol, Jonathan. *Savage Inequalities*. New York: Crown, 1991.

Kuhn, Thomas S. *The Structure of Scientific Revolutions*. 2nd ed., enlarged. Chicago: University of Chicago Press, 1970.

Kumar, Krishan. *Prophecy and Progress*. Harmondsworth, England: Penguin, 1978.

Laclau, Ernesto. "Metaphor and Social Antagonisms." In Cary Nelson and Lawrence Grossberg, eds. *Marxism and the Interpretation of Culture*. Chicago: University of Illinois Press, 1988.

Laclau, Ernesto. "Universalism, Particularism, and the Question of Identity." *October* 61 (1992): 83–90.

Laclau, Ernesto, and Chantal Mouffe. "Post-Marxism without Apologies." *New Left Review* 166 (1987): 79–136.

Laclau, Ernesto, and Chantal Mouffe. *Hegemony and Socialist Strategy*. New York: Verso, 1985.

Lash, Scott. *Sociology of Postmodernism*. Boston: Routledge, 1990.

Lash, Scott, and Jonathan Friedman, eds. *Modernity and Identity*. Cambridge: Basil Blackwell, 1992.

Lather, Patti. "Postmodernism and the Politics of Enlightenment." *Educational Foundations* 3, 3 (Fall 1989): 7–28.

Lather, Patti. *Getting Smart*. Boston: Routledge, 1991.

Levin, Harry. "What Was Modernism?" In *Refractions*. New York: Oxford University Press, 1966.

Lyotard, Jean-François. *Instructions Païennes*. Paris: Galilée, 1977.

Lyotard, Jean-François. *Rudiments Païens*. Paris: Union Générale d'éditions, 1977.

Lyotard, Jean-François. "Presentations." In *Philosophy in France Today*, ed. Alan Montefiore. Cambridge: Cambridge University Press, 1983.

Lyotard, Jean-François. *The Postmodern Condition: A Report on Knowledge*. Trans. Geoff Bennington and Brian Massumi. Foreword by Fredric Jameson. Minneapolis: University of Minnesota Press, 1984.

Lyotard, Jean-François. "Interview," with Georges Van Den Abbeele." *Diacritics* 14, 3 (Fall 1984): 16–23.

Lyotard, Jean-François. *The Differend: Phrases in Dispute*. Trans. Georges Van Den Abbeele. Minneapolis: University of Minnesota Press, 1988.

Lyotard, Jean-François. "An Interview with Jean-François Lyotard" (with Willem van Reijen and Dick Veerman). *Theory, Culture and Society* 5 (1988): 277–309.

Lyotard, Jean-François. *The Lyotard Reader*, ed. Andrew Benjamin. Cambridge: Basil Blackwell, 1989.

Lyotard, Jean-François. *Heidegger and "the Jews."* Trans. Andreas Michel and Mark Roberts. Minneapolis: University of Minnesota Press, 1990.

Lyotard, Jean-François. *The Postmodern Explained to Children: Correspondence 1982–1985*. Sydney: Power Publications, 1992.

Lyotard, Jean-François. *Libidinal Economy*. Bloomington: Indiana University Press, 1993.

Lyotard, Jean-François. *Political Writings*. Trans. Bill Readings and Kevin Paul Geiman. Minneapolis: University of Minnesota Press, 1993.

Lyotard, Jean-François. "On the Strength of the Weak." In *Toward the Postmodern*, ed. Robert Harvey and Mark S. Roberts. New Jersey: Humanities Press, 1993.

Lyotard, Jean-François, and Jean-Loup Thébaud. *Just Gaming*. Trans. Wlad Godzich. Minneapolis: University of Minnesota Press, 1985.

Macey, David. *The Lives of Michel Foucault*. London: Hutchinson, 1993.

Marable, Manning. *The Crisis of Color and Democracy*. Maine: Common Courage Press, 1992.

McLaren, Peter. "Postmodernism, Post-Colonialism and Pedagogy." *Education and Society* 9, 1 (1991): 3–22.

McLaren, Peter. "Schooling and the Postmodern Body: Critical Pedagogy and the Politics of Enfleshment." In *Postmodernism, Feminism and Cultural Politics*, ed. Henry Giroux. New York: Bergin and Garvey, 1991.

McLaren, Peter. "Multiculturalism and the Postmodern Critique: Towards a Pedagogy of Resistance and Transformation." *Cultural Studies* 7, 1 (January 1993): 118–46.

McLaren, Peter. *Life in Schools*. 2nd. ed. Boston: Longman, 1994.

Miller, James. *The Passion of Michel Foucault*. New York: Simon & Schuster, 1993.

Morin, Edgar. "The Student Commune." In *Reflections on the Revolution in France, 1968*, ed. Charles Posner. Harmondsworth, England: Pelican, 1968.

Mouffe, Chantal. "Hegemony and New Political Subjects: Towards a New Concept of Democracy." In *Marxism and the Interpretation of Culture*, ed. Cary Nelson and Lawrence Grossberg. Chicago: University of Illinois Press, 1988.

Mouffe, Chantal. "Citizenship and Political Identity." *October* 61 (1992): 33–45.

Nicholson, Carol. "Postmodernism, Feminism, and Education: The Need for Solidarity." *Educational Theory* 39, 3 (1989): 197–206.

Nietzsche, Friedrich. *Daybreak*. Trans. R. J. Hollingdale. Cambridge: Cambridge University Press, 1982.

Nietzsche, Friedrich. *On the Genealogy of Morals*. Trans. and ed. Walter Kaufmann. New York: Vintage Books, 1969.

Nietzsche, Friedrich. "Thus Spoke Zarathustra." In *The Portable Nietzsche*. Trans. Walter Kaufmann. New York: Penguin Books, 1976.

Nietzsche, Friedrich. *The Gay Science*. Trans. Walter Kaufmann. New York: Vintage Books, 1974.

Nuyen, A. T. "Lyotard on the Death of the Professor." *Educational Theory* 39 (1992): 25–37.

Nuyen, A. T. "Rorty's Hermeneutics and the Problem of Relativism." *Man and World* 25 (1992).

Paglia, Camille. *Sex, Art, and American Culture*. New York: Vintage Books, 1992.

Peters, Michael. "Techno-Science, Rationality, and the University: Lyotard on the 'Postmodern Condition.' " *Educational Theory* 39, 2 (Spring 1989): 89–105.

Peters, Michael. "Re-reading Touraine: Postindustrialism and the Future of the University." *Sites* 23 (Spring 1991): 63–83.

Peters, Michael. "Performance and Accountability in 'Post-Industrial Society': The Crisis of British Universities." *Studies in Higher Education* 17, 2 (1992): 123–39.

Peters, Michael. "Radical Democracy, the Politics of Difference and Education." In *Critical Multiculturalism: Uncommon Voices in a Common Struggle*, ed. Barry Kanpol and Peter McLaren. New York: Bergin and Garvey, 1994.

Peters, Michael. "Philosophy and Education: 'After' Wittgenstein." *Philosophy and Education: Accepting Wittgenstein's Challenge*, ed. Paul Smeyers and James Marshall. Dordrecht: Kluwer, in press.

Peters, Michael, James Marshall, and Bruce Parr. "The Marketization of Tertiary Education in New Zealand." *Australian Universities' Review* 36 (1993): 34–39.

Pignatelli, Frank. "Towards a Postprogressive Theory of Education." *Educational Foundations* 7, 3 (1993): 7–26.

Poster, Mark. *Existential Marxism in Post-War France*. Princeton, N.J.: Princeton University Press, 1975.

Poster, Mark. "The Future According to Foucault: The Archaeology of Knowledge and Intellectual History." In *Modern European Intellectual History: The Appraisais and New Perspectives*, ed. D. Lacapra and S. Kaplan, 137–52. Ithaca, N.Y.: Cornell University Press, 1981.

Purpel, David. *The Moral and Spiritual Crisis in Public Education*. New York: Bergin and Garvey, 1989.

Quine, Willard. *Word and Object*. Cambridge, Mass.: MIT Press, 1960.

Raulet, Gérard. "Structuralism and Post-Structuralism: An Interview with Michel Foucault." *Telos* 53 (1983): 119–206.

Rawls, John. *A Theory of Justice*. Cambridge, Mass.: Harvard University Press, 1971.

Readings, Bill. *Introducing Lyotard: Art and Politics*. London: Routledge, 1991.

Readings, Bill. "Foreword: The End of the Political." In Jean-François Lyotard, *Political Writings*. Trans. Bill Readings and Kevin Paul Geiman. Minneapolis: University of Minnesota Press, 1994.

Rorty, Richard. *Philosophy and the Mirror of Nature*. Oxford: Basil Blackwell, 1980.

Rorty, Richard. "Hermeneutics, General Studies and Teaching." *Selected Papers from the Synergos Seminar* 2 (1982).

Rorty, Richard. *Consequences of Pragmatism: Essays, 1972–1980*. Minneapolis: University of Minnesota Press, 1982.

Rorty, Richard. "Habermas and Lyotard on Postmodernity." In *Habermas and Modernity*, ed. Richard Bernstein. Cambridge: Polity Press, 1985.

Rorty, Richard. "The Old-Time Philosophy: The Case against Allan Bloom on Philosophy and Democracy." *The New Republic* 198, 14 (1988): 28–33.

Rorty, Richard. "The Dangers of Over-Philosophication: Reply to Arcilla and Nicholson." *Educational Theory* 40 (1990): 40–44.

Rorty, Richard. "Feminism and Pragmatism." *Michigan Quarterly Review* 30, 2 (1991): 231–32.

Rorty, Richard. "Is Derrida a Transcendental Philosopher?" In *Essays on Heidegger and Others*. Cambridge: Cambridge University Press, 1991.

Safran, W. *The French Polity*. New York: MacKay, 1977.

Schulte-Sasse, Jochen. "Imagination and Modernity: The Taming of the Human Mind." *Cultural Critique* 5 (Winter 1986–87): 23–48.

Schulte-Sasse, Jochen. "Modernity and Modernism, Postmodernity and Postmodernism: Framing the Issue." *Cultural Critique* 5 (Winter 1986–87): 5–22.

Shapiro, Svi. *Between Capitalism and Democracy*. New York: Bergin and Garvey, 1990.

Spanos, William V. "The Apollonian Investment of Modern Humanist Education: The Examples of Matthew Arnold, Irving Babbitt, and I. A. Richards." *Cultural Critique* 1 (Fall 1985).

Touraine, Alan. *The Movement of May*. Trans. Leonard Mayhew. New York: 1971.

Touraine, Alan. *Post-Industrial Society*. Trans. Leonard Mayhew. New York: Random House, 1971.

Vattimo, Gianni. "Verwindung: Nihilism and the Postmodern in Philosophy." *SubStance* 16, 2 (1987).

Weber, Samuel. *Institution and Interpretation*. Minneapolis: University of Minnesota Press, 1987.

Weiler, Kathleen. *Women Teaching for Change.* New York: Bergin and Garvey, 1987.

Welch, Sharon. *Communities of Resistance and Solidarity: A Feminist Theology of Liberation.* Maryknoll, New York: Orbis Books, 1985.

West, Cornel. "The New Politics of Difference." In *Out There: Marginalization and Contemporary Cultures,* ed. Russell Ferguson, Martha Gever, Trinh T. Minh-ha, and Cornel West, 19–36. Cambridge: MIT Press, 1990.

West, Cornel. "Decentering Europe: A Memorial Lecture for James Snead." *Critical Quarterly* 33, 1 (Spring 1991): 1–19.

West, Cornel. *Beyond Eurocentrism and Multiculturalism,* vol. 1 *Prophetic Thought in Postmodern Times* and vol. 2 *Prophetic Reflections: Notes on Race and Power in America.* Maine: Common Courage Press, 1993.

Winch, Peter. *Trying to Make Sense.* Oxford: Basil Blackwell, 1987.

Wittgenstein, Ludwig. *Tractatus Logico-Philosophicus.* Trans. D. F. Pears and B. F. McGuiness, with Introduction by Bertrand Russell. London: Routledge & Kegan Paul, 1961.

Wittgenstein, Ludwig. *Philosophical Investigations.* Trans. G.E.M. Anscombe. Oxford: Basil Blackwell, 1953; repr. of English text, 1972.

Yeo, Fred. "The Conflicts of Differences in an Inner City School: Experiencing Border Crossings in the Ghetto." In *Education, Democracy and the Politics of Difference,* ed. Barry Kanpol and Peter McLaren. New York: Bergin and Garvey, 1994.

Index

About the Contributors

WILLIAM BAIN is presently finishing his dissertation, "Nietzsche, Bakhtin, Foucault: Politics of Identity and the 'Culture' of Multiculturalism," in Cultural Foundations of Education at Syracuse University. He has coauthored essays on education and postmodernism in *Educational Theory*, *Educational Foundations*, and *International Third World Studies Journal and Review*. One of the coauthored essays, "Postmodern Conditions: Rethinking Public Education," has recently appeared in a Portuguese translation. His research interests include the problematics of modernism, postmodernism and poststructuralism and a focus on questions of identity, meaning, order, difference, and culture.

J. M. FRITZMAN, an assistant professor of philosophy at Northern Illinois University, has research interests in social and political philosophy and in nineteenth- and twentieth-century European philosophy. Fritzman has published articles in such journals as *American Philosophical Quarterly*, *Clio*, *Educational Theory*, *International Philosophical Quarterly*, *Praxis International*, and *Rhetorica*.

JOHN HINKSON is a senior lecturer in the School of Education at La Trobe University, Australia. His research interests center upon the changing relationships among education, the mass media, the economy, and politics. He is the author of *Postmodernity: State and Education* (1991) and numerous articles published in a variety of journals, including the newly established series *Arena Journal*, for which he is currently convenor of the editorial board.

BARRY KANPOL is assistant professor in education at Penn State University. He is the author of *Towards a Theory and Practice of Teacher Cultural Politics: Continuing the Postmodern Debate* (1992) and (with Peter McLaren) coeditor of the recent collection *Critical Multiculturalism: Uncommon Voices in a Common Struggle* (1994). As a critical educator he has contributed a number of articles to a variety of international journals in education.

JEAN-FRANÇOIS LYOTARD is professor emeritus at the University of Paris at Vincennes and professor of French and Italian at the University of California at Irvine. He is also a council member at the Collège International de Philosophie and the author of numerous works, several of which have appeared in English, notably *The Postmodern Condition: A Report on Knowledge* (1984), *Just Gaming* with J.-L. Thebaud (1985), *The Differend: Phrases in Dispute* (1988), *Peregrinations: Law, Form, Event* (1988), *Heidegger and "the Jews"* (1990), *The Postmodern Explained to Children* (1992), and *Political Writings* (1993).

JAMES MARSHALL is professor of education and dean of the Faculty of Education at the University of Auckland, New Zealand. His interests are in educational philosophy and the educational implications of the work of Michel Foucault. He is the author of a number of books and monographs, including *What Is Education?* (1981), *Positivism or Pragmatism? Philosophy of Education in New Zealand* (1987), and *Why Go to School?* (1988). In addition, he has coauthored three books in education and contributed to a wide range of international journals in educational philosophy, social theory, policy, and administration. He is coeditor of a forthcoming collection on Ludwig Wittgenstein and education, as well as the author of a forthcoming book on Foucault and education.

PETER McLAREN formerly held the positions of Renown Scholar-in-Residence and director of the Center for Education and Cultural Studies in the School of Education and Allied Professions at Miami University of Ohio. He is presently associate professor in the Graduate School of Education, at the University of California, Los Angeles. He has served as educational correspondent for a teachers' union in his native Canada and since 1985 has been active in urban educational reform in the United

States. Author of numerous books and articles on critical educational theory, including the Canadian best-seller *Cries from the Corridor: The New Suburban Ghettos* and *Life in Schools*. In addition to lecturing extensively in Latin America and Europe, he coedits two publication series dealing with critical social theory and critical pedagogy (with Henry Giroux for SUNY Press, and Joe Kincheloe for Westview Press). He is also the coeditor with Colin Lankshear of *Critical Literacy: Politics, Praxis and the Postmodern* (1993) and *Politics of Liberation: Paths from Freire* (1994).

CAROL NICHOLSON is professor of philosophy at Rider University, Lawrenceville, New Jersey. Her research interests are in the history of philosophy, philosophy of education, and interdisciplinary humanities. Her publications include "Teaching on Uncommon Ground: The Ideal of Community in the Postmodern Era" (*Education and Society*), "Postmodernism, Feminism, and Education: The Need for Solidarity" (*Educational Theory*), and "Postmodernism and the Present State of Integrative Studies" (*Issues in Integrative Studies*).

A. T. NUYEN is currently senior lecturer in philosophy at the University of Queensland. His interests include the philosophy of social issues, the philosophy of David Hume and Immanuel Kant, and contemporary French and German philosophy. He has published in numerous international journals, including those in philosophy of education, such as *Educational Theory* and the *Journal of Thought*.

MICHAEL PETERS is senior lecturer in the education department at the University of Auckland, New Zealand. His research interests are in the areas of educational philosophy and policy, with a particular focus on poststructuralism. He has contributed to a number of edited collections and to a wide range of international journals, including *Educational Theory, Educational Philosophy and Theory, French Cultural Studies, Studies in Higher Education, Discourse, Policy Sciences*, and *Public Administration*.

BILL READINGS teaches in the comparative literature department at the University of Montreal. He is the author of *Introducing Lyotard: Art and Politics* (1991) and coeditor of *Postmodernism across the Ages* (1993) and *Textuality* (1994). He also edited and translated *Political Writings* Jean-François Lyotard. He is currently completing a book entitled *Beyond Culture: The Posthistorical University*.

ISBN 0-89789-373-5

90000>

EAN

9 780897 893732

HARDCOVER BAR CODE